THE BUDDHA

THE BUDDHA

His Life Retold

• *ROBERT ALLEN MITCHELL* •

PARAGON HOUSE
NEW YORK

First edition, 1989

Published in the United States by

Paragon House
90 Fifth Avenue
New York, NY 10011

10 9 8 7 6 5 4 3 2

Designed by Virginia Norey

Library of Congress Cataloging-in-Publication Data
Mitchell, Robert Allen.
The Buddha : his life retold / Robert Allen Mitchell. — 1st ed.
p. cm.
ISBN 1-55778-151-6
1. Gautama Buddha. 2. Buddhists—India—Biography. I. Title.
BQ882.M57 1989
294.3'63—dc19
[B] 89-3304
CIP

Manufactured in the United States of America

The paper used in this publication meets the minimum requirements of American National Standard for Information Sciences—Permanence of Paper for Printed Library Materials, ANSI Z39.48-1984.

CONTENTS

VI. *SPREAD OF THE DOCTRINE*

VII. *AT KAPILAVASTU*

VIII. *FOUNDING OF THE JETAVANA MONASTERY*

IX. *THE LAST VISIT TO KAPILAVASTU*

X. *THE SECOND SIX YEARS OF TEACHING*

XIV. *THE PLOT OF DEVADATTA*

XV. *JOURNEY'S END*

XVI. *THE GREAT DECEASE*

PREFACE

The multilayered story of the life and teachings of the Buddha has been told and retold through the centuries in diverse forms: in the soaring stone images of the Ajanta and Ellora caves in India; in the towering stone-cut sculptures of the world-famous caves of Yun-kang and Lung-men in China; in the paintings, murals, statues and other Buddhist artifacts of the Tun-huang caves; and in the powerful stone sculptures of Borobudor in Indonesia. That same inspiring story can also be heard in the oral traditions of the Buddhist East and West. Most accessible, of course, are accounts of the Buddha's life as recorded in numerous biographies in a variety of languages, not excluding English, of course.

Given the immense quantity of written material available on the life of Buddhism's founder, the skeptical reader may justifiably ask, "How different is this book from the others?" For one thing, THE BUDDHA: HIS LIFE RETOLD encompasses material not available in any other book in English of which I am aware. But there are other compelling reasons. It is a truism that every generation seeks what it is prepared to find, and today Americans are more inclined to accept the myth, fable, and allegory with which many of the events of the Buddha's life are entwined. More and more modern readers are persuaded that a myth is not an untrue story simply because it violates certain scientific notions of what is possible and what is not possible, but is a story that conceals truths and experiences so majestic, so profound that they cannot be encompassed within mere fact. Such acceptance opens wide the doors of perception to the richness of the saga of the Buddha's life and times. The increasing recognition of the power of myth to help us understand the world and ourselves is borne out by a recent statistic. Two hundred thousand copies of renowned mythologist Joseph Campbell's book THE POWER OF MYTH, based on a series of interviews between Campbell and television journalist Bill Moyers, were sold within a comparatively short time of the book's publication.

Other intriguing circumstances impelling a closer look at the Buddha's life and what it means for us today can be seen in the discoveries of certain scientists on the nature of the universe and man's place in it. These discoveries, oddly enough, have conferred on much of the Buddha's teachings a contemporary relevance. Who would have believed that prominent scientists would concede that 2,500 years ago a mystic, Gautama the Buddha, had gained through intuition and introspection an understanding of the nature of the universe and man's relation to it that anticipated their own empirical discoveries of the same truth?

The perplexity of at least one scientist in the face of the powers of transcendental perception is evident from a paper on the holographic model of the universe, by the neurophysiologist Karl Pribram (as quoted by Renee Weber, professor of philosophy at Rutgers University, in her article "The Holographic Model and Esoteric Traditions, *The Quest,* Winter 1988). He asks, "How is it possible that mystics 3,000 years ago have plagiarized what we scientists are doing today?" Weber adds, "He was really perturbed about this."

How closely does the holographic model of the universe as espoused by scientists Karl Pribram and David Bohm, to name two, resemble the Buddha's Insight of truth? Let us briefly compare them, quoting from Weber's perceptive article:

> *It would be correct then to state the maximum claim for the idea of the holographic universe, namely that in some deep level of being, the whole is enfolded within each part. And that includes not only object and object, which is the domain of physics at the moment; it also includes subject and object, which is the domain of psychology and philosophy of science; it is the knower facing the known; it includes most particularly subject and object. And that is what happens to interest [the physicist] David Bohm increasingly, namely the transcendence of an isolated, distorted, and hence falsified notion of ourselves as separate from one another, to a domain—one energetic domain—which he calls the consciousness of mankind, which has its roots in the inward layers of the implicate order, and anchored in matter so fine that it can only function as a unitive and not as a fragmented kind of entity.*
>
> *The Buddha put it more simply:*
>
> *Verily, I declare unto you that within this very body, mortal though it be and only a fathom high, but conscious and endowed with mind, is the world and the waxing thereof and the waning thereof, and the way that leads to the passing away thereof.*

In other words, each of us is both a part of the universe and at the same time the whole.

Other remarkable parallels between the Buddha's view of man and the universe and the views of contemporary science on the same subject can be pinpointed, but such a detailed comparison would take us beyond the scope of this Preface. What is increasingly clear, however, is that the new is much closer to the old than many had imagined. One may read THE BUDDHA: HIS LIFE RETOLD with these fascinating similarities in mind, or one may ponder the deep revelations lying beyond the outer vestments of the myth and fable that encircle this captivating account of the Buddha's life and teaching.

Robert Allen Mitchell, the author of THE BUDDHA: HIS LIFE RETOLD, was born in Bar Harbor, Maine, on October 24, 1917. He attended the University of Maine but left when his father died after a long struggle with cancer. Since the family had no medical insurance and the fees for his father's illness were considerable, the family was obliged to sell their home to pay the medical bills. As a consequence, Mitchell and his mother were forced to move into a small rustic summer camp in the rural section of Bar Harbor, where they lived in poverty for the rest of their lives.

Mitchell was an extremely intelligent and well-read person—he carried on a correspondence with Albert Einstein—and was also a prolific writer of short stories, spending many hours in the Bar Harbor summer home of the late novelist Mary Roberts Reinhardt, who reviewed his work and encouraged him.

Now, twenty five years after his death in 1964, his book is published. The manuscript itself was found in Mitchell's mother's home after her death in 1972. It was brought to me for evaluation by Ben Taylor, a student of mine, who had received it from Daniel J. Alexander, a distant relative of Robert Mitchell. I found the manuscript to be the most comprehensive biography of the life and teaching of the Buddha that I have read in English.

Roshi Philip Kapleau
Rochester, New York
Spring, 1989

INTRODUCTION

This is the life story of Prince Siddhārtha Gautama, universally known as the *Buddha.* The story of the Buddha's eighty years on earth constitutes one of the most remarkable of human documents. Not only was Prince Siddhārtha successful in attaining his Ideal, but his tremendous spiritual achievement resulted in the establishment of a religious system which has exerted an incalculably profound and gracious influence upon the lives of men for the past twenty-five centuries.

The great Ideal sought and attained by the Buddha is the eternal Dharma, or Truth, which he taught, and which conducts to Nirvāṇa, the *summum bonum* of his system. As a religious system formulated in human terms (i.e. "Buddhism"), the Dharma represents the daring discoveries of a master metaphysician who attacked the deepest problems of life with a spiritually inspired intellectuality and with a fearless confidence born of experience and wisdom. Considered from the practical point of view as a bold diagnosis of man's spiritual ills and a heroic prescription for their cure, the Buddha's Doctrine may well be regarded as the loftiest product of the human quest for Truth and "Rightness."

To divorce the teachings of the Buddha from an account of his life would not be wholly wise. In a special sense, the Buddha and his Dharma are one; the experience of Buddha-Dharma. Such is the inescapable imprint of Buddha's warm and forceful personality, and such is the time-defying power of his unequalled intellect and unique spiritual consciousness.

The present volume includes many of the Buddha's more important discourses interspersed with historical and legendary narrative material. Drawn from both Pāli and Sanskṛt sources, most of the material selected for inclusion has been greatly abridged. The present story is accordingly a *version,* not a collection of translations; but even so, the ancient texts have been transcribed with an eye for accuracy and with a sympathetic feeling for the flavor of the originals.

In spite of the preponderance of Pāli material in this book, proper names and Buddhist technical terms have all been turned into their more catholic Sanskṛt forms. Pāli, a dialect akin to the Māgadhī actually spoken by Buddha, is the "Greek" of the Buddhist canon, while Sanskṛt (of a late and generally impure sort) is its "Latin." Aside from the fact that much of the contents of the Pāli *Tripiṭaka* existed also in at least one Sanskṛt *Tripiṭaka* (Tibetan doctors aver that both were translated from a Prākṛt original), the use of Samskṛt spelling is preferred by Buddhists of all schools except the Theravādins of southern Asia.

For a scholarly discussion of Buddhist schools and canons of sacred literature, the reader is referred to Dr. Edward J. Thomas's *History of Buddhist Thought* (Barnes & Noble, New York, 1951), a companion volume to his equally authoritative *Life of Buddha as Legend and History* (Routledge & Kegan Paul, London, 1949).

R. A. MITCHELL

I

SOME FORMER LIVES OF BUDDHA

• BUDDHA'S FORMER • EXISTENCE AS SUMEDHA

Prologue

Lord Buddha comes into the world like a rain cloud to shed the life-giving Teaching upon all creatures; and having appeared in the world, he manifests Truth in accordance with Reality, saying:

> *Without beginning are the beings that hurry on from life to life in the current of time according to their deeds! Without end are the beings that wander on from world to world, reaping as they sow! And painful is birth again and again!*

I come to refresh all beings whose bodies are bent with pain:
I bring felicity to the weary, bestowing happiness and rest.
Hearken to me, O gods and men! I am the Tathāgata, the
Lord of all, who appears in this world to liberate!

The Story of Sumedha, the Holy Youth Who was Reborn in India After 100,001 Eons as the Buddha Śākyamuni

Once upon a time there lived a brahmin youth named Sumedha in a town called Amara in a world of long ago, a world that used to be. So long ago was that time that it cannot easily be reckoned in years, centuries, or millennia. It was a hundred thousand world-cycles and four immensities ago.

"Is there any escape from this wretched round of birth and death?" thought Sumedha to himself. "Is there a Place of Safety where birth and death are vanquished by immortality?"

Now Sumedha, reflecting upon the ills of life and the misery of repeated rebirth, overcame his doubt and thought: "There is, there must be, an escape from all this woe and pain! I'll make the search! I'll discover the Way that leads to freedom and release!"

And thinking thus, he gave away all his wealth to the poor and entered upon the life of a religious recluse.

Homeless, with possessions gone, Sumedha went to a hill in a snow-capped mountain range and built for himself a hermitage of poles and leaves. And in no long time, but after strenuous efforts, Sumedha the ascetic became a master of morality and meditation, possessor of high psychic powers.

Now, one day the people of a border country, their faces bright with joy, passed through the mountain fastness where Sumedha lived in solitude. On being asked the reason for their journey, they replied: "A mighty Buddha has appeared, Dīpaṅkara, Lord of all the world! We have invited him to preach to us; and we go to clear the way for him, the path, the track to travel on!"

At the sound of the word *Buddha* (meaning "Enlightened-One"), Sumedha's heart leaped up in exultation.

"A Buddha!" he exclaimed. "Now is the time to sow good seed—I must not let this opportunity slip by! Give me, pray, a task to do, so that I, with you, may help clear the way!"

The delighted people gladly took Sumedha along with them; and when, at last, they had prepared the path, came Dīpaṅkara accompanied by an entourage of four hundred thousand Arhats (Saints), unspotted, perfected, and possessing the Six High Powers.

Then the people greeted that mighty sage, that Perfect One, with shouts and the beating of drums. But at that very moment Sumedha chanced to spy a muddy place that still remained in the path of the Buddha.

"If only I can keep the mire from touching him," thought Sumedha, "great merit will certainly result."

Thereupon Sumedha laid himself face down in the mud exclaiming, "Let the Buddha with all his disciples tread upon me!"

While he lay there upon the ground, a multitude of thoughts flashed through his mind. He considered first that he might attain Arhatship and burn up all his faults that very day. "But why," he reflected further, "should I enter Nirvāṇa without aiding others? I'll first achieve omniscience and become a Buddha! I'll arrest the whirlpool of birth and death! I'll climb the sides of Dharma's ship and convey both men and gods to Yonder Shore!"

Dīpaṅkara, knower of all worlds, stepped up to where Sumedha lay and stayed his foot. And turning his face of radiant glory to the crowd, the world-honored Buddha declared: "Behold this ascetic and mark the austerity of his discipline! Innumerable eons hence this very recluse will become a supreme Buddha and revolve the Wheel of Dharma in the world even as I do today!"

Pleased with the Buddha's words, the people cheered, saying, "If we fail to grasp the Dharma now, if we miss Lord Dīpaṅkara's words, we can count on standing face to face with this other in time to come!"

After Dīpaṅkara had moved on, Sumedha raised himself up, his mind enraptured with ecstatic joy.

"Yes, a Buddha I shall surely be," he said, "for the Buddhas speak nothing but the truth!"

And as he embarked upon the Path of Bodhisattva by making the great vow to become a Buddha, the earth quaked in exultation, and the inhabitants of ten thousand universes thundered forth a glad and mighty shout: "You have made the great vow; great signs are seen: a Buddha you shall surely be! Just as the rivers in every land find their way to ocean's deeps, may gods and men in every world find their way to you!"

Returning to his mountain hermitage, the Bodhisattva pondered the Ten Perfections as the great highway traveled by all Bodhisattvas on the way to the Supreme Enlightenment of Buddhahood, namely:

1. *Generosity*
2. *Morality*
3. *Renunciation (of worldly ties)*
4. *Wisdom*
5. *Energy*
6. *Patience*
7. *Truthfulness*
8. *Resolution (to save all beings)*
9. *Loving friendliness*
10. *Equanimity*

And while he reflected upon these Ten Perfections, their nature and essence, ten thousand universes again trembled in uproar, and the ground shook like the ponderous, revolving wheel of an oil mill. Rapid indeed was Sumedha's progress upon the path to Buddhahood; and never swerving from his high resolve, he fulfilled during innumerable rebirth all the conditions of the Bodhisattva's high career, even to making the Five Great Donations, to wit:

1. *The gift of one's wealth*
2. *The gift of one's child*

3. *The gift of one's wife*
4. *The gift of royal rule*
5. *The gift of one's life*

• THE STORY OF VIŚVAṆTARA •

In the course of his rebirths, the Bodhisattva was reborn many eons ago as Prince Viśvaṇtara, son of King Viśvāmitra, a ruler blessed with wealth, prosperity, and a peaceful reign. And young Viśvaṇtara, advancing into manhood, gained worldwide fame for his excessive generosity.

One day the Bodhisattva Viśvaṇtara drove out from the royal city to a pleasure park in a splendid chariot gleaming with jewels, gold, and silver. And a band of brahmins versed in the Vedas met him and said: "O youth of the noble caste, throughout the whole world you are renowned as one who gives all things away. It would be fitting, therefore, if you would make us a present of your chariot."

On hearing these words, Viśvaṇtara swiftly alighted from the chariot and presented it to the brahmins with joyful heart.

"As I have given away the chariot with the greatest pleasure," he said, "so may I, by giving away the triple world, become possessed of the highest supreme Enlightenment!"

On another occasion Viśvaṇtara was riding on a sacred white elephant, and this was also desired by certain brahmins. The Bodhisattva gave it to them with great joy.

Now, when the people heard that the Bodhisattva had given away the white elephant, they became angry and demanded that King Viśvāmitra banish Prince Viśvaṇtara from the country. And having no choice in the matter, the king obeyed his subjects and sent his son away.

Because he was incapable of refusing requests, and was soon to have nothing left to give, Viśvaṇtara pronounced a solemn vow that he would devote the rest of his life to religious meditation in a distant forest. And bidding farewell to his father the king and to his wife Madrī, the Bodhisattva made haste to depart.

But Madrī, fearful of being parted from her husband, joined the palms of her hands and entreated the Bodhisattva to take her with him.

"Parted from you, O lord, I am not capable of living a moment longer. And why? As the sky when it is deprived of the moon, as the earth when it is deprived of water, so is the wife who is deprived of her husband. O lord, so long as I am able, I shall follow you wherever you go."

Then the Bodhisattva turned to his father and bowed low in reverence.

"O father," he said, "be pleased to forgive my fault, the giving away of the elephant. As I am now going forth to the forest with my wife, my son, and my daughter, your treasury, O king, will not become empty."

The king, choked by grief at the parting, exclaimed with tremulous voice: "O my son, renounce your practice of generosity and remain here with us!"

"The earth with its mountains will be overthrown sooner than I can turn aside from my giving," replied Viśvaṇtara.

After saying these words and turning back a large retinue of devoted followers by reminding them that separation from all things near and dear is inevitable, the Bodhisattva gave away all his wealth and departed with his wife and two children for the penance-forest in a chariot drawn by steeds of royal breed.

When the Bodhisattva had journeyed three hundred yojanas, a brahmin accosted him with a request for the chariot. Madrī was incensed thereat, and addressed the brahmin with angry words.

"O merciless brahmin, do you feel no pity when you see the prince fallen from his royal estate?"

But Prince Viśvaṇtara cautioned Madrī to find no fault with the brahmin, saying: "If there were no people of that sort, greedy and longing for possessions, charity would be curtailed. As generosity and the other Perfections comprise the highest virtue, the Bodhisattvas constantly attain to the highest Wisdom."

After the Bodhisattva had bestowed the chariot and horses upon the brahmin with great joy, he took little Prince Kṛṣṇa upon his shoulder while Madrī likewise took little Princess Jālinī. And at length they settled in the penance-forest, living on fruits, edible roots, and water.

Now one day, when Madrī had gone to collect food, a brahmin came to Viśvaṇtara and said: "O prince of the noble caste, your fame for giving has spread all over the world. As I have no slave, it is only fitting that you give me your two children."

Viśvaṇtara was stunned by this request. He considered the feelings of his bright-eyed, beloved children and of his wife, Madrī; but in the end he yielded to the brahmin's importunities and laid aside his attachment to his children.

Now, when the two children saw that their father was about to give them away, they seized his feet, crying, "O father, will you give us away before our mother returns?"

The Bodhisattva then succumbed to grief; and his face was wet with tears as he embraced his children and said: "O children, there is no unkindness in my heart, but only merciful compassion. As I have manifested virtue for the salvation of the whole world, I must give you away to attain the highest Enlightenment; and, myself having attained quiescence, I may save the worlds which lie devoid of support in the ocean of woes."

When little Kṛṣṇa and Jālinī perceived that their father's resolve was unshakable, they made obeisance to him and asked forgiveness for any faults they may have committed. And then the brahmin took them away.

Madrī, meanwhile, had set out for the hermitage; and as she carried her roots and fruits, inauspicious omens seized her heart with terror. Wild animals hindered her progress, and sorrowful wailing notes pervaded the forest.

"As the birds utter mournful cries, as my heart trembles, as the earth quakes, both my children have surely been given away!"

With a hundred thousand similar thoughts of disaster, she hastened toward the hermitage. Entering, she looked sadly around; and not seeing her children, she followed with sinking heart the tracks they had left on the ground. Not finding them, she laid aside her roots and fruits, embraced her husband's feet, and cried with tears of anguish: "O lord, where have the children gone?"

"A brahmin came to me full of hope," replied Viśvaṇtara. "To him have I given the two children."

When he had spoken these words, Madrī fell to the ground like a fawn pierced by a poisoned arrow.

"Shaped like young lotuses, slender as young gazelles, what sufferings are my children now undergoing in the power of cruel strangers?"

Then Madrī, looking upon the saplings which the children had planted and tended, touched them tenderly and said: "The children fetched water in small pitchers, and dropped water upon the leaves. You, O trees, were cared for by my children as though you were sentient beings."

And farther on, when she saw the young gazelles with which the children used to play, she sadly said: "The young gazelles have come looking for their playmates, searching among the plants, and not finding them."

"O Madrī!" exclaimed Viśvaṇtara, "it was hard to give them away! I have given for the deliverance of the world the children whom it was hard to give!"

When Madrī had recovered her strength of mind, she declared: "I will not be a hindrance to you. If you wish to give me away, too, give me without hesitation."

Now, when Śakra, king of the gods, perceived the marvelous endurance of the Bodhisattva and the patience of Madrī, he descended from his heaven-world and appeared at the hermitage in the form of a brahmin to test the Bodhisattva. Said Śakra to Viśvaṇtara: "Give me as a slave this lovely woman, fair in all her limbs, unblamed by her husband, prized by her race!"

Madrī was filled with anger by this request.

"O shameless one, full of craving, do you desire her who is not lustful like you, O rubbish of brahmins, but delights in righteousness?"

As the Bodhisattva Viśvaṇtara looked upon her with compassionate heart, Madrī said to him, "I have no anxiety for myself: my only concern is for you. How are you to exist when remaining alone?"

"Because I seek the height which transcends the endless anguish of the universe," replied the Bodhisattva, "no complaint must escape my lips,

O Madrī. Follow this brahmin, therefore, without complaining. I will remain in the hermitage, living in the manner of the gazelles."

Then, turning to the brahmin, he said, "Receive, O brahmin, this my dear wife, loving of heart, obedient, and charming."

And when Madrī was being led away by the brahmin, overcome by pain at being separated from her husband and children, she moaned, "Oh, what crime have I committed in my previous existence that now, like a cow whose calf is dead, I am lamenting in an uninhabited forest?"

Śakra forthwith assumed his true form, glowing with surpassing radiance, and comforted Madrī. And after returning her to Viśvaṇtara, the god deluded the mind of the greedy brahmin and caused him to lead the two children to the city of their grandfather, King Viśvāmitra, where they were sold as slaves.

When the royal ministers saw this, they purchased the children and took them to King Viśvāmitra. So sorry were the king and his people for having exiled Prince Viśvaṇtara, that messengers were sent to summon home the Bodhisattva and his wife Madrī.

Now, when King Viśvāmitra had come to the end of his years, the ministers and all the people of the country installed the Bodhisattva as their sovereign. And so Viśvaṇtara, then king, lived happily for many years with Madrī and their two children, Kṛṣṇa and Jālinī. And after he had given presents of various kinds to religious recluses, brahmins, the poor and needy, his friends and relatives, and to all his acquaintances and servants, King Viśvaṇtara uttered this solemn pronouncement: "Charity is the most excellent of virtues. With a heart free from passion I have given away my children and my wife, and thereby obtained power over gods and men both in this life and in the next."

The Viśvaṇtara existence was the last existence of the Bodhisattva in a terrestrial world before his rebirth as Prince Siddhārtha Gautama, the latest in the succession of supreme Buddhas to appear on earth.

• IN THE HEAVEN OF THE TUṢITA GODS •

When the Bodhisattva died as King Viśvaṇtara, the conditions which go to make a Buddha had all been fulfilled. As a result of his merit, he was reborn as a god in Tuṣita Heaven. That was an immensity of time ago, forasmuch as the Bodhisattva's life as a Tuṣita god was of long duration.

While the Bodhisattva was still dwelling in Tuṣita Heaven, the "Buddha Uproar," as it is called, occurred. Now, there are three Uproars which take place in the world, the Cyclic Uproar (heralding the end of the world), the Buddha Uproar (presaging the imminent arising of a Buddha in the world), and the Universal-Monarch Uproar (signaling the advent of a ruler of the whole world).

When the gods of ten thousand world-systems took note of the Buddha Uproar, proclaimed by the Four Celestial Kings, they ascertained which particular being was to attain Buddhahood and approached him, beseeching him to persevere in his high aspiration.

"Sir, it was not to acquire the glory of a ruler of the gods or a ruler of men that you fulfilled the Ten Perfections," said the emissaries of those gods to the Bodhisattva. "It was surely to win omniscience in order to save the world that you fulfilled them. Sir, the time for your assumption of Buddhahood has arrived."

But the Great Being made five observations before assenting to the wish of those gods. In the first observation he asked himself whether it was the proper time to be reborn on earth. It is not the right time when the length of men's lives is more than a hundred thousand years because, in that case, mortals forget about birth, old age, and death, and a Buddha's preaching about transience, misery, and the absence of substantive reality would fall upon deaf ears. Also, it is not the right time when men's lives are less than a hundred years. And why is that? Because mortals are then so exceedingly corrupt that exhortation makes no impression on them.

Now at that particular time the length of men's lives was between a hundred and a hundred thousand years, so the Bodhisattva observed that it was the right time for his last birth. Next he made observations concerning the continent, the country, the family, and the mother-to-be.

"Sirs," he said to the gods, "you are right: the time for my Buddhahood has come."

Then, surrounded by the gods of Tuṣita Heaven, and dismissing all the other gods, he entered the Nandana Grove of the Tuṣita capital to die. And while listening to a recitation by the gods of his vast store of merit, his flowers began to fade, his complexion became pale, and he passed away from Tuṣita Heaven to arise in the womb of Queen Māyā of the house of Gautama among the Śākyas in Kapilavastu.

II

BIRTH AND INFANCY OF PRINCE SIDDHĀRTHA

• BIRTH OF THE BODHISATTVA •

Nowhere in all Jambudvīpa (India) were the midsummer festivities gayer, more joyous, than in Kapilavastu, the chief city of the tiny Śākyan kingdom nestled in the rolling foothills of Himālaya, the abode of snows whence arose the little river Rohiṇī which wound its sinuous way through the city.

The Śākyas were ruled in those days by King Śuddhodana Gautama, whose two wives were sisters, the older named Māyā and the younger, Prajāpatī. Now, Queen Māyā had taken vows of abstinence and chastity.

Abstaining from strong drink and resplendent with garlands and perfumes, Queen Māyā took part in the festivities for the six days previous to the Āṣāḍha full moon. And on the seventh day of the feast she rose up early, bathed in flower-scented water, and sent couriers to the people with four hundred thousand pieces of money as alms to the needy.

Drowsiness overcame the beautiful queen very suddenly that morning; and she could not forbear lying down to rest upon the royal couch in her elegantly furnished chamber. Soon she found herself in the lotus-land and this was her dream.

Queen Māyā dreamed that the Four Celestial Kings raised her, together with the couch, and conveyed her over the Himālayan range to the high tableland of Tibet. And having arrived at a spot beyond the lofty peaks, they set her down under a jewel-spangled tree and stood respectfully at one side.

Then the wives of the Four Celestial Kings came and conducted her to a shimmering mountain lake in which they bathed her to remove every human stain. And after clothing her in divine garments, the goddesses anointed her with heavenly perfumes and decked her with celestial flowers.

Nearby was a silver mountain surmounted by a golden mansion. Now, the four gods and their wives prepared a divine couch with its head to the east; and upon it they laid Queen Māyā.

A star blazing with supernal splendor descended from Tuṣita Heaven; and then a superb white elephant was to be seen wandering about on the hill. Approaching from the north, the magnificent animal plucked a white lotus with his silvery trunk and, trumpeting loudly, he entered the golden mansion.

Walking around his future mother's couch three times, keeping his right side toward it, he struck Queen Māyā on her right side and disappeared, mysteriously entering her womb. And thus the Bodhisattva was conceived in the womb of Queen Māyā on the full moon day of Āṣāḍha.

Now at the moment when the Bodhisattva made himself incarnate in his mother's womb, the atoms constituting ten thousand world-systems vibrated, all at the same instant, and a measureless light shone irradiant over all. Good omens were made manifest: the blind received their sight, as if from a yearning to behold the glory of the Great Being; the deaf heard the sound; the dumb uttered praise of the Great Being; the deformed were straightened; the crippled were healed; prisoners in chains were freed from bondage.

In the hells the fires went out; hunger and thirst were allayed in the realm of earthbound ghosts; wild animals ceased to be afraid; the illness of all who were sick was alleviated; all men began to speak kindly to one another.

Beasts of burden gave voice to gentle emotions; musical instruments sounded forth though no one played them; bracelets jingled of themselves; the skies became clear; cool, soft breezes wafted pleasantly; wells and springs became filled with pure water; birds nested; the sea became fresh and covered with lotuses of every color; flowers blossomed everywhere; the trees burst into bloom, and exquisite lotuses broke through the rocks and blossomed forth by sevens.

Celestial flowers rained down from the sky, and celestial music filled the heavens; the ten thousand universes of the chiliocosm revolved and rushed close together like a bouquet of flowers, becoming, as it were, a wreath of worlds, as fragrant and resplendent as a mass of garlands, or as a sacred altar decked with flowers.

Queen Māyā awoke with a start, astonished by her marvelous dream; and on the next day she related it to King Śuddhodana.

"A Great Being like frosted silver and exceeding the sun and moon in radiance, a lovely elephant as strong as thunderbolts entered my womb. Then I beheld universes like globes of silver fire shining brightly, I heard countless gods and goddesses singing hymns of praise to him as I lay there in the manse of gold. With tranquil mind I knew the bliss of trance divine.

"It would be well, O king, to summon brahmins quickly and tell this dream to them that they may inform us whether it presages good to me or misfortune to the family."

Śuddhodana immediately summoned sixty-four eminent brahmins and told them the dream.

"It is honor, not calamity, that is coming to the house of Gautama," replied the brahmins. "A son is going to be born to you. And if he lives the household life, he will become a great king, a universal monarch; but if he leaves the household life and retires from the world, he will become a Buddha, a remover in the world of the veil of ignorance."

"Are you certain of that?" asked the king.

"Yes, O king, the signs are unmistakable. The earth quaked mightily this full moon day. An immeasurable light spread through ten thousand world-systems. The blind received their sight as if from a desire to see the Great Being, and the deaf received their hearing as if from a desire to hear the music sounding from on high. The heavens rained down flowers, and the fires in all the hells went out."

Queen Māyā carried the Bodhisattva in her womb for ten lunar months (two hundred eighty days); and when the day of her delivery had arrived, she journeyed forth from Kapilavastu to Devaḍaha, the city of her relatives. Now, between the two cities and belonging to the inhabitants of both was a pleasure grove of śāla trees called Lumbinī Garden.

At that particular season the grove was one mass of flowers from the roots of the trees up to the topmost branches. And among the blooms bees of many colors hummed in swarms, and among the boughs various kinds of birds sported, warbling sweetly.

The moment Māyā saw the beauty of Lumbinī, she desired to enter it and disport herself in the midst of that paradise of color and perfume. Expressing her wish to the courtiers of her retinue, she alighted from her golden palanquin and entered the park with a number of female attendants, tripping gaily from tree to tree while birds of brilliant plumage followed her like divine attendants appointed by the gods.

Coming to the foot of a magnificent śāla tree, Queen Māyā was strangely thrilled by its heavenly beauty. She stretched out her hand and seized a flower-laden branch; but as she stood there playfully looking up to the sky with open mouth, she was shaken by the pains of childbirth.

And at the moment of birth, the gods exclaimed: "Rejoice, O queen, a mighty son has been born to you!"

No sooner had these words resounded through the sky when a warm rain began to fall softly: and the rain was followed by a shower of celestial flowers.

Queen Māyā was still standing under the towering śāla tree when her maids discovered her with a baby boy of radiant golden color clasped lovingly to her breast.

"A charming baby, a prince indeed!" cried the people joyfully when they saw Queen Māyā's son. And while they were worshiping the holy child with offerings of flowers and rare perfumes, innumerable celestial voices chanted in concert: "Great Being, hail! There is no one who is your equal, much less your superior! Hail, O Jewel in the lotus, hail!"

And the earth itself began to thunder and quake and roar, crying from its depths: "Great Being, you are chief in all the world!"

As eventide had not yet fallen, Queen Māyā and her train returned with the newborn prince to the palace at Kapilavastu instead of going on to her native city of Devaḍaha.

And thus was the Bodhisattva delivered from the womb of Māyā Gautamī on the full moon day of Vaiśākha.

• PROPHECIES OF BUDDHAHOOD •

Just as the sixty-four eminent brahmins who interpreted Queen Māyā's dream had prophesied that the son of King Śuddhodana would become either a universal monarch or a Buddha, so also did Asita, a swarthy ascetic who had come to the palace in Kapilavastu to see the newborn prince.

The king, holding the Bodhisattva in his arms, began to move the holy infant before Asita in a gesture of obeisance; but the golden feet of the Bodhisattva planted themselves in the old ascetic's matted hair. For in all the world there was no one worthy of the Bodhisattva's reverence—indeed, if the king had succeeded in causing the infant to bow, Asita's head would have split in seven pieces!

"Permit me, O king, to hold the child," said Asita.

Taking the boy in his arms, the brahmin sage smiled as he saw at a glance the marks of a great man on the tiny body.

"Truly marvelous is this person who has appeared in the world!" declared Asita as he handed the baby back to Śuddhodana. And pressing the palms of his hands together, the old sage worshiped the Bodhisattva, sighing deeply as the tears rolled down over his cheeks.

When Śuddhodana saw Asita weeping, he was filled with alarm, and all his court with him.

"Our good friend the ascetic smiled but a moment ago," whispered the Śākyan nobles, "and now he has begun to weep!"

"Why do you shed tears and sigh?" cried Śuddhodana in distress. "Is any misfortune in store for the boy?"

Seeing the sorrowful faces of the Śākyas, the sage addressed them with a voice filled with emotion.

"No misfortune is to befall the child, O king: no ordinary person is he. If he dwell in a house, he will become ruler of all the world; but if he renounce the worldly life, he will surely become a Tathāgata, a Fully Enlightened Buddha, a widely proclaimed Teacher of gods and men."

"Then why do you weep?"

"I am old, O king," Asita replied, "aged and advanced in years; and this boy will doubtless attain supreme complete Enlightenment. And having attained it, he will turn the Wheel of Dharma which has not been turned by anyone else in this world for countless ages. He will teach the Dharma for the welfare and happiness of the world.

"As an udumbara flower at some time and place arises in the world, even so, after the passing of incalculable centuries, holy Buddhas arise in the world. This boy, O king, will take innumerable beings across the ocean of birth and death to the Other Shore and establish them in eternal Life, but I, being old, shall not live to see that Buddha-Jewel. He will preach the Āryan Dharma that leads to peace and Nirvāṇa in this very life, but I shall not live to hear it. Great, O king, is my loss!"

And so the sage Asita, having prophesied with certainty that the baby prince would be a Buddha in the world, departed.

On the fifth day after the birth of the Bodhisattva, the rite of giving a name to the holy child was to be performed. The royal palace was prepared by anointing the grand pavilion with different kinds of perfume and by scattering different kinds of flowers over the floor. And one hundred and eight brahmins had been invited for the name-giving ceremony.

As soon as the brahmins were comfortably seated, they were served a delicious pudding of whole rice grains boiled in milk and sweetened with honey. And when they had finished eating, King Śuddhodana entered their presence with Lady Prajāpatī, Queen Māyā's sister, who was tenderly carrying the infant Bodhisattva.

Queen Māyā was herself confined to her chamber, for, since the birth of the Bodhisattva, she had become grievously ill.

"What, O king, is to be the boy's name?" asked the head priest.

"Let him be called 'Siddhārtha,'" replied King Śuddhodana.

Ceremonial water was then sprinkled upon the head of Prince Siddhārtha Gautama.

Then eight brahmins (Rāma, Dhadhya, Lakṣaṇa, Manti, Kauṇḍinya, Bhodhya, Svayāma, and Sudatta) who were well versed in the art of prophesying fortunes from a consideration of bodily marks and characteristics stepped forward and examined the Bodhisattva carefully. Seven of the eight each raised two fingers and gave a double interpretation, saying:

"If a man possessing such marvelous marks and characteristics continue in the household life, he becomes a universal monarch; but if he retire from the world, he becomes a Buddha, a Supremely Awakened One."

The youngest of the eight brahmins, a mere youth whose family name was Kauṇḍinya, raised only one finger and gave but a single interpretation.

"I see nothing to make him stay in the household life," said Kauṇḍinya. "He will undoubtedly become a Buddha and save the world from ignorance and pain."

Now, King Śuddhodana became increasingly disturbed by predictions of Buddhahood for his son. The Śākyas were a race of warriors; and Śuddhodana, as their chieftain, was determined that Prince Siddhārtha should one day become a ruler of men, even a king of all the earth. The very thought that his own son might enter the religious life, calling nothing his own and begging his daily bread, filled the proud sovereign with dismay.

"What makes you so sure that there is nothing here to detain my son from embarking upon the life of a religious mendicant?" demanded Śuddhodana of the young brahmin.

"Several characteristics, O king; thirty-two in all, and four in particular," replied Kauṇḍinya. "Do you see the tiny circlet of white hairs on his forehead between the eyebrows? And the protuberance of the top of his head? And his black body hairs curling to the right? And the fine golden color of his skin? Without any doubt at all, the Four Signs will induce the prince to renounce the worldly life."

"The Four Signs?" asked the king with dread in his voice. "Pray, brahmin, name the four!"

"An old man, a sick man, a dead man, and a monk."

Śuddhodana rose to his feet, eyes flashing with anger.

"From this time forth," he commanded, "let no such persons approach the prince! It will never do for my son to become a Buddha! Prince Siddhārtha is destined to exercise sovereign rule and authority over all the great continents together with their thousands of attendant isles!"

But the hundred and eight brahmins shook their heads and went away.

Later that same day eighty thousand Śākyan clansmen assembled in the royal palace, and in the presence of King Śuddhodana each dedicated a son to the Bodhisattva, saying: "Whether the young prince become a Buddha or a king, we will each of us give a son, so that if he become a Buddha he shall be followed and surrounded by monks of the noble caste, and if he become a king, by warriors of the noble caste."

Now on the seventh day after the birth of the Bodhisattva, his mother died and was reborn as a goddess in the realm of the Tuṣita gods.

When Queen Māyā passed away, the physician at her bedside declared: "She, poor girl, was not strong. A hemorrhage has drained her life away."

A certain brahmin sage, overhearing the physician's words, added: "The mothers of Buddhas always die seven days after having brought forth their illustrious sons. For the womb that has been occupied by a Bodhisattva in his last birth is like the shrine of a temple, and can never be occupied again."

The king procured nurses for the Bodhisattva, women of lovely form and free from all blemish; but it was chiefly Lady Prajāpatī, the departed queen's sister, who nursed and cared for the holy child. And so Prince Siddhārtha of the house of Gautama increased in stature, well nurtured, protected from the world, and surrounded by an immense retinue in regal splendor.

• PRINCE SIDDHĀRTHA'S • MARRIAGE TO YAŚODHARĀ

As the years went by, Prince Siddhārtha became increasingly given to deep thought, delighting in solitude and meditation. It is said that on a certain occasion, when the young prince had been taken by his nurses to watch farmers plowing, he sat alone under a roseapple tree in deep meditation. And when the nurses were ready to take the Bodhisattva home, they noticed that the shadows of the other trees had turned with the sun, but the shadow of the roseapple had not moved.

King Śuddhodana, anxious lest the prince renounce the world and forsake royal rule, devised many kinds of pleasures and amusements for his son. And to protect the Bodhisattva insofar as possible from the Four Signs predicted by the brahmin Kauṇḍinya at the name-giving ceremony, the king built three luxurious palaces for his son, namely, one for summer, one for the rainy season, and the third for winter.

The three palaces with their costly pavilions and elegantly ornamented porticoes, with their multitudinous galleries and thousands of tinkling bells on every roof, were set in the midst of vast gardens and parks with exquisite flower-scented bowers and innumerable clear ponds dotted with lotuses among which swans of many colors glided gracefully.

In these palaces the young Bodhisattva lived surrounded by royal splendor and immersed in luxurious enjoyments, existing like a god in a lush paradise of pleasure. Bevies of ravishingly beautiful dancing girls entertained him continually, while an army of servants attended his every whim.

And yet the Bodhisattva failed to find true happiness in worldly pleasures.

Now, when the Bodhisattva reached the age of sixteen years, King Śuddhodana sent to the best Śākyan families letters in which he wrote: "My son the prince is grown up, of age; and I intend to establish him in the kingdom. Do you, therefore, send the most attractive girls that have grown up in your house to this house."

But the Śākyan chieftains replied to the king, saying: "The young man Siddhārtha is wholly given over to pleasure, merely handsome and good only for looking at. He is untrained in any manly art. What could he do if war were to break out? How will he be able to protect a wife? We will not send our daughters."

The king was exceedingly disappointed; but Siddhārtha declared that he did not need to train himself in the arts so dear to his relatives.

"Let the crier go about the city beating the drum to announce that I will demonstrate my proficiency. On the seventh day from today I will show my skill."

Thereupon King Śuddhodana commanded the town crier to proclaim this news to all the people of Kapilavastu according to the Bodhisattva's request. And on the seventh day Prince Siddhārtha went to the tournament grounds and surpassed the prowess of the most expert archers of the realm. Conforming to the custom of the world, the Bodhisattva displayed feats of skill which could not be equalled by anyone.

Witnessing the manifold knightly accomplishments of Śuddhodana's son, the Śākyas became favorably disposed toward the black-haired youth. With one mind each chieftain arrayed his own daughter and sent her to the royal household—in all, several thousand girls skilled in dancing, singing, and music.

And at that time a wife was given to Siddhārtha, the beauteous Yaśodharā, daughter of a Śākyan chieftain named Daṇḍapāṇi. It was truly said that Yaśodharā's charm and grace were surpassed only by her passionate adoration of the handsome young prince.

The following thirteen years slipped by uneventfully in the palaces of Prince Siddhārtha. ONLY THE MYSTERIOUS YEARNING OF HIS HEART AND THE SILENT CALLING OF THE WAY HINDERED THE BODHISATTVA FROM PEACE OF MIND.

III

THE GREAT RENUNCIATION

• THE FOUR SIGNS •

When the Bodhisattva was twenty-nine years old, Princess Yaśodharā was far gone with child. And on the morning of a beautiful day when winter had been vanquished by summer, Yaśodharā addressed the prince, saying: "Go, beloved husband, to the park of the summer palace and enjoy the trees and flowering plants which are now coming into bloom. I shall remain here in Kapilavastu, for the time of my delivery draws near."

Prince Siddhārtha accordingly summoned Chandaka, his charioteer, and proceeded to the park in an elegant chariot drawn by four white horses of royal breed.

As the Bodhisattva passed through a village of gardeners not far from

Kapilavastu, a decrepit old man, bent of body, leaning on a staff, toothless and gray-haired, stumbled out into the road.

The horses neighed with fright as Chandaka tightened the reins to avoid running down the tottering old man.

"Chandaka!" cried the prince in astonishment. "What kind of man is that? Never before have I seen a man in such a deplorable condition!"

"It is an old man, master," replied Chandaka, "a man who has seen many years come and go."

"But his face—see how wrinkled it is! Was he born in that unfortunate state?"

"No, master, he was once as young and blooming as you are now."

"Are there many more such old persons in the world?"

"Yes, master. It is the course of nature that all who are born must grow old and feeble if they do not die young."

"I, also, Chandaka?"

Chandaka lowered his head out of deference to the Bodhisattva. "You also, master."

The ardor of youth fled at once from the prince. "Shame on birth, since to everyone born old age must come! Return to the palace, Chandaka!"

And so the prince returned to his father's palace in Kapilavastu.

King Śuddhodana, astonished by his son's hasty return, summoned the charioteer.

"What happened on the way? Why has my son returned so quickly?"

"He has seen an old man, O king," answered Chandaka, "and because he has seen old age he desires to seek out the nature of birth and Death."

"Do you want to kill me, man, that you say such things? We must not let the prince enter the religious life. We must not allow the prophecies of the brahmin soothsayers to come true."

The next day the Bodhisattva again desired to go to the park; and the king; learning of this, stationed guards all along the road. But despite these preparations, Siddhārtha's eyes fell upon a sick man, suffering and very ill, fallen in his own excrements by the roadside.

"Chandaka!" cried the Bodhisattva. "Stop the chariot at once!"

When Chandaka failed to stop, Siddhārtha took the reins from the charioteer's hands. And after the chariot had been turned around, the prince drew to the side of the road where the sick man was.

"What, Chandaka, has that man done that his eyes are not like others' eyes? nor his voice like the voice of other men?"

"He is what is called sick, master."

"Sick? Are all people liable to sickness?"

"Yes, master."

"Then I, too, could become such as this, I, the glory of the Śākyas! Let us return to the palace: enough of going to the park!"

Notwithstanding his discovery of human misery, the Bodhisattva set out for the third time on the following morning.

The trip was uneventful until the chariot had reached the outskirts of the gardeners' village. There a corpse was being carried to a funeral pyre by weeping relatives.

Prince Siddhārtha looked upon the scene with impatience, not knowing what to make of it. But perspiration broke out on Chandaka's forehead as he silently prayed to the gods to withhold the sight of death from the prince.

The gods, however, were of a different mind. Like an invisible hand, a sudden gust of wind swooped down upon the bier and ripped away the pall in fluttering tatters.

Prince Siddhārtha's mouth opened in horror when his gaze fell upon the dead body. Could *that* once have been human? Could *that* even have been alive?

"And to think," gasped the prince, "that that vile body was once a thing of delight to its owner, a source of fleeting pleasures! Is the man dead, Chandaka, hopelessly and irretrievably dead?"

"His relatives and friends will not see him any more," replied Chandaka, "nor will he see them."

"It has become clear to me, Chandaka, that death is universal. I, too, am subject to death, not beyond the sphere of death. Now what if I, being subject to old age, sickness, and death, were to investigate the nature of birth, likewise the nature of old age, sickness, and death? What if I, having seen the wretchedness of mundane existence, were to seek out the Unborn, the Undying, the supreme peace of Nirvāṇa?"

When the Bodhisattva returned to the palace, he related his experiences to King Śuddhodana and Lady Prajāpatī and informed them that he intended to renounce the worldly life and become a solitary ascetic.

"Why should I pursue that which is subject to birth, decay, old age, and rebirth? Why shouldn't I, with my eyes open to the perils which these things entail, pursue, instead, the consummate peace of Nirvāṇa which knows neither disease nor death, neither rebirth nor decay, neither sorrow nor impurity?"

Both his father and his foster mother burst into tears when they heard these words, and they begged the prince to remain at home, content with the pleasures of the world. But Siddhārtha went to his chambers disappointed and with a heavy heart.

Early in the morning of the fourth day, the Bodhisattva set out again for the pleasure park of the summer palace. And as the chariot approached the park, the prince caught sight of a religious recluse walking by the side of the road.

"Who, Chandaka, is that man clad in a simple yellow robe, his head shaved, his face radiant with peace and joy?"

"That man," replied the charioteer, "is a monk, one who has gone forth from the household life and lives on food he has begged. He is one who is thorough in the religious life, thorough in the peaceful life, thorough in good actions, thorough in meritorious conduct, thorough in harmlessness, thorough in kindness to all living beings."

"A monk!" exclaimed the Bodhisattva. "Never before have I seen such happiness and inner peace shining forth from the face of a man! Is it possible, friend Chandaka, that I, too, might find rapture and peace of mind by leaving the world, by becoming such as he and living on food I have begged?"

"We are approaching the summer palace, master."

"Friend, I beg you to tell me! Why, pray, do men leave the world?"

"For the sake of subduing and calming themselves," said Chandaka, "and for attaining Nirvāṇa."

NIRVĀṆA! "Happiness" or "Extinction" as one looks at the world! On hearing the word *Nirvāṇa,* the Great Being was delighted; and taking pleasure in the thought of abandoning the world, he bade Chandaka to drive on into the park.

• THE GREAT RENUNCIATION •

Prince Siddhārtha arrived safely at the summer palace. A great crowd of courtiers, musicians, and dancing-girls pressed forward to sweep the prince into a whirl of pleasure. The Bodhisattva accordingly spent most of the day sporting in the beautiful gardens and groves of the park, meanwhile partaking of the choice dainties which had been prepared for him: but his mind was not on amusements.

Late in the afternoon the Bodhisattva bathed and adorned himself, saying, "This is my last adornment." No sooner had these words left his lips when the gods showered him with celestial mandārava flowers and raised a cry of exultation which sounded like thunder gamboling carefree among the soaring peaks of snowcapped Himālaya.

Meantime, Princess Yaśodharā had brought forth a son; and messengers sent from the royal palace announced the good news to the Bodhisattva.

"An impediment *(rāhula)* has been born, a fetter has been born," declared the Bodhisattva with a sigh. King Śuddhodana, when told of Siddhārtha's remark, exclaimed: "My grandson's name shall be Rāhula from this very day!"

Prince Siddhārtha returned to Kapilavastu in his splendid chariot with a pomp and magnificence of glory that enraptured the minds of all the people.

Standing on the balcony of her palace, a young noblewoman named Kṛṣā Gautamī feasted her eyes on the handsomeness and majesty of the Bodhisattva as he rode through the streets of Kapilavastu. And when the Great Being had come beneath her balcony, Kṛṣā's pleasure and delight so inspired her that she gave voice to a joyous utterance:

> *Happy (nirvṛto)* indeed the mother,
> Happy, too, the father,

Surely happy the woman
Who possesses this husband sublime!

The Bodhisattva, hearing the word *nirvṛta* ("happy" or "extinct"), was pleased with *nirvāṇa* ("happiness" or "extinction"), and he stopped and seized the word.

The Bodhisattva thought, "She certainly knows whereof she speaks! On seeing a handsome offspring the heart of a mother attains nirvāṇa, the heart of a father attains nirvāṇa, the heart of a wife attains nirvāṇa. This is what she says. NOW, WHEN WHAT IS EXTINGUISHED *(NIRVṚTA)* IS THE HEART MADE HAPPY *(NIRVṚTA)?"*

And he whose mind was already becoming averse to passion thought, "When the fires of greed, hatred, and delusion are extinguished, that is Nirvāṇa! When lust, conceit, false belief, and all the other passions that poison the spirit are extinguished, that is Nirvāṇa! She has taught me a valuable lesson, for Happiness *(Nirvāṇa)* is what I am searching for. It behooves me to quit the household life this very day and fare me forth in quest of Extinction *(Nirvāṇa)*. I shall send this lady a teacher's fee!"

Taking the priceless pearl necklace from his neck, he sent it to Kṛṣā Gautamī. But Kṛṣā, thrilled as she had never been thrilled before, wrongly imagined that the prince had fallen in love with her and had sent her the necklace as a token of his affection.

The Great Being went at once to his chamber in the royal palace and lay down upon his couch of state. Seductive women, charmingly adorned, immediately gathered around the prince with sweet-toned musical instruments and endeavored to arouse amorous passions in him with dance, song, and instrumental music.

The Bodhisattva's newfound aversion to passion, however, left him indifferent to enticing melodies and rhythmically swaying bodies. He soon fell asleep from boredom.

The women, seeing the prince sleeping, exclaimed: "Well, now, just look at him! He for whose sake we were performing has fallen asleep! Girls, what is the use of our wearying ourselves any longer?"

Thereupon they threw their instruments upon the floor and lay down.

Meantime, the lamps fed with sweet-smelling oil continued to burn.

The Bodhisattva awoke with a start. Suddenly the oppressiveness of his luxurious surroundings seized his heart; and when his eyes passed over the women of his seraglio sleeping on the floor with their musical instruments scattered about them, he was repelled.

"How like a cemetery filled with dead bodies impaled and left to rot!"

Some of the women reeked of stale sweat, others had saliva trickling down their twitching faces, some were muttering and snoring, and some, whose costumes had fallen apart, lay naked in disgusting postures.

"Having heard the sound of Nirvāṇa, having given ear to Nirvāṇa, having beheld supreme Nirvāṇa, it behooves me to go forth upon my retirement this very night!"

Commanding Chandaka the charioteer to saddle the swift horse Kanthaka, the Bodhisattva went silently to Princess Yaśodharā's chamber to take one last look at little Prince Rāhula, his newborn son. Then he went down to the stable and approached his horse, saying: "My dear Kanthaka, save me now; and when I have become a Buddha I will save the world of gods and men!"

Hearing these words, Chandaka burst into tears and fell at Prince Siddhārtha's feet in entreaty.

"Pray do not go forth, O master! Pray do not reject the kingdom or forsake parents, child and wife!"

"It is too late for asking that, Chandaka," replied the Great Being. "From this day forward I am the Ascetic Gautama."

"Then, sire, take me with you on your retirement!"

The Bodhisattva agreed to take Chandaka with him a certain distance, but not beyond that point. Mounting his steed and grasping the reins firmly in his hands, the Great Being bade Chandaka mount behind him.

Then, at the stroke of midnight, Kanthaka flew swiftly as the wind over the streets of Kapilavastu: and just as he came to the gate on the south side of the city, the earth began to rumble and shake, swinging the massive gate ajar. And so it was that the Bodhisattva renounced the world on the full moon day of Āṣāḍha when he was twenty-nine years of age.

As soon as he was beyond the city limits, a chill night wind gathered up a bog mist from which the voice of Māra, the tempter, spoke to Gautama's heart.

"Turn back, Siddhārtha, go back to your palace! For on the seventh day from now the wheel of empire will appear to you, and you shall rule over all the great continents with their thousands of attendant isles. Now is the time to turn back, O prince!"

"Who are you who speaks thus to me?"

"I am the spirit of the world, the generator of life's restless cravings, the disposer of death and resurrection in the sphere of change and grasping. Indeed, prince, I am powerful!"

"Māra, I knew that the wheel of empire was on the point of appearing to me; but I will have no part of a thing like that. On the contrary, I am about to cause the universe to thunder with my assumption of Buddhahood!"

"What an ambitious stripling you are, friend Gautama!" replied Māra. "Do you presume to escape my power, the power of your secret desires, the force of your own craving for sensate existence? Well, now, sir, you are going to be watched! The very first time that you have a lustful, malicious, or cruel thought, I shall know it, and I shall catch you!"

And like the ever-present shadow of a man's conscience, ready to accuse, the Evil One followed after, always on the watch for some slip.

The Bodhisattva traveled southeastward through the night and arrived at dawn at a rivulet called Anomā in the principality of the Mallas. Dismounting, he entered the village of Anomiyā and obtained the eight requisites of a religious recluse (three robes of patched, saffron-dyed cotton, a bowl for alms-gathering, a razor, a needle, a belt, and a water strainer).

When he had returned, the Great Being cut his hair off with his sword, diadem and all, and assumed the Yellow Robe, that most excellent vesture, that symbol of sainthood and retirement from worldly life. And to Chandaka he gave his princely raiment and costly ornaments, saying: "I now take my leave of you, good friend. Return to Kapilavastu and inform my father and my foster mother that I am well."

Chandaka did obeisance to his former master; and keeping his right side toward the Bodhisattva out of respect, he sorrowfully departed for the country of the Śākyas.

But the horse Kanthaka, who had overheard Gautama's conversation with Chandaka, was unable to bear his grief at the thought: "I shall not see my master any more!" When he had passed out of the Great Being's sight, his heart burst, and he was reborn in the Heaven of the Thirty-Three Palaces as the god called Kanthaka.

At first the grief of Chandaka had been but single, but now he was afflicted with a second sorrow in the death of Kanthaka. And so poor Chandaka returned to Kapilavastu weeping and wailing.

IV

THE QUEST FOR ENLIGHTENMENT

• GAUTAMA'S PROMISE TO BIMBISĀRA •

Left alone and owning nothing in the world except the meager requisites of a religious recluse, the Bodhisattva wandered about until he had come to the mango grove Anupiyā in Mallan territory. He spent a full week there in the joy of having retired from the world.

"Encumbered is the household life," he reflected, "houses are abodes of dust. Faring forth is freedom in the open air!"

And having gone forth, the Ascetic Gautama abstained from the doing of evil deeds and the speaking of wrongful talk.

Thus purified, he continued southeast to the bustling metropolis of Rājagṛha, capital city of the great kingdom of the Magadhas, then ruled by Śronika Bimbisāra, a king righteous and kind.

Having arrived in Rājagṛha, Gautama begged for food from house to house; and all the city was thrown into a commotion by the sight of so handsome a personage making the rounds like an ordinary mendicant.

One day King Bimbisāra, standing on the roof of his palace, chanced to glimpse the Great Being begging food on the street below. Observing the princely demeanor of the Bodhisattva, he turned to his attendants and commanded them to find out where the handsome young ascetic was dwelling.

Now, after Gautama had collected sufficient food for the day's sustenance, he made his way to Paṇḍava Hill, one of the five hills of Rājagṛha. And when he had arrived at his hermitage, he sat down facing the east and prepared to eat his meal.

Looking at the wretched scraps of food in his bowl, Gautama became nauseated, feeling as though his stomach were on the point of coming out through his mouth. Never before had he seen such miserable fare. But in the midst of his distress at that repulsive food, he began to admonish himself.

"Siddhārtha, although you were born into a family having plenty to eat and drink, and into a station of life where you lived on fragrant third-season rice served with various sauces of the finest flavors, yet when you saw a monk clad in garments taken from the rubbish heap you said, 'Oh, when shall I be like him and eat food which I have begged? Will that time ever come?' And then you retired from the world. Now that your wish has come true, and you have given up everything, what, pray, is this that you are doing?"

After he had remonstrated with himself in this way, his disgust subsided, and he ate his meal.

Now, King Bimbisāra's messengers had discovered the Bodhisattva's dwelling place by following him to Mount Paṇḍava; and immediately upon their return to the royal palace with news of their discovery, Bimbisāra set out for the hill by way of the chariot road.

Drawing near to the Bodhisattva, the king exchanged greetings and sat down.

"Sir, you are young, a fellow in the prime of manhood," declared

Bimbisāra. "I also perceive that you are of the noble caste. Such a one as yourself deserves the wealth I bestow upon those who accept positions in my command. Pray tell me something about yourself."

"There is a country on Himālaya's snowy slopes, O king, its people endowed with wealth and valor, settlers in Kośala borderland. By clan they are Āryas of solar race, Śākyas by birth, O king. From such a family I have gone forth, having no longing for worldly things. Seeing the wretchedness of lusts and passions, looking upon renunciation as peace, I am faring forth to strive: and Nirvāṇa is my goal."

And Gautama refused the king's offers of wealth and high position.

"Truly," replied Bimbisāra, "you are certain to become a Buddha. When that happens, your first journey must be to my kingdom. Having won Enlightenment, you must come back and teach me the doctrine you discover."

"Surely, O king, there is no doubt of my winning Enlightenment. And having won it, I shall return and teach you the Dharma."

Having made this promise to Śrenika Bimbisāra, the Bodhisattva set out across the river Gaṅgā (Ganges) and proceeded north to Vaiśālī, chief city of the Vṛjis.

• THE SEVERE AUSTERITIES •

The Ascetic Gautama soon learned that the world was overcrowded with diverse religions. Some religious devotees tormented themselves, with the thought of avoiding by such practices the ripening of unfavorable karma. Others prayed to a god in the hope that he would deliver them from the effects of their sins and bring them to rebirth in a heaven-world. And still others sought emancipation through mental discipline and through good works and attention to ceremonial rites. Which, if any, of these methods of salvation was the true, the right, the efficacious one? Gautama did not then know, for he had yet to attain the omniscience of the Great Awakening.

"Look at the people frantically grasping and clinging," he thought, "pursuing what is subject to impermanence and sorrow, subject to the round of rebirth. Himself subject to impermanence, suffering, and rebirth, man pursues ties no less subject thereto with blind and avid appetite. Being myself subject to these evils, should not I, with my eyes open to the perils which these things entail, pursue instead the consummate peace of Nirvāṇa which knows neither impermanence nor sorrow, and is beyond the sphere of rebirth? But how am I to begin?"

At Vaiśālī Gautama found a learned ascetic, Ārāda Kālāma, who taught a method of one-pointed concentration and deep meditation.

"My doctrine is such that an intelligent man can quickly master it and learn to abide in it," said Ārāda.

And Ārāda's words were true, for in no long time Gautama mastered all that Ārāda had to teach. But that was not enough.

"How far, friend Kālāma, does this doctrine of yours conduct?" Gautama asked his teacher.

"It conducts to the Sphere of Nothingness," replied Ārāda.

"Well, friend, I have mastered your doctrine. I am able to attain the Sphere of Nothingness."

At these words Ārāda was filled with delight and satisfaction.

"We are fortunate to have with us a man like you, friend Gautama! You have accomplished everything that I have accomplished! Come now, friend, the two of us will devote ourselves to teaching this group."

Gautama considered it a great honor to be set equal to his teacher, but he declined Ārāda's offer. For Ārāda's doctrine conducting only to the Sphere of Nothingness did not lead to absence of passion, tranquility, higher knowledge, Nirvāṇa.

With these thoughts the Bodhisattva abandoned Ārāda Kālāma's doctrine and made his way back to Magadhan country still questing for Truth.

In Rājagṛha Gautama found another religious sage having an assembly of pupils. This accomplished ascetic, Rudraka Rāmaputra (Rudraka "Son of Rāma"), trained the Bodhisattva much as Kālāma had done, except that Rāmaputra's doctrine conducted past the Sphere of Nothingness to the Sphere of Neither-perception-nor-nonperception.

Gautama quickly mastered this more difficult doctrine; and Rāmaputra was so nearly overwhelmed with admiration that he proposed to set the Bodhisattva above him as teacher. But Gautama declined, sadly realizing as before that he had failed to find a man who could teach him the path to the uttermost peace of Nirvāṇa.

After he had wandered some distance southwest of Rājagṛha, Gautama settled down by the river Nairañjanā near the little town of Gayā in the Magadhan army-township called Uruvilvā.

"This is truly a delightful spot," he reflected. "What a pleasant grove, and what a lovely river of clear water flowing by! And close at hand is a hamlet in which to beg alms-food! This is surely the proper place for the striving of a clansman intent on striving for his welfare!"

There the Great Being began to practice austerities in the hope of learning the truth about existence and mankind's ills. So great was his skill and purity that in just a few years his fame as a holy man had spread throughout the length and breadth of India.

And it came to pass that word of Gautama's severe austerities reached the country of the Śākyas and the ears of Kauṇḍinya, the brahmin who, as principal spokesman for the hundred and eight brahmins at the name-giving ceremony, had predicted only one possible destiny for Śuddhodana's son—the attainment of Buddhahood. So Kauṇḍinya decided to follow the Great Ascetic, as Gautama was called by the people; and he took four of his friends with him.

When the "Band of the Five" consisting of Kauṇḍinya, Bhadrika, Vāṣpa, Mahānāma, and Aśvajit reached Uruvilvā township, they asked the Bodhisattva how he had been faring since his retirement from the world. Thereupon the Great Being enumerated to them his manifold austerities and announced his intention to continue striving until he had attained Nirvāṇa. The five brahmins became the Bodhisattva's disciples that very day and proceeded to imitate the austerities practised by their master.

Gautama then began to practice self-mortifications even more severe than the preceding ones, first attempting to destroy obsessive desires by rooting out discursive thought. Time and again the Great Being set his teeth together and pressed his palate with his tongue in an effort to force his consciousness down; and the agony of the struggle was so excruciating that sweat poured from his armpits.

His energy was strenuous and unyielding in spite of the terrible suffering. The quality of unconfused mindfulness was indeed established; but his body, overwhelmed by the stress of pain, could not sustain the exercise. And because the agonizing sensations had failed to overpower discursive thought, Gautama abandoned the practice.

He then restrained his breathing, holding his breath until a roaring sound arose in his ears and grievously sharp and painful sensations arose in his head. Even this method failed; and at length he fell to the ground as if deprived of life, not regaining consciousness until some time afterward.

Abandoning that method, Gautama tried living on the most meager diet imaginable—a small quantity now and then of the juice squeezed from beans and peas.

"Perhaps by this method I can attain superhuman excellence of insight, that truly Āryan knowledge transcending mortal things," said Gautama to Kauṇḍinya.

"Do as you think best, Master Gautama," replied Kauṇḍinya. "We five will take care of you."

Thus the experiment began. Day followed day, and Gautama's body became extremely thin: and soon he reached a state of utter physical exhaustion.

His limbs with their joints resembled knotgrass in their sparseness. The mark left by his bottom was like a camel's footprint. Through little food the bones of his spine were like a row of spindles, and his ribs stuck out like the rafters of an old shed. Just as in a deep well the waters may be seen sparkling in the depths, so in the depths of his eye-sockets did the luster of his eyes seem sunken. And as an unripe gourd cut off from the stalk is shriveled by wind and sun, so was the skin of his head shriveled through little food.

Gautama had all but sacrificed his life to his experiment. For many weeks he lay on the ground a withered, discolored caricature of the handsome youth who had set out from Kapilavastu nearly six years before to win supreme Enlightenment. So pitifully emaciated was his body that people came to stare at him out of curiosity.

"Look," the onlookers exclaimed, "the Ascetic Gautama is becoming discolored—his skin looks like that of a mangura fish! Surely, he cannot live much longer!"

Gasping for breath, the Bodhisattva whispered to Kauṇḍinya.

"Whatever sudden, sharp pains have been suffered by ascetics in the past or in the present, at most they have not suffered more than this!"

Thinking that Gautama had meant that Enlightenment was near at hand, Kauṇḍinya went at once to his four companions and said, "When the Ascetic Gautama arrives at the Dharma, he will teach it to us."

But then the Bodhisattva began to conceive a dissatisfaction with painful self-mortifications, for he knew that the attainment of Nirvāṇa was as far away as ever.

"What useless anguish of body-mind," he thought, "what a waste of time and effort! I have spent six years like a man trying to tie the air into knots!"

Gautama then realized that only intelligent meditation conjoined with purity of life could lead to the uttermost Peace that surpasses the beatitude of even the highest of the gods.

"What a deluded fool I should be if I were to become suspicious and disdainful of the happy state which exists apart from sensual desires and evil ideas! It will not be easy for me to reach that state of ease with my body utterly exhausted, however. Suppose, now, that I take nourishing food."

Thereupon Gautama called for the brahmins to take him into his hut and prepare for him a gruel made of rice begged in the village. But when the Band of the Five saw their master eating substantial food, they became indignant.

"See how pleasure-loving the Ascetic Gautama has become! He has given up striving and eats householders' food! It would be useless for us to look for any benefit from such a fellow: let us take our leave and have nothing more to do with him."

With these complaints the Band of the Five left in disgust and started out in a northwesterly direction toward Vārāṇasī (Benares), chief city of the Kāśīs.

Gautama nevertheless continued to eat full meals, begging his food after the custom of religious mendicants. Strength and vigor soon returned to his body, his complexion resumed its fine color, and the handsomeness of his features was in every respect restored. But Gautama, rejected by his disciples, knew full well that his greatest struggle lay ahead.

• SUJĀTĀ'S OFFERING •

At that time there lived in Uruvilvā a young highborn woman named Sujātā. When she had reached the age for marriage, she prayed to a certain banyan tree, saying: "O God of the Tree! If I get a husband of equal rank with myself, and my firstborn is a son, I will make a yearly offering to you worth a hundred thousand pieces of money."

Her fervent prayer was answered favorably; and she attributed her good fortune to the god who lived in the banyan.

Wishing to make her offering on the full moon day of Vaiśākha, she prepared a sweet gruel of rice boiled in rich, creamy milk freshly drawn. Then she bade her servant girl Pūrṇā to get everything in readiness at the holy place.

Now Gautama, having bathed and attired himself, had come early in the morning to that same banyan tree to await the proper hour to go begging in the village. And when he had seated himself he thought, "Today is my thirty-fifth birthday. Methinks the day will prove auspicious."

Then came Pūrṇā who saw the Great Being garbed in yellow robes sitting at the foot of the tree contemplating the eastern quarter of the world. Thinking that the Bodhisattva was the god of the tree come down in material form to receive Sujātā's offering, she ran back to tell her mistress of the matter.

Sujātā was overjoyed by Pūrṇā's news, and went herself to present the offering. Placing the rice gruel in a golden dish worth a hundred thousand pieces of money, and carrying some flower-scented water in a golden vase, she drew near to Gautama, bowing reverently as she approached.

Sujātā placed the dish of milk rice in the hand of the Great Being; but as she did so, he looked at her, and she perceived that he was not the god, but a religious recluse.

"Accept my donation, Lord, and feel free to go wherever it pleases you," she said, bowing low. "May your wishes prosper like my own."

Caring no more for her golden dish than if it had been a dead leaf, she went back to her house.

Taking the golden dish, Gautama arose from his seat and went to the bank of the Nairañjanā River and ate the milk rice which had been prepared as a religious offering. Then the Bodhisattva, after bathing in the river, rested in a nearby grove of blooming śāla trees.

Now, very late that afternoon, just as the rays of the westering sun gilded the trees with a prodigal burst of glowing color, Gautama rose up like a lion bestirring himself and set out on the way back to his forest hermitage. And there, on the road which the wind had paved with fragrant flowers, the Bodhisattva met a grasscutter by the name of Svastika. And when Svastika saw the Great Being, he gave him eight handfuls of the sweet-scented grass he was carrying.

The Bodhisattva took the grass, intending to make with it a seat for sitting in deep meditation.

In Gautama's forest grove hermitage near Gayā there was a spreading pipal tree; and on coming to it the Bodhisattva regarded it with an eye of supernormal intuition and perceived that the pipal was a "Bodhi tree"—a tree under which a Bodhisattva might sit to attain the transcendental Wisdom of Buddhahood.

He took his bundle of grass and shook it out under the tree to form a seat on the eastern side of the tree trunk. And he seated himself cross-legged upon the mat of grass which had assumed a shape so perfect that not even the most skillful painter or carver could have designed it. This was indeed the Diamond Throne of Enlightenment!

• THE ASSAULTS OF MĀRA •

Seated facing the east upon the Diamond Throne under the Bodhi tree, the Bodhisattva uttered a mighty resolution, saying: "Let only skin and bones remain, let the flesh and blood of this body dry up, but I shall never abandon this seat until I have attained the supreme and absolute Enlightenment, the omniscience of Buddhahood!"

Then the voice of Māra, the Evil One, began to make itself heard in all the doubts and fears that had hidden themselves in the back of Gautama's mind.

"How presumptuous of Siddhārtha, abandoned by his disciples, to assume the cross-legged posture on the Seat of Wisdom! Śuddhodana's son is desirous of passing beyond my control; but I will never allow it!"

With great swiftness dense clouds swept over the sky to blot out the scarlet glories of the sunset; and beads of perspiration gathered on the Bodhisattva's brow as the light of day grew dim.

Flashes of lightning accompanied by angry rumblings veined the gray gloom with a fearful tracery of flickering brilliance. A blinding, searing bolt suddenly exploded in front of Gautama; and a tall tree, its trunk split lengthwise, fell crashing to earth in flames.

"Māra!" exclaimed the Bodhisattva.

A powerful throbbing at once assailed the Great Being, shaking his body violently. The foliage of the Bodhi tree, rustling softly only a moment before, began to hiss in the hot wind like the echo of a million screams. And the very earth groaned and opened up before the Great Being in fissures, trembling like quicksand.

"Even the beneficent deities, shaken out of their complacency by the fury of Māra, have forsaken the world!" declared the Bodhisattva. "Śakra has fled to the rim of the galaxy, and Great Brahmā has transposed himself back to his Brahma-world! But how is this, that the gods have become visible to me, that I can see what they are doing?"

Then said Māra to his army of demons: "Comrades, the son of Śuddhodana is far greater than any other man. We shall never be able to fight him in front: we shall attack him from behind."

The Great Being looked around and saw the angry flood of Māra's army rushing upon him.

"Here is this Māra-host of doubts and waverings exerting great power against me, who am alone with no one to uphold me with a word of encouragement. But I have the Ten Perfections like old retainers long cherished at my board. And now the veil of mystery regarding my past existences is being swept away like dust from my eyes! It behooves me, therefore, to make the Ten Perfections my shield and my sword and to strike a blow with them that will destroy my misgivings and vanquish the army of Māra!"

Remaining seated cross-legged on the Diamond Throne made of the scented grass Svastika had given him, the Great Being addressed Māra, saying:

"Friend of the lazy and careless, there is no need to be found in me for any additional work of merit. Confidence, heroism, and wisdom—I have them all, and will, energy, and discretion, also. I see no one in the world, with its gods and men, who can shake me from my zeal. Behold a being who is pure!

"O Māra, Lust is your first battalion, your second is called Discontent. Your third is Hunger and Thirst, your fourth is Craving. Your fifth is Sloth and Torpor, your sixth is known as Fear. Your seventh battalion is Doubt, and your eighth is Hypocrisy and Cant.

"Gain, fame, honor, and glory ill-won, the exalting of oneself and the condemning of others,—such, Māra, is your force, the black scourge that heroes, not cowards, overcome. Behold, I am wearing armor! Better to me is death in battle than to live defeated!"

At these words Māra attempted to frighten and drive Gautama away with a whirlwind, a cloudburst, a shower of meteors, and a dense blackness, but to no avail. The wind which could have uprooted trees did not cause even the edge of the Bodhisattva's robe to flutter. The rain did not wet him: and the cinders that fell from the sky scattered themselves at the Bodhisattva's feet and changed into flowers and incense. And the darkness vanished like a shadow in sunlight when it reached the radiant figure of the Bodhisattva—such was the power of the Great Being's merit.

Unable to dislodge the Bodhisattva by these stratagems, Māra drew near to the Great Being and said, "Get up from this seat, Siddhārtha! It does not belong to you, but to me!"

"O Māra, you have not fulfilled the Ten Perfections," replied the Great Being, "nor have you made the Five Great Donations. You are not striving for the welfare of the world, or for Enlightenment. This seat does not belong to you, but to me."

Unable to restrain his rage, Māra hurled his discus; but when the Bodhisattva reflected on the Ten Perfections, the discus was transformed into a canopy of flowers.

"Māra, who is your witness to your having made donations?"

"All these, as many as you see here, are my witnesses."

And immediately Māra's demons cried one and all: "I am his witness, I am his witness!"

Then said Māra to the Great Being, "Siddhārtha, who is your witness to your having made donations?"

"Your witnesses are animate beings," replied the Bodhisattva, "and I have no animate witnesses present. However, disregarding the donations which I gave in other past existences, the great donations which I gave in my life as Prince Viśvaṇtara shall now be testified to by the solid earth, even though inanimate."

And stretching forth his right hand toward the earth, Gautama touched the ground with the tips of his fingers.

"Are you witness or are you not to my having given great donations in my Viśvaṇtara existence?"

A mighty thundering at once arose from the depths of the solid earth; and an invincible roar overwhelmed the armies of Māra with the tremendous utterance: "I, EARTH, BEAR YOU WITNESS!"

The clouds then began to disperse, calm came again to the countryside, and the last ruddy rays of sunset painted the treetops. The storm had subsided as quickly as it had come; and the Great Being found himself quite alone, still seated on the Diamond Throne under the Bodhi tree. And although he had been shaken during the brief conflict, a new strength then came to him, and he was suffused with a serenity more profound than he had ever experienced before.

• THE GREAT SUPREME • PERFECT ENLIGHTENMENT

Night had fallen, and the full moon peeped over the trees of the forest as if from a desire to behold the Great Being. And while the Bodhi tree sprinkled coral-red sprigs of bloom upon his robes as though doing homage to him, the Bodhisattva attained and abode in the four Absorptions of the fine-material sphere:

1. Detached from sensual desires and unwholesome thoughts, he entered the First Absorption, which is accompanied by reasoning and discursive thought, born of detachment, and filled with rapture and happiness.

2. After the fading away of reasoning and discursive thought, and by the gaining of inward tranquility and one-pointedness of mind, he entered into a state free from reasoning and discursive thought, the Second Absorption, which is born of concentration and filled with rapture and happiness.

3. After the fading out of rapture, he abode in equanimity—clearly conscious, mindful, and experiencing that feeling of which the Aryas say, "happy lives the man of equanimity and attentive mind,"—and thus entered the Third Absorption.

4. After the rejection of pleasure and pain, and through the cessation of previous joy and grief, he entered into a state beyond pleasure and pain, the Fourth Absorption, which is purified by equanimity and attentiveness.

a. Then beginning in the first watch of the night, with mind purified and concentrated, the Great Being directed his mind to the remembrance of his former existences up to hundreds of thousands of births, up to many cycles of dissolution and evolution of the universe.

"There I was of such and such a name, family, station of life, and livelihood," Gautama realized. "Such pleasure and pain did I experience; and passing away from there I was reborn elsewhere. Thus do I remember all of my many former existences with their special modes and details."

b. Then in the middle watch of the night the Great Being directed his mind to the passing away and rebirth of beings. With superhuman vision he saw them dying and being reborn, low and high, in happy or wretched existences according to their karma.

"Those beings who lead evil lives in deed, word, or thought," he realized, "who hold to false views and acquire unfavorable karma thereby, are reborn in a state of misery and suffering in hell. But those beings who lead good lives in deed, word, or thought, who hold to right views and acquire favorable karma thereby, are reborn in a state of joy and bliss in heaven."

c. Then in the last watch of the night the Great Being directed his mind to the complete destruction of the "Poisons," thereby acquiring a Wisdom in conformity with the reality of the Four Aryan Truths, namely, Suffering, its Cause, its Cessation, and the Path which leads to its cessation.

And as he thus knew and thus perceived, his mind was completely emancipated from the Poison of lust (sensual desire), from the Poison of existence-infatuation (the desire for continued sensate existence or for annihilation at death), from the Poison of false view (delusion and superstition), and from the Poison of ignorance (of the Four Aryan Truths).

And as the Great Being reflected on the Four Aryan Truths, his Fully Awakened Mind fathomed the twelve Causes in the chain of Dependent Origination.

"This being present as cause, that arises. This not being present as cause, that does not arise."

In the past life (he realized):

1. *There is ignorance.*
2. *Ignorance conditions the predisposing mental formations.*

In the present life:

3. *The predisposing mental formations condition discriminative consciousness.*
4. *Discriminative consciousness conditions mind-and-body.*
5. *Mind-and-body conditions the six senses.*

6. *The six senses condition contact.*
7. *Contact conditions feeling.*
8. *Feeling conditions craving.*
9. *Craving conditions attachment.*
10. *Attachment conditions the process of becoming.*

In the future life:

11. *The process of becoming conditions rebirth.*
12. *Rebirth conditions decay and death, likewise sorrow, lamentation, pain, grief, and despair.*

"Thus does this entire mass of suffering arise. But on the complete fading out and cessation of ignorance, this entire mass of suffering comes to an end."

And so the Great Being acquired in the last watch of the night the knowledge of the destruction of pain and the Path leading thereto. Ignorance was dispelled, Wisdom arose. Darkness was dispelled, Light arose.

Gautama had then attained the uttermost Wisdom, the perfect omniscience of Supreme Enlightenment. Nirvāṇa had at last been won: Siddhārtha Gautama had become an Utterly Perfect One, a Peerless Lord, a Supreme Buddha—Sugata, the Happy One. As a Tathāgata ("Successor of the Buddhas of Old"), Gautama was "Śākyamuni Buddha," the latest in the succession of Supreme Buddhas who have appeared at rare times in the worlds of beings.

And just as the first glimmer of dawn brightened the eastern sky, Gautama breathed forth that solemn utterance which, in essence, is said to be uttered by all the Buddhas upon their attainment of omniscience: "LOOKING FOR THE MAKER OF THIS HOUSE I HAVE RUN THROUGH A COURSE OF MANY BIRTHS, NOT FINDING HIM; AND PAINFUL IS BIRTH AGAIN AND AGAIN. BUT NOW, MAKER OF THIS HOUSE, YOU ARE SEEN! YOU SHALL NOT CONSTRUCT THIS HOUSE AGAIN! ALL YOUR RAFTERS ARE BROKEN, YOUR RIDGEPOLE IS SHATTERED! HAVING SUNDERED THE BONDS OF CRAVING, LIBERATION IS WON!"

These words had scarcely fallen from his lips when ten thousand world-systems quaked and thundered with the Great Being's attainment of Buddhahood. Flowers sprang up everywhere, exhaling perfume like celestial incense; and in the depths of the cosmos the pitch-black hells, which not even the light of seven suns had formerly been able to illuminate, were then flooded with radiance. And thus ended Gautama's six-year search for Truth.

The Perfect One remained sitting at the foot of the Bodhi tree for several days experiencing the bliss of Nirvāṇa's freedom. He pondered the arising and ending of all causes with the knowledge that he himself was completely emancipated from all fetters, both human and divine. For him rebirth had been destroyed; the holy life had been successfully pursued; DONE WAS ALL THAT NEEDED TO BE DONE.

V

THE WHEEL OF DOCTRINE TURNS AGAIN

• THE TEMPTATION •

Rising from the Diamond Throne at the foot of the Bodhi tree, the Buddha went to a certain banyan tree called the "goatherd's banyan" and sat in meditation there. Now, a certain brahmin priest of haughty disposition happened to be passing by; and when he saw Gautama he stopped and asked, "Tell me, which are the qualities that constitute a brahmin?"

"Friend, a man does not become a brahmin because of his caste or outward appearance," replied the Perfect One. "A highborn man may be arrogant and wealthy; but the poor man who is free from all attachments,—him do I call a brahmin.

"What is the use of your matted hair, vain man? What bearing does your raiment of goatskins have on the religious life? Within you there is ravening, but only the outside do you make clean. But the brahmin who has banished his evil traits, is free from pride, self-restrained and spotless—it is he alone who may claim the name of brahmin."

On hearing these words the brahmin went away, making no reply.

Then the Tathāgata went to a tree named for the serpent-king Mucalinda, and sat at its foot for several days again experiencing the bliss of freedom and release.

Now just at that time a great mass of clouds appeared out of season, and rain fell in dense sheets, driven hither and thither by cold winds.

"This has come about through the power of Māra," thought Śākyamuni. "He still seeks to dissuade me from the Holy Life."

Then appeared Māra before the eyes of the Buddha. By the use of thought-power the Evil One revealed all the kingdoms of the earth in all their glory and diversity to the Tathāgata's mind.

"See the glory of the world, the wealth of its cities, the number of its inhabitants. All this can be yours, Siddhārtha, if only you will abandon your meditation and devote yourself to almsgiving and other good works."

Buddha answered nothing.

"Think, Siddhārtha, is it right that you repudiate clan and family, and abandon child and wife? Is it not cowardly, this thing that you have done? How will you reply to the people who will find fault with you?"

Again the Exalted One answered nothing.

Māra, then becoming enraged, caused the water of the clouds to inundate the Tathāgata. But Mucalinda the serpent-king issued from his abode and spread his hood over the Perfect One's head so that not a single raindrop splashed upon the Tathāgata's body.

Failing to disturb Buddha's serenity by this tactic, the Evil One then made use of his last and most dangerous weapon. Through the power of mental creation, Māra caused three enticing female forms to appear.

"These are my daughters, Siddhārtha. Are they not beautiful and desirable? Take note, O prince, that they are beckoning for you to come and sport with them."

Then the Perfect One opened his mouth to speak.

"O Māra," he said, "there is One whose victory no one in the world can wrest away, One whom no desire, ensnaring and poisonous, can lead astray. By what path can you lead the Trackless?

"The kingdoms of the world and their glory which you have shown me, O Evil One, I renounced when I aspired to Buddhahood. Come, look at this world glittering like a royal chariot! Fools are absorbed in it; but the wise refuse even to touch it. Better than sovereignty over all the earth, better than lordship over all worlds, better, even, than going to heaven, is entering the stream that conducts to Nirvāṇa, the first step in holiness. If by abandoning a trifling happiness one gains a vision of a great happiness to come, the wise man will abandon the small happiness and pursue the great.

"Which do you think is better, the donation of wealth that perishes or the donation of that complete salvation which has nothing lacking and no limit? Verily, whatever gift of alms a man may make for a whole year to gain merit, the whole of it is not worth a farthing compared with reverence shown to the righteous.

"Have I repudiated clan and family as you say? What is my clan but the helmsman clan of Arhats who have crossed the ocean of life to the Farther Shore? Who are my ancestors but the Buddhas of olden times in whose footsteps I follow? Who are my child and wife but the teachings of the liberating Dharma? Only fools, Māra, censure the wise.

"I see through your three daughters, Evil One! The first is Tṛṣṇā (Craving), the second is Arati (Discontent), and the third is Rāga (Greedy Desire). I would not touch them even with my foot.

"O Māra, you have acted foolishly in trying to tempt me. Having attained Nirvāṇa, I am beyond temptation. I am Chief without superior. I have conquered all; I know all, and in all conditions of life I am free from taint. I have left all; and through the destruction of ignorance and craving I am free. Having myself supremely understood, whom should I indicate as my teacher?"

Thereupon Māra, dejected, let his lute slip down and passed from sight.

• THE DECISION TO TEACH •

After Māra had departed, Śākyamuni thought, "I have gained the Dharma which is profound, hard to perceive, transcendent, beyond the sphere of intellection, subtle, intelligible only to the wise: but this world of men is intent on its attachments, enfettered and blinded. It will therefore be difficult for mankind to understand the principle of origination by way of cause. It will be a hard task for the common people to comprehend the cessation of all composite things, the renunciation of all attachment to rebirth, the extinction of craving, the absence of passion, the winning of the Eternal Life of Nirvāṇa.

"Verily, if I were to teach them the Dharma and they did not understand it, it would be a weariness and vexation to me. Would it not be better if I were to spend the rest of my days in bliss and pass away into Nirvāṇa with the Dharma undivulged?"

When the god Brahmā perceived that the Tathāgata was averse to teaching the Dharma, he said with a voice of thunder: "Let my Lord the Perfect One teach the Dharma! For there are beings in the world whose sight is but little clouded with the dust of passion. They are perishing through not hearing the Dharma."

Buddha then looked upon the world with superhuman vision and saw that what Brahmā said was true: there were many intelligent beings who perceived peril in repeated rebirths and lived in fear of the ripening of evil deeds.

When the Perfect One reached the decision to teach the Dharma, he answered Brahmā, saying: "Open for such is the door to the Deathless State! Let them who have ears cast off their old, imperfect creeds! Conscious of danger in Dharma's profundity, Brahmā, I did not want to teach the Doctrine of Doctrines to men."

Buddha first thought of teaching the Dharma to Ārāda Kālāma and Rudraka Rāmaputra, his first teachers, as they were learned and wise and versed in pure living; but the knowledge arose that both of those worthies had previously died. Then he decided to teach the Dharma to the Band of the Five headed by Kauṇḍinya.

With divine vision surpassing that of men, the Tathāgata perceived that the five brahmin ascetics who had been his disciples were dwelling near Vārāṇasī in the Deer Park (Mṛgadāya) in the Place of Holy Men (Ṛṣivadana). And so, having remained in Uruvilvā as long as he wished, the Happy One set out in a northwesterly direction for Vārāṇasī in the country of the Kāśīs.

On the way he met a naked ascetic by the name of Upaka who greeted him courteously and asked whom the Great Being followed in retiring from the world. The Perfect One replied:

All wisdom's mine. Whom should I follow?
I have no teacher anywhere:
My equal nowhere can be found.
In all the world of gods and men
No one to rival me exists.

Victors like me are all of those
Who have vanquished depravity's poisons.
Conquered by me are evil things;
Hence a Victor am I, Upaka.

To set revolving pure Dharma's Wheel
I go to Vārāṇasī in Kāśī-land;
And in this blinded world I'll beat
The drum of Deathless Immortality.

• THE "TURNING-OF-THE-WHEEL" DISCOURSE AT VĀRĀṆASĪ •

Days later when the Perfect One had arrived at Ṛṣivadana in the Mṛgadāya a few miles east of Vārāṇasī, chief city of the Kāśīs, the five ascetics who had been Gautama's disciples did not rise to meet him when they saw him. Thinking that Gautama had given himself over to luxurious living, they agreed among themselves not to rise in respect nor to take his bowl and robe.

"We will merely set a seat for him; and if he wishes, he may sit down."

But so majestic was the Enlightened One's appearance, that the five brahmins were unable to hold to their agreement. One of them took Gautama's bowl and robe, another spread a seat for him, and another brought water for washing his feet. But when the Perfect One announced his Buddhahood, the brahmins would not believe him.

"Your stern austerities failed to enable you to transcend human limitations," they said. "How, then, now that you live in abundance, have given up striving and have devoted yourself to a life of luxury, can you have transcended human limitations and gained superhuman, truly Āryan knowledge and insight?"

"Monks," replied Śākyamuni, "the Tathāgata does not live luxuriously, nor has he given up striving. The Tathāgata, O monks, is an Arhat, a Supreme Buddha. As the Tathāgata speaks, so he does; as he does, so he speaks. Moreover, whatever the Tathāgata proclaims and teaches between the day of his Enlightenment and the day on which he passes utterly away—all that is truly so and not otherwise.

"Monks, in the cosmos with its universes and worlds, with its gods and men, the Tathāgata is all-conquering and unconquerable, all-seeing, superior to all. Confess, O monks, have I ever before spoken to you as I have spoken today?"

"Never before, Lord."

Thus Buddha succeeded in winning over the Band of the Five; and while the five monks took turns going for alms-food, the Awakened One exhorted and taught his disciples, saying: "Open your ears, O monks! The Kingdom of Righteousness is established once again: deliverance from death has been found!

"There are two extremes which should not be followed by one who strives for salvation. Which are the two? On the one hand, devotion to the pleasures of sense—a low, unāryan practice, vulgar, degrading, ruinous, and without any benefit. On the other hand, self-mortifications and penances—painful, gloomy, and without any benefit.

"Avoiding these two extremes, the Tathāgata has discovered that

Middle Way which leads to insight and wisdom, which conduces to tranquility, supreme Enlightenment, Nirvāṇa.

"Verily, O monks, it is the Āryan Eightfold Path, namely, Right View, Right Thought, Right Speech, Right Action, Right Livelihood, Right Effort, Right Attentiveness, Right Concentration.

"Why must beings suffer so much, O monks? It is by not understanding, not grasping, the Four Āryan Truths that we have had to wander so long in this weary round of rebirth, both you and I. And what are the four?

"The Āryan Truth about Suffering, the Āryan Truth about the Cause of Suffering, the Āryan Truth about the Cessation of Suffering, and the Āryan Truth about the Path that leads to the Cessation of Suffering.

I. "What, monks, is the Āryan Truth about Suffering? Birth is suffering, old age is suffering, sickness is suffering, death is suffering, likewise sorrow, lamentation, pain, grief, and despair. Contact with the unpleasant is suffering, separation from the pleasant is suffering, unsatisfied desire is suffering. In a word, the five craving-producing aggregates of mind-and-body (corporeality, feeling, perception, predisposing mental formations, and discriminative consciousness) are suffering.

II. "What, monks, is the Āryan Truth about the Cause of Suffering? Verily, suffering originates in that rebirth-causing craving which is accompanied by sensual pleasure and which seeks satisfaction now here, now there—craving for sensual pleasures, craving to be born again, craving to be annihilated.

III. "What, monks, is the Āryan Truth about the Cessation of Suffering? Verily, it is passionlessness, the complete destruction of this craving for sensual pleasures, for becoming, and for annihilation; the forsaking and relinquishing of this craving, the harboring no longer of this craving.

IV. "What, monks, is the Āryan Truth about the Path that leads to the Cessation of Suffering? Verily, it is this Āryan Eightfold Path of Right View, Right Thought, Right Speech, Right Action, Right Livelihood, Right Effort, Right Attentiveness, and Right Concentration. Pay close attention, monks, and I will expound and analyze the Āryan Eightfold Path for you.

1. "What, monks, is Right View? To view in accordance with reality suffering, its cause, its cessation, and the Path leading to its cessation.

2. "What, monks, is Right Thought? Thoughts free from sensuality, ill will, and cruelty.

3. "What, monks, is Right Speech? Speech free from deceit, malice, abuse, and silliness.

4. "What, monks, is Right Action? Action free from killing, stealing, adultery, lying, and the use of intoxicants. (These are the Five Precepts of Right Action.)

5. "What, monks, is Right Livelihood? When the Āryan disciple avoids an evil trade—soothsaying, trickery, usury, trading in weapons, in living beings, in meat, in intoxicants, and in poison—and gets his living by right and honorable means.

6. "What, monks, is Right Effort? There are four Right Efforts. Herein a disciple puts forth energy, incites his mind, and struggles (1) to prevent the arising of bad thoughts that have not yet arisen, (2) to dispel bad thoughts that have already arisen, (3) to develop good thoughts that have not yet arisen, and (4) to maintain good thoughts that have already arisen.

7. "What, monks, is Right Attentiveness? There are four Fundamentals of Attentiveness. What are they? Herein a monk abides self-possessed and attentive, contemplating, according to reality, (1) the body, (2) feelings, (3) the mind, and (4) thoughts, seeing all as composite, ever-becoming, impermanent, and subject to decay.

8. "What, monks, is Right Concentration? One-pointedness of Mind is concentration. Now, a monk, gaining one-pointedness of Mind (as through breathing exercises or special meditations), enters and abides in the four Fine-Material Absorptions and the four Immaterial Absorptions.

The Fine-Material Absorptions

1. Detached from sensual desires and unwholesome thoughts, he enters the First Absorption, which is accompanied by reasoning and discursive thought, born of detachment, and filled with rapture and happiness.

2. After the fading away of reasoning and discursive thought, and by the gaining of inward tranquility and one-pointedness of mind, he enters into a state free from reasoning and discursive thought, the Second Absorption, which is born of concentration and filled with rapture and happiness.

3. After the fading out of rapture, he abides in equanimity—clearly conscious, attentive, and experiencing that feeling of which the Āryas say, 'happy lives the man of equanimity and attentive mind'—and thus enters the Third Absorption.

4. After the rejection of pleasure and pain, and through the cessation of previous joy and grief, he enters into a state beyond pleasure and pain, the Fourth Absorption, which is purified by equanimity and attentiveness.

The Immaterial Absorptions

5. Through having completely transcended all perceptions in the fine-material sphere, and through the vanishing of sense-perceptions, and rising above the idea of multiform phenomena—at the idea 'space is boundless', he attains and abides in the Sphere of Boundless Space.

6. Through having completely transcended the Sphere of Boundless Space, at the idea 'consciousness is infinite' he attains and abides in the Sphere of Infinite Consciousness.

7. Through having completely transcended the Sphere of Infinite Consciousness, at the idea 'nothing really exists' he attains and abides in the Sphere of No-thingness.

8. Through having completely transcended the Sphere of Nothingness, he attains and abides in the Sphere of Neither-perception-nor-nonperception.

"WHETHER BUDDHAS ARISE OR NOT, O MONKS, IT REMAINS A FACT AND THE FIXED AND NECESSARY CONSTITUTION OF CONDITIONED EXISTENCE THAT ALL ITS CONSTITUENTS ARE IMPERMANENT, PRODUCTIVE OF PAIN, AND DEVOID OF REALITY. BUT WHEN A BUDDHA ARISES, HE DISCOVERS, PROCLAIMS, AND TEACHES THIS FACT. NOW, WHOEVER KNOWS AND UNDERSTANDS THESE THREE CHARACTERISTICS OF FINITE EXISTENCE—TRANSIENCE, SUFFERING, AND IMPERSONALITY—BECOMES IMMUNE TO PAIN. THIS IS THE WAY OF PURITY; AND THE WISE AND MORAL MAN WHO KNOWS THE MEANING OF THESE THINGS SHOULD QUICKLY CLEAR THE WAY THAT CONDUCTS TO NIRVĀNA'S BLISS.

"But keep in mind, monks, that the Buddhas only point out the way: you yourselves must make the effort. Not to commit moral offense, to do good, and to cleanse one's heart—this is the teaching of all the Buddhas."

Now when the Perfect One had set the Wheel of Dharma revolving, the gods of heaven and earth raised a mighty shout of exultation. Ten thousand worlds shook, shuddered, and trembled; and a boundless light of immeasurable intensity appeared, surpassing the divine radiance of the gods.

• THE FIRST DISCIPLES •

Kauṇḍinya instantly perceived the Dharma, and thus was henceforth called Ājñāta-Kauṇḍinya (Kauṇḍinya, Possessor of Highest Wisdom). And Buddha accepted him as the first monk of the Saṅgha (Order of Monks) with the words, "Come, monk, well proclaimed is the Dharma! Lead the life religious for making a complete end of pain!"

Then Buddha addressed the other four ascetics, saying: "If the followers of another teacher were to ask you, 'Is it in order to be reborn in heaven that the Ascetic Gautama leads a holy life?' wouldn't you be ashamed of that preposterous idea?"

"Yes, Master."

"Then it would appear to me that you are ashamed of and detest the idea of life in heaven, heavenly beauty and happiness, heavenly glory and power. But much more, O monks, should you be ashamed of and detest evil deeds, evil speech, and evil thoughts."

Themselves subject to death and rebirth, the four ascetics then understood the wretchedness of all that is subject to death and rebirth, and, like Ājñāta-Kauṇḍinya, attained Nirvāṇa. And they likewise donned yellow robes and entered the Saṅgha.

The Perfect One then preached to the five monks on the absence of the True Self in anything that the senses or the mind can grasp.

"O monks, the thing variously called thought and mind and discriminative consciousness is the very same thing to which the ignorant common people cling, thinking, 'this is my self.' It would be better, monks, if they were to approach the body, rather than the mind, as the self. The body is seen enduring for many years, but this thing variously called thought and mind and discriminative consciousness, this by night and day dissolves as one thing and reappears as another.

"As a monkey faring through jungle and forest catches hold of a bough, and having let go takes hold of another, even so does this thing variously called thought and mind and discriminative consciousness, this by night and day dissolves as one thing and reappears as another.

"The body, monks, is not the self. For if it were, it would not be subject to disease, and it would be exactly as we might wish it to be. So also with feelings, perceptions, predisposing mental formations, and discriminative consciousness. For if, monks, the consciousness were the self, it would not be subject to anguish, and it would be exactly as we might wish it to be.

"Monks, what do you think? Is the body permanent or perishable?"

"Perishable, Lord," answered the monks.

"And that which is perishable, does it cause pain or lasting happiness?"

"It causes pain, Lord."

"But is it correct to regard what is perishable and painful as 'this is my ego, this is my soul, this is my true self'?"

"Certainly not, Lord."

"As with body, monks, so also with feelings, perceptions, predisposing mental formations, and discriminative consciousness. Would it be correct to regard any of these aggregates, perishable and painful, as 'this is my ego, this is my soul, this is my true self'?"

"That is impossible, Lord."

"Well, monks, that being the case, he who is able to see all things as they really are will regard all bodies, feelings, perceptions, predispositions, and discriminative consciousnesses, be they past, present, or future, be they internal or external, gross or subtle, far or near, as 'none of these is my ego, none of these is my soul, none of these is my true self.'

"Considering this, O monks, the wise Āryan disciple turns away from body, feelings, perceptions, predispositions, and discriminative consciousness. Turning away from them, he becomes free from craving; through being free from craving, he becomes emancipated; and in him who is emancipated the knowledge arises: 'I am free; rebirth is exhausted; lived is the life religious; nothing more remains to be done; there is no more of life under finite conditions.' "

Thus spoke Śākyamuni Buddha; and well pleased were the monks with his words. Now at that time there were six Arhats in the world: the Buddha, Ājñāta-Kauṇḍinya, Bhadrika, Vāṣpa, Mahānāma, and Aśvajit.

• THE STORY OF YAŚAS; • THE "SENDING FORTH"

At that time there lived in Vārāṇasī a noble youth named Yaśas, son of a wealthy guildmaster. Having secretly overheard a few words of the Perfect One's discourses in the park called Mṛgadāya, he conceived a disgust for his life of idle luxury.

One morning shortly after dawn, Yaśas ran away from home and went to the Deer Park where Buddha, having risen early, was walking in the open air. Seeing Yaśas approaching from afar, the Perfect One sat down on a seat which had been prepared for him.

"How oppressive, how afflicting is the household life!" exclaimed Yaśas as he drew near to the Exalted One.

"But life in the open air, Yaśas, is not oppressive, not afflicting. Come, Yaśas, sit down, and I will teach you the Dharma."

Having saluted the Master with due obeisance, Yaśas sat down at one side. Buddha then talked to him about almsgiving, morality, heaven, the wretchedness of lusts, and the blessings of renunciation; and when the Tathāgata saw that the mind of Yaśas was prepared, susceptible, elated, and happy, he expounded the Four Āryan Truths. And as a clean cloth free from stains readily takes the dye, so in Yaśas arose the pure, unstained insight that everything subject to birth is also subject to dissolution.

Now, Yaśas' parents, unable to find their son, became anxious and sent out messengers to search for him. The guildmaster himself set out for the Deer Park in Ṛṣivadana; and when Buddha saw the guildmaster approaching, he made Yaśas invisible by an exercise of supernormal power.

When the guildmaster came to the Perfect One, he said, "Perchance the reverend Master has seen my son Yaśas, who ran away from home."

"Well, householder, sit down, and perhaps you can see Yaśas nearby."

Then the Tathāgata instructed the guildmaster in the Dharma; and so marvelously compelling were Buddha's words that the guildmaster obtained clearness of mind with all his doubts and uncertainties dispelled.

"Wonderful, Lord!" he exclaimed. "It is just as if one were to set up what had been overturned, or to reveal what had been hidden, or to show the way to the lost, or to dispel darkness with a lamp! To the Buddha I go for refuge! To the Dharma I go for refuge! To the Saṅgha I go for refuge! May the Perfect One accept me as a lay-disciple from this day forward as long as life shall last!"

The Vārāṇasī guildmaster was thus the first to become a Buddhist by uttering the Threefold Refuge.

Meantime, Yaśas, who had listened to the instruction given to his father, attained Arhatship. Buddha, realizing what had happened, then caused Yaśas to become visible to his father's sight. And as Yaśas was then free from attachment, he could not possibly return to the lower life of the world, but was ordained as the sixth member of the Saṅgha having Śākyamuni Buddha as its head.

Thus the Dharma began to illuminate the world with the light of salvation. And when, in a few weeks, the number of Arhats had increased to sixty-one, the Perfect One empowered them to ordain others who wished to enter the Saṅgha. He sent them forth as missionaries, saying: "O monks, you are released, as I, from all human bondage and from all divine enslavement. Go forth, O monks, and wander about for the gain of many, for the happiness of many, out of compassion for the world, for the welfare, for the gain, for the happiness of gods and men. Let not any two of you go together.

"Proclaim, O monks, the glorious Dharma, lovely in its beginning, lovely in its middle, and lovely in its end, both in the spirit and in the letter. Preach a life of holiness, perfect and pure. There are pure-minded beings in the world who are perishing through not hearing the Dharma. Such as they will become knowers of the Dharma.

"This is the only Way; there is no other that leads to the purification of insight. Just as a lily grows to full sweet-scented perfection even on a heap of rubbish by the roadside, so must you, O disciples, outshine the blinded worldling by your knowledge even among those who are mere living rubbish.

"Go, now, monks, while the season is ripe. As for myself, I intend to return to the army-township of Uruvilvā to teach the Dharma there."

VI

SPREAD OF THE DOCTRINE

• THE JOURNEY TO URUVILVĀ; • DISCOURSE ON KARMA

*O*n his way to Uruvilvā, the Perfect One sat down in a forest grove to rest. Now, in that very grove was a sporting party of thirty princes, twenty-nine of whom were accompanied by their wives, and the thirtieth by his mistress.

While the princes and their consorts were making merry, the courtesan ran away with some of the young men's jewel-studded cloaks. Searching for her, the young men asked the Tathāgata if he had seen where the woman had gone.

"Which do you think is better, young men," answered Buddha, "to go looking for a woman or to go in search of yourselves?"

"I suppose, sir," answered one of the men, "that it is better to go in search of ourselves."

The princes and their wives then sat down while the Perfect One preached the Dharma to them. All were converted: the princes entered the Saṅgha as monks, and the women took refuge in Buddha as lay disciples.

Soon afterwards Śākyamuni was sitting cross-legged under a banyan when a brahmin by the name of Droṇa chanced to see him. The noble figure of the Buddha sitting in the posture of meditation under the tree was thought by Droṇa to be the materialization of a divine being.

Drawing near to the Tathāgata with reverent feelings of awe, Droṇa asked: "Is your reverence a god, perhaps?"

"I am certainly not a god," replied the Perfect One.

"Then your reverence is perhaps a gandharva or a yakṣa?"

"I am indeed neither a gandharva nor a yakṣa."

"Then is your reverence perhaps only a human being?"

"Indeed, brahmin, I am not a mere human being."

"But, your reverence!" exclaimed Droṇa in bewilderment. "If you are not a god, nor a nonhuman being, nor a mere human being—what, pray, can you be?"

"Those tendencies which would have made me a god, or a nonhuman being, or a human being," explained the Perfect One, "have been thoroughly given up, completely rooted out, like the stump of a palm tree, and are incapable of reappearing.

"O brahmin, just as a lotus, born in the water, grown up in the water, raises itself above the water and stands there without being polluted by the water—in the same way, O brahmin, though I was born in the world and grew up in the world, did I transcend the world; and having transcended the world, I live as one who is not polluted by the world. As BUDDHA should you know me, O brahmin!"

And Droṇa there and then worshiped him who is infinitely superior to the gods, even the highest.

Continuing on the road to Uruvilvā, the Tathāgata met a brahmin student by the name of Śubha. On seeing the Perfect One, Śubha exchanged courteous and cordial greetings with him and sat down at one side.

"Now what, Master Gautama, is the reason why differences are seen among human beings—some of low birth, some of high; some stupid, some intelligent; some of bad health, others healthy and strong, and so on?"

"Beings, student," replied Buddha, "are the heirs of karma. Karma distributes beings according to birth, capabilities, health, and so forth. That is why human beings differ so widely in condition and station.

"Even an evildoer can experience happiness until his evil deed ripens; but when it ripens he experiences torment. Even a good man can experience evil things until his good deed ripens; but when it ripens he experiences happiness.

"Not in the sky, not in the depths of the sea, not if one hides in mountain caves, is there known a place in all the world where a man might escape the aftermath of an evil deed or not be overcome by death.

"A being, student, is the master of his destiny. Oneself is lord of oneself—who else could be the lord? By oneself the evil is done, by oneself one suffers. By oneself the evil is left undone, by oneself one is purified. *The pure and the impure stand and fall by themselves: no one can purify another.*

"Reflect well, student. There is the case of a person who takes life, cruel, with bloodstained hands, given to striking and killing, and having no mercy upon living things. When the karma of that person is worked out and completed, with the dissolution of the body at death he is reborn in a state of woe, in an unhappy condition of life, or in hell.

"Then there is the case of a person who has put aside harming and the taking of life, who has renounced the use of deadly weapons, and dwells mild-mannered, full of kindliness, and compassionate for the welfare of all living things. When the karma of that person is worked out and completed, with the dissolution of the body at death he is reborn in a state of happiness, in a felicitous condition of life, or in heaven."

• THE "FIRE SERMON" AT GAYĀŚĪRṢA •

When Buddha had reached the district of Uruvilvā, he took residence in the hermitage of Uruvilvā-Kāśyapa, the leader of five hundred fire-worshiping ascetics. The Perfect One preached and converted all of them, whereupon Uruvilvā-Kāśyapa and his disciples threw their sacrificial utensils into the river Nairañjanā.

At a little distance downstream dwelt Uruvilvā-Kāśyapa's two brothers, Nadī-Kāśyapa (Kāśyapa of the River) and Gayā-Kāśyapa, having three hundred and two hundred disciples, respectively. Now, when these two saw the utensils floating by, they thought that some misfortune had befallen their elder brother, and they hastened to inquire.

Buddha also converted Uruvilvā-Kāśyapa's two brothers to the Dharma; and at last the three Kāśyapa's, together with their thousand pupils, cut off their hair, put on saffron robes, and joined the Exalted One's Saṅgha.

The Tathāgata then proceeded to Gayāśīrṣa (Gayā-Head) with the great assembly of monks. And it happened that a forest fire was just then playing over slopes of the Vindhya Hills. When the Master saw the scarlet flames greedily devouring the jungle and belching forth angry billows of murky smoke, he bade the monks be seated.

"All things, O monks, are on fire," he said. "The eye is on fire; visible forms are on fire. Impressions received by the eye are on fire, and whatever sensation—pleasant, unpleasant, or neutral—that originates in dependence on impressions received by the eye is also on fire.

"Likewise, monks, the ear, sounds, impressions received by the ear, and all sensations based on impressions received by the ear are on fire. The nose, odors, impressions received by the nose, and all sensations based on impressions received by the nose are on fire. The tongue, tastes, impressions received by the tongue, and all sensations based on impressions received by the tongue are on fire. The body, tangibles, impressions received by the body, and all sensations based on impressions received by the body are on fire. The mind, ideas, impressions received by the mind, and all sensations based on impressions received by the mind are on fire.

"And with what are all these things on fire?

"Verily, with the fire of delusion, with the fire of passion, with the fire of hatred are they on fire, with birth, old age, sickness, death, sorrow, lamentation, misery, grief, and despair are they on fire.

"Perceiving this, O monks, the intelligent Āryan disciple conceives an indifference toward the sense organs, their objects and impressions, and the sensations based on those impressions. And in conceiving this indifference he becomes shorn of craving, and by the absence of craving he becomes free. Realizing his freedom, he realizes that he has transcended all possible modes of finite existence and has attained Nirvāṇa."

On hearing these words, all of the thousand monks, together with the three Kāśyapa's, attained Nirvāṇa; that is to say, they became Arhats.

• BUDDHA'S PROMISE • TO BIMBISĀRA FULFILLED

Recalling his promise to King Bimbisāra of Magadha, made when he was yet a Bodhisattva in quest of Enlightenment, Buddha journeyed with the thousand Arhats to the Magadhan capital Rājagṛha.

Śrenika Bimbisāra and all the people of Rājagṛha went to the grove where the Perfect One was staying; and when they saw Uruvilvā-Kāśyapa there, they argued among themselves as to whether the Perfect One was Kāśyapa's disciple or not. So the Perfect One addressed Kāśyapa in the presence of the people, asking him why he had discarded his sacrificial utensils. Kāśyapa replied that when he had perceived the moral stain involved in fire sacrifice, he had ceased to take pleasure in it. And then, bowing his head at the Exalted One's feet, he said: "My teacher, Lord, is the Perfect One. I am his disciple."

Buddha then addressed the people with a discourse on almsgiving, morality, heaven, the wretchedness of the passions, the three Unwholesome Roots of greed, hatred, and delusion, and the blessing of rejecting worldly ties.

"Do not be afraid of doing good deeds!" he admonished the people. " 'Good deeds' is merely another name for happiness, for what is pleasant, charming, dear, and delightful."

And then he told the people that, as a result of deeds of charity, self-control, and good manners in former lives, he, himself, had been reborn many times as a god—even as a Brahmā, an unconquerable conqueror, as gods go. Then the Tathāgata declared: "Now, if beings knew, as I know, the ripening of sharing gifts, they would not enjoy the use of gifts without sharing them, nor would the taint of stinginess obsess the heart and there remain. Even if it were their last possession, their last morsel of food, they would not enjoy its use without sharing it, if there were anyone to receive it.

"Whatever motives people have for doing good works with a view to favorable rebirth, all of them are not worth a sixteenth part of that loving-friendliness which is the heart's release. Loving-friendliness alone shines and burns and flashes forth in surpassing them just as the radiance of the moon shines and burns and flashes forth in surpassing the radiance of the stars."

When Śākyamuni saw that the mind of the multitude was prepared and free from bias, well-disposed and elated, he preached the praiseworthy Dharma of all the Buddhas, namely, Anguish, its Cause, its Extinction, and the Path leading to its extinction.

And many of the people, including King Bimbisāra, understood then and there that craving is the cause of rebirth, while karma determines the mode and condition of the future life. They understood, too, that when craving is destroyed, rebirth is ended and Nirvāṇa gained—the Secure Refuge, the Shelter, the Place of Safety, Power, Bliss, Happiness, the Supreme Good, the Worthiest Goal, Supreme Reality, the one and only Truth, the eternal, hidden, and incomprehensible Peace.

King Bimbisāra, perceiving the Dharma with all his doubts and perplexities gone, bowed before the World-Honored One and said: "Formerly, Lord, when I was yet a prince, I made five wishes. The first: 'May I be consecrated king!' The second: 'May an Arhat, a Buddha, come to my kingdom!' The third: 'May I have the opportunity of worshiping such a Lord!' The fourth: 'May that Lord instruct me in the Buddha-Dharma!' The fifth: 'May I understand the Dharma when it comes to pass that I shall hear it!' Until today, Lord, only my first wish had been fulfilled; but now all of them have come true!

"May the Perfect One receive me as a lay disciple from this day forward as long as life shall last! May the Perfect One accept a meal from me tomorrow together with this great company of monks! May the Perfect One accept my pleasure park, the Veṇuvana (Bamboo Grove) in Kalandaka-Nivāpa (the Squirrels' Feeding Ground), as the site of a monastery which I intend to build for the Perfect One and his Saṅgha!"

• ŚĀRIPUTRA AND • MAUDGALYĀYANA BECOME DISCIPLES

At that time a wandering ascetic by the name of Sañjaya was dwelling at Rājagṛha in company with two hundred and fifty disciples. Two of this company, Upatiṣya Śāriputra and Kolita Maudgalyāyana, had made an agreement that the first to attain Nirvāṇa was to tell it to the other.

Now, it also happened that the venerable Aśvajit, one of the Band of the Five whom Buddha had converted to the Dharma at Vārāṇasī, was making the rounds of Rājagṛha for alms.

The moment Śāriputra caught sight of Aśvajit, his spirits rose.

"That surely must be a true Arhat, or else a monk who has entered the Path which conducts to Arhatship. I will follow him; and when the opportunity presents itself, I will ask him whose doctrine he follows."

As soon as Aśvajit had finished making his rounds, winning the hearts of men by his sober and friendly mien, Śāriputra approached him courteously and asked the question he had in mind.

"Friend," replied Aśvajit, "there is a mighty Sage of the Śākyas who is my Master. To follow the Dharma taught by this Master, I have retired from the world."

"But what," asked Śāriputra, "is your teacher's doctrine?"

"I am not good at speeches," said Aśvajit. "It would be difficult for me to explain the whole Dharma; but I can give you the gist of it."

"Why waste words? It is the gist of it that I want!"

The venerable Aśvajit then recited to Śāriputra an exposition of the Dharma in a verse:

Of things proceeding from a cause
Their cause the Tathāgata reveals,
And also how things cease to be.
All this the Great Ascetic teaches.

On hearing this verse there arose in the mind of Śāriputra a clear knowledge of the whole Dharma. He paid his respects to Aśvajit and hurried back to his hermitage where Maudgalyāyana was. And Maudgalyāyana, seeing the radiance of Śāriputra's face, knew that his friend had attained Nirvāṇa.

When Śāriputra recited Aśvajit's verse to him, Maudgalyāyana also attained Nirvāṇa. The two friends then told the matter to Sañjaya's disciples, with the result that all but a few of them abandoned Sañjaya's teaching and went over straightway to the Tathāgata. But Sañjaya, himself, refused to recognize Śākyamuni as a worthy teacher. In a fit of rage he suffered a stroke, hot blood pouring from his mouth.

When Buddha saw coming toward him the band of converts headed by the wise and patient Śāriputra and the mighty and deep Maudgalyāyana, he prophesied:

These two good friends are coming,
Kolita Maudgalyāyana and Upatisya Śāriputra.
They shall be my jewel-pair of disciples,
The chief, an excellent pair.

The two who were to become the Perfect One's chief disciples—Śāriputra, "General of the Dharma," and Maudgalyāyana, "Chief of those possessing supernormal powers"—were ordained by Buddha himself, and likewise all those who had accompanied them.

After the monastery had been built by King Bimbisāra in the Veṇuvana, another famous disciple entered the Order, Mahā-Kāśyapa, that is to say, Kāśyapa the Great. He, through a practical joke of letter-carriers, had been forced to marry a girl whom he did not love. Both he and Bhadrā, his bride, deciding to renounce the world, went their separate ways. Mahā-Kāśyapa chose Lord Buddha as his Master; and he became renowned as "Chief of those who undertake extra austerities."

• ŚUDDHODANA'S INVITATION TO BUDDHA •

News of the Perfect One's teaching was carried over all Jambudvīpa, that Roseapple Land of India, and even to the northern country of the Śākyas. Now, although King Śuddhodana was amazed and delighted by his son's success, he still held fast to the hope that Prince Siddhārtha would give up the religious life and return to Kapilavastu to assume royal rule.

Śuddhodana Gautama accordingly dispatched a royal minister accompanied by a retinue of courtiers to Rājagṛha to invite Buddha to visit Kapilavastu.

At the time of the minister's arrival in the Veṇuvanārāma (Veṇuvana Monastery), the Perfect One was preaching a discourse to a congregation of monks. And on hearing the words of the Perfect One, both the royal minister and his retinue were converted to the Dharma; and each and every man joined the Saṅgha. Soon all of them attained the highest goal, Nirvāṇa; and because Arhats are indifferent to worldly things, they neglected to transmit Śuddhodana's invitation to his illustrious son.

Again and again King Śuddhodana sent messengers to the Magadhan capital, and each time the same thing happened: the Śākyan nobles renounced the world, shaved their heads, and assumed the yellow robe of the Saṅgha.

At long last Śuddhodana requested a young noble named Kālodāyin, who had been a playmate of Prince Siddhārtha, to bring the Ten-Powered One back to Kapilavastu.

"You are of the same age as he," said Śuddhodana, "you are akin to me, and my affection for you is well known. My son will heed your words."

"If I, O king, may also join the Ten-Powered One's Saṅgha, then I will bring him hither," replied Kālodāyin.

"Very well, assume the garb of an ascetic if you insist. But whatever you do, show me my son. Bring him back that his own kith and kin may hear him preach the Dharma. If my son could now see the magnificence of my peaceful kingdom and the contentedness of my subjects, he will surely accept the throne he spurned nearly ten years ago."

Now when Kālodāyin had completed his journey to the country of the Magadhas and had come to the Veṇuvana monastery, he thought: "It is not yet time for the Perfect One to return to Kapilavastu. When the rains have come, clothing the earth with verdure, then it will be the proper time."

Joining the Saṅgha, Kālodāyin attained Arhatship and spent his time in meditation until the first rains had brought forth fresh foliage and the brilliant glory of blossoming shrubs. And put in mind of his promise to King Śuddhodana by the beauties of nature, he approached the Tathāgata and said:

Now crimson glow the trees, dear Lord, and cast
Their ancient foliage in quest of fruit.
Like crests of flame they shine irradiant,
And rich in joy, great Hero, is the hour.

Verdure and blossom-time in every tree,
Where'er we look delightful to the eye,
And every quarter breathing fragrant airs,
While petals falling, yearning comes for fruit:
'Tis time, O Hero, that we set out hence.

Not over hot nor over cold, but sweet,
O Master, now the season of the year.
O let the Śākyas and the Kolyas
Behold thee with thy face set toward the west,
Crossing the border river Rohiṇī.

Surely a hero lifts to lustrous purity
Seven generations past wherever he be born.
And so methinks can he, the Vastly Wise, the God
Of Gods. In thee is born in very truth a Seer.

Śuddhodana is named the Mighty
Prophet's sire,
And mother of the Buddha was our Queen Māyā.
She, having borne the Bodhisattva in her womb,
Found, when the body died, delight in Tuṣita.

Considering that salvation would come to many by his going, Buddha consented by his silence to return to Kapilavastu; and Kālodāyin, having perceived the Perfect One's assent, preceded him to the Śākyan capital.

King Śuddhodana failed to recognize Kālodāyin, shorn and yellow-robed; so his former courtier revealed his identity by saying: "I am a son of Buddha, Achiever of the impossible, the Holy, the Peerless, the Perfect One. The father of my Father are you, great Śākyan chief; and through the Dharma you, Śuddhodana Gautama, are my grandfather."

VII

AT KAPILAVASTU

• BUDDHA SNUBBED BY THE ŚĀKYAS •

The snowcapped peaks of Himālaya reared up in the north as Buddha and a company of twenty thousand Arhats walked along the mud-caked road leading to Kapilavastu. Soon they were inside the city limits, crossing the little river Rohiṇī over a rustic bridge that creaked and trembled under the rumbling wheels of farmers' ox-carts.

The houses of the city were decorated with flowering branches and garlands in honor of Śākyamuni; and crowds attired in festive garb flocked toward the illustrious son of their monarch to accord him a royal welcome. Royal ministers were on hand to conduct the Perfect One and his monks to a monastery which had been built for them in the Nigrodhārāma (Banyan Park).

When Buddha and the twenty thousand Arhats were settled in the monastery, King Śuddhodana and his court, together with many hundreds of his noble relatives, entered Banyan Park to pay their respects.

"My dear son!" exclaimed Śuddhodana, his voice choked by emotion. "How I have longed for this auspicious day! Tell me, Siddhārtha, how are you faring? Are you well and happy?"

"O king, I fare well and happily," said Buddha, "and to see you face to face is a joy such as only a son can understand."

The king embraced his son affectionately; but the Perfect One's failure to kneel in filial respect disturbed him.

"Of course you are to occupy your old apartments in the palace while your disciples remain in the monastery," said Śuddhodana. "Your son Rāhula and Princess Yaśodharā are waiting to welcome you."

"As for Rāhula and Yaśodharā, O king," replied Buddha, "I shall pay my respects to them both in due time. But these monks you see here are my true sons: it is not fitting that I dwell apart from them amid regal splendors."

Śuddhodana felt a flush of annoyance rise to his cheeks.

"This is not the country of the Magadhas, Siddhārtha! This is your own kingdom, and these are your own people. My old age might be easier to bear had you not run away from the responsibilities of royal rule to emulate the brahmins!"

Devadatta, a cousin of the Perfect One, then turned to the assemblage of Śākyan nobles and said: "My good sirs, is a man who has chosen the yellow rags of beggary instead of royal rule likely to surround himself with warriors instead of monks? Truly, the son of the king must first renounce this philosophical madness of his before ascending the throne!"

The Śākyan nobles muttered assent to Devadatta's words; but the Tathāgata held himself erect with the dignity and serenity of a Supreme Buddha while his kinsmen stared at him with disapproval in their eyes.

The venerable Kālodāyin could endure the awkward situation no longer.

"Good sirs!" he cried in a loud voice, "the Master has come hither by your king's invitation that you might hear the Dharma from him who discovered it!"

"Yes, Siddhārtha," said the king, "do by all means explain to us the Dharma. Friend Kālodāyin has already told us somewhat concerning it, and it seems most commendable—do not kill, steal, and so forth. But since we hear these things all the time from the brahmin teachers, pray waste no words. Better for you to exchange those yellow garments for royal vesture and help us plan defenses against the Kolyas who threaten to attack our peaceful land!"

The Blessed One then turned his face from Śuddhodana and looked upon his disciples.

"O monks, I do not see any other single obstacle, hindered by which humanity for a long, long time fares up to heaven and down to hell and wanders on from world to world, like this obstacle of ignorance.

"Here, monks, I discern persons of corrupt mind to be such because I compass their thoughts with my thought. And if at this very moment these persons were to meet their end, they would go just as they are into hell according to their karma. What is the reason for that? Their corrupt minds, monks."

Hearing these words of condemnation, the sullen Śākyan nobles turned their backs upon the Light of the World and made ready to return to their dwellings. But at that very moment Buddha performed the "miracle of the pairs" and astonished the people.

Knowing that nothing short of a spectacular display of supernormal power would suffice to soften the proud hearts of the Śākyas, the Tathāgata ascended into the air while flames of fire issued upwards from his body and torrents of water poured down. Then the flames went downward while the water went up toward the sky. Next, fire came from the right side of his body, and water from the left. Then the fire and water changed sides.

After twenty-two variations of pairs had been exhibited, Śākyamuni exercised his supernormal powers to create the illusion of a jeweled promenade in the sky along which he walked.

Coming down from the sky, Buddha told the people the story of his existence as King Viśvaṇtara, which preceded his birth as a god in Tuṣita Heaven. And then King Śuddhodana and all the nobles realized that they beheld, not just a man, not a mere god or god's messenger, but a Buddha Supreme.

• CONVERSION OF THE ROYAL FAMILY •

The following day the Perfect One and his disciples made the rounds of the city, begging alms-food from house to house. Now it happened that Princess Yaśodharā, looking out upon the street from a window of the royal palace, saw the Great Being begging food in the manner of a religious mendicant. And being filled with wonder at the sight, she informed the king that she, too, would put on yellow robes and live on simple food.

But Śuddhodana was indignant. He hurried from the palace into the morning sunlight of the street where he found his son begging food.

"My son," cried Śuddhodana with dismay, "why do you disgrace me so, asking for gifts like a homeless beggar?"

"This has always been the custom of my Ancestors," replied Buddha.

"Your ancestors! How can your speak as you do? Our lineage is the noble lineage of Mahāsammata; and not one noble has ever abased himself so far as to beg his daily bread!"

"That royal lineage is your lineage, O king," said the Perfect One, "but mine is the Buddha-lineage of Dīpaṅkara. The Buddhas of the past did even as I am doing, and the Buddhas who are to come in future time will also do as I am doing."

And standing there in the street, Śākyamuni addressed the king with a verse.

Away with languor—be alert and practice Dharma!
Dharma-farers live happily in this world and the next.

On hearing this verse the king, mind illumined by the first glimmer of insight, became a Stream-Entrant and realized the first step on the Path to Nirvāṇa. Taking the Sugata's begging bowl, Śuddhodana conducted Buddha together with the monks to the royal palace where they were accorded honors and treated to a meal.

After the meal was finished, the Tathāgata gladdened the nobles of the royal court with a discourse on religion, converting all of them to the Āryan Dharma. Then all the women of the royal household, with the sole exception of Yaśodharā, came to Lord Buddha and worshiped him. Prajāpatī, the Great Being's aunt and foster mother, was the first of these women to be converted to the Dharma.

When Yaśodharā was asked by her attendants to pay her respects to the Great Being, she said, "If I mean anything at all to him, my husband will come to me of his own accord; and having come into my presence, I will worship him as it pleases me."

When the Tathāgata heard of this, he addressed the king, saying: "Do not hold it against her. The king's daughter-in-law may do reverence to me as she wishes."

Thereupon the Perfect One went to Yaśodharā's chamber, accompanied by Śāriputra and Maudgalyāyana, and sat on a seat placed near the door.

Yaśodharā was dressed, not in the costly finery befitting her royal station, but in the simple yellow robes of a nun. Her face, no longer adorned by cosmetic artifice, seemed very young and guileless.

"When I saw you this morning wearing yellow robes, my Lord," she said, "I, too, put on yellow robes. When they told me, after I saw you begging food, that you eat from a beggar's bowl, I, too, resolved to eat from a bowl. When I heard that you had renounced a luxurious bed, I, too, resolved to lie on a narrow couch. When I knew that you had given up garlands and perfume, I, too, gave them up."

Then she sank down before him, weeping as she clasped his ankles and placed his feet upon her head, doing reverence to him according to her desire. And when she had finished doing so, Buddha praised her, telling her that she had been faithful and devoted to him not only in that life, but also in former existences.

"You were my wife Madrī in my Viśvaṇtara existence; and the assistance you gave me then to reach the consummation of Bodhisattvahood has reaped for you an inexhaustible store of merit."

The following day Nanda, the Perfect One's half-brother, was to be crowned king. Royal celebration was in progress: bands of musicians were playing, and military exercises were taking place. And that same day was also the occasion of Nanda's marriage.

"Come, your reverence," said Nanda to the Tathāgata, "and confer a blessing upon my bride and myself by accompanying us to the parade ground to watch the strength of the Śākyas in military display."

Buddha explained that it is not fitting for Arhats to witness military parades and war games; but he handed Nanda his bowl while he pronounced a formula of good luck. Then the Perfect One returned to the Nigrodha monastery without taking back his bowl, for Nanda had neglected to give it back to him.

Nanda, accordingly, followed the Tathāgata to the monastery; and when he had returned the bowl, the Tathāgata said: "Well, Nanda, are you going to leave the world?"

"Yes, Lord," stammered Nanda without thinking, "I am going to leave the world!"

The Perfect One then instructed Śāriputra to confer full ordination upon Nanda. Thus Nanda became a monk; and thus Nanda's bride lost her groom, and the Śākyan kingdom a crown prince.

• LITTLE RĀHULA BECOMES A MONK •

Rāhula, the Tathāgata's ten-year-old son, was next in line for the throne.

After seven days had elapsed, Yaśodharā adorned Rāhula with princely robes delicately embroidered in rich colors and studded with thousands of flawless jewels. And taking Rāhula to the door of the great pavilion where Buddha and the monks of the Saṅgha had been invited by the king to eat the morning meal, she said: "Do you see, dear, that golden-colored Ascetic, looking like Brahmā, and attended by thousands of monks? He is your father, who would now be king had he not left the world. Go and ask him for your inheritance and say to him that you are heir apparent, and that when you are crowned king you will be a universal monarch in need of wealth; for the son is the owner of what belonged to the father."

But the Perfect One, having finished his meal, got up and returned to the monastery, and behind him followed little Rāhula.

Rāhula followed his father like a shadow, and even entered into the monastery with the Perfect One. And to his son Buddha said: "Why did your mother send you to me, Rāhula?"

"She sent me to request my inheritance, Ascetic. I shall some day be king and need the wealth that I have come to ask of you."

"You demand of me an inheritance which is subject to decay and leads to suffering, Rāhula," replied the Tathāgata. "Such a one I have no longer to bestow. But the Āryan wealth which I gained under the Tree of Wisdom shall be yours. This will make you the owner of an inheritance beyond this world, an inheritance which no one can take away from you."

And Buddha told Śāriputra to admit Rāhula to the Saṅgha.

"Rāhula," the Perfect One declared, "whenever you have a desire to do any deed whatever of body, speech, or thought, you should first consider whether it conduces to the harm of either yourself or others. If it does, then it is wrong, painful in result; and you should refrain from doing it. You should hold back from it or, if you are unable to do so, you should disclose and confess it so as to come to restraint in future time.

"If, on the other hand, you desire to do a deed of body, speech, or thought that does not conduce to the harm of either yourself or others, and you know it to be a good deed, happy in result; then, Rāhula, such a deed should be done by you. For by doing good deeds you can go along in joy and delight, training yourself night and day in states that are right."

After the ordination of Rāhula, King Śuddhodana came to the Perfect One in a state of agitation.

"When, Lord, you abandoned the world, it was no small pain to me. Sorrow seized me again when Nanda did so, and again when Rāhula did so. Grant, Lord, that the Āryan disciples may not confer ordination upon a son without the permission of his mother and father."

Śākyamuni granted his father's request by making a new rule, namely, that youths under twenty years of age should not be given full ordination without their parents' consent.

• ĀNANDA AND • DEVADATTA ENTER THE SAṄGHA

The next day eighty thousand nobles visited Buddha. These were the sons whom the Śākyan chieftains had dedicated to Śuddhodana's illustrious son at the name-giving ceremony to form a retinue for him when he should become either a Buddha or a universal monarch. The eighty thousand were given full ordination into the Saṅgha headed by Śākyamuni Buddha.

And so the Perfect One departed from Kapilavastu with one hundred thousand ordained disciples: and he led his monks south on the road to Magadha.

It happened, however, that two of Śākyamuni's cousins, Ānanda and Devadatta, had delayed entering the Saṅgha. Taking with them four wellborn companions (Mahānāma, Aniruddha, Bhṛgu, and Kimbila), and accompanied by their barber Upāli, they set out from home as though they were going to a pleasure park to sport.

After going a long way from Kapilavastu, the noble youths removed all their jewels and handed them over to Upāli to take back. But Upāli had not gone far on the road home when he became apprehensive of the anger of the Śākyas. Hanging the bundle of jewelry on a tree, he rejoined the six nobles; and after much pleading, they permitted him to accompany them.

The group of youths caught up with the Master and the company of monks at Anupiyā, the same mango grove in Mallan country where the Exalted One had rested for a week at the time of his retirement from the world.

Approaching the Tathāgata, the six noble youths requested that Upāli, the barber, be admitted to the Saṅgha first in order that their clannish Śākyan pride might be humbled through having their former servant as their senior. Buddha consented, ordaining Upāli first, and afterward the six.

Then Ānanda, seeing that many of the monks had already become Arhats, felt disappointed that he had failed to attain Nirvāṇa at once: and he went to Buddha to ask the reason.

But the Tathāgata, knowing what was in Ānanda's mind, turned to the noble youth and said: "Ānanda, good moral habits have the absence of bad conscience as their goal and good result. The absence of bad conscience has delight as its goal and good result. Delight has joy, joy has calm, calm has ease, ease has contemplation, contemplation has knowledge and insight, knowledge and insight have equanimity, and equanimity has Nirvāṇa as its goal and good result. Thus, Ānanda, good moral habits lead on gradually to the Highest."

Among the monks who had attained Nirvāṇa there was one named Bhadrika, a hunchbacked dwarf, repulsive in appearance, generally scorned by the less enlightened monks, and the butt of jokes.

Shortly before the Perfect One departed from Anupiyā, the venerable Bhadrika fell into the habit of resorting to forest solitudes, there giving utterance to the exclamation, "Ah, 'tis bliss!"

Now, many of the monks who had heard that oft-repeated exclamation supposed that Bhadrika had become discontented with the religious life and was yearning for the old life when he had enjoyed royal luxuries. The monks reported the matter to Buddha; and Buddha summoned Bhadrika and questioned him in the hearing of the entire congregation.

"What, Bhadrika, is the significance of your saying, 'Ah, 'tis bliss'? What motive, Bhadrika, prompts you to utter that exclamation?"

"Formerly, Lord," replied Bhadrika, "when I enjoyed the pleasures of a royal household, I lived apprehensive, anxious, and afraid even though guards were stationed both inside and outside my palace. But now, Lord, as I resort to forest solitudes, I am without apprehension, without anxiety and fear. I live at ease, alert, and as light at heart as some wild creature. This was the motive I had for exclaiming, 'Ah, 'tis bliss!' "

Then the Tathāgata, pleased with Bhadrika's reply, said to the monks: "O monks, Bhadrika is highly gifted, of a lofty nature. It is no easy thing to win the goal for which he left the household life—that uttermost Goal of Nirvāṇa wherein he now abides, having come to know it thoroughly for himself and to realize it."

At last the great company of monks began to resume the journey to the Magadhan capital of Rājagṛha, the thousands of yellow robes looking from a distance like globules of liquid gold flowing gently along the winding road.

VIII

FOUNDING OF THE JETAVANA MONASTERY

• ANĀTHAPIṆḌADA'S BARGAIN •

The first leaden clouds of the rainy season scurried across the sky on the wings of the monsoon which had begun to blow steadily against the southern battlements of Himālaya; and vegetation, which had lain dormant during the withering dryness of the hot season, greened suddenly, as if by magic, and sprang to life in rank growth as Earth thirstily imbibed the first refreshing showers.

The Tathāgata and a large congregation of monks, including the chief disciples, were staying at that time in the Sītavana (Cool Grove), which was situated on the outskirts of Rājagṛha, and not far from the Veṇuvana (Bamboo Grove) in Kalandakanivāpa (the Squirrels' Feeding Ground).

Many thousands of monks, however, were scattered far and wide over all the land, braving all weathers and enduring all hardships to preach the Dharma which is lovely in its beginning, lovely in its middle, and lovely in its end. As Śākyamuni once said, "The gift of Dharma surpasses all other gifts; the flavor of Dharma surpasses all other flavors; delight in Dharma surpasses all other delights: the destruction of craving conquers all suffering."

Now at that time certain brahmins, members of heretical sects, found fault with Buddha and his Saṅgha and condemned the roaming about of the monks in all seasons.

"Roaming as they do in the rainy season, they tread down the grass and trample to death many a tiny life!"

When some of the Perfect One's monks overheard the people grumbling and arguing among themselves, they reported the matter to the Master.

"In order not to offend the people," replied Buddha, "you and I might well observe a period of retreat during the rains, not journeying afar except in cases of urgent necessity. But if the Saṅgha so desires, it may abolish this rule of discipline at its own discretion."

And thus began the custom of *varṣa,* the three-month "retreat" during the rainy season.

After the period of retreat, when the rays of the sun began to grow longer and the sky assumed the lovely splendor of autumn, a certain wealthy householder of Śrāvastī, Sudata by name, but known from his great generosity as Anāthapiṇḍada ("Giver of alms to the unprotected"), had come to Rājagṛha on some business or other. And during his stay in Rājagṛha, he met Lord Buddha and became converted.

Anāthapiṇḍada confessed to the Tathāgata that even though business had burdened his mind with cares, he enjoyed his work as an investor and applied himself to it diligently.

"Should I give up my work, Lord, and renounce the world?"

"A person who possesses riches and uses them wisely and correctly is a blessing to his fellow men," replied Śākyamuni. "No, Sudata, it might be well for you to remain a lay disciple and continue to apply yourself diligently to your enterprises. There are other men, of different temperament, whom I advise to enter the Saṅgha for training in the religious life."

So pleased was Anāthapiṇḍada with Lord Buddha's words that he prepared a meal for the Perfect One and the monks, cooking and serving the food with his own hands. And when the meal was finished, Anāthapiṇḍada sat down beside the Master and said: "May the Perfect One, I beg, consent to spend the next rainy season at Śrāvastī."

"The Tathāgatas, householder, delight in solitary places," declared the Exalted One.

"I see, O Lord! I understand, O Happy One!"

Then the Tathāgata stirred and gladdened Anāthapiṇḍada with an exposition of Dharma; and when the discourse was concluded, he rose up and returned with the monks to the Sītavana Monastery.

Now, the householder Anāthapiṇḍada was a man of influence: he had many friends and acquaintances who thought highly of him and who were ever anxious to please him. So when he had finished his business in Rājagṛha, and had departed for Śrāvastī, the chief city of Kośala country, he made requests of the people all along the way to prepare for the coming of Lord Buddha.

"Good people, build rest houses, get lodgings ready, prepare offerings of food, for a Buddha has arisen in the world. That Perfect One will soon pass along this road, having been invited by me to spend the next rainy season at Śrāvastī."

When Anāthapiṇḍada reached Śrāvastī, he surveyed the city all about, thinking, "Now where can the Perfect One dwell so that he will not be too far from town and not too near? in a place conveniently situated and easy of approach for people who wish to see him? not overly frequented by day and free from noise and din at night? a place sheltered from the wind, remote from the abode of men, and suitable for solitude?"

Then Anāthapiṇḍada directed his attention to the grove owned by young Prince Jeta, observing that it fulfilled all the requirements. He accordingly bought the park, but not without difficulty, for Jeta-Rāja remarked: "The park is not for sale unless it be covered over with gold pieces."

Anāthapiṇḍada devoted the remainder of his wealth (for to cover the park with gold had taken many cartloads of money) to the building in Jeta Grove of lodgings and cells for the monks, storerooms, service halls, rooms for fires, sundry conveniences, toilets, promenades, wells and well houses, bathing rooms and dressing rooms, and pools and pavilions. Thus was established the Jetavana Monastery, and thus was all the material wealth of Anāthapiṇḍada exchanged for merit—the kind of wealth which may be taken with one beyond this world.

• ON THE WAY TO THE NEW MONASTERY •

Forasmuch as the rainy season was close at hand, Buddha and many of the monks who were staying with him at Rājagṛha set out on the road which led northwest to Śrāvastī in Kośala country.

As the little hamlet of Mātula came into view, the venerable Śāriputra ventured to ask a question of the Sugata.

"The Conqueror who shall follow you as Buddha—what will he be like, and when is he to come?"

"I will tell you, Śāriputra," replied Buddha. "Long after me, at a time far distant in the future, there shall arise in the world a Tathāgata named Maitreya ("the Kindly One"), an Arhat, a Perfectly Enlightened One endowed with wisdom and righteousness, a Sugata, a Knower of all worlds, unsurpassed as a guide for mortals who seek guidance, a Teacher of gods and men, a Perfect One, a Buddha even as I am now.

"He, by himself, shall realize and know thoroughly the cosmos with its various universes of worlds even as I now, by myself, realize and know thoroughly all worlds. He shall proclaim the Dharma, and he shall make known the higher life in all its purity even as I do now. He shall lead a Saṅgha even as I do now, a Brotherhood having a thousand monks for every hundred monks in the Saṅgha which I lead."

As Śākyamuni explained the matter to Śāriputra, the venerable Maudgalyāyana, Ānanda, and several other monks gathered around to listen to Buddha's teaching. And as it was the heat of the day, the monks seated themselves under the leafy canopy of trees which afforded them shelter from the searing rays of the sun.

"Make of yourselves islands, monks," taught the Master, "work hard, be wise! Live as islands to yourselves, as refuges to yourselves: take no other refuge. Live with the Dharma as your lamp, with the Dharma as your refuge. Meditate on the components of mind and body, seeing them as they really are, remaining energetic, self-possessed, and attentive to overcome worldly hankering and dejection.

"Realizing that all composite things are impermanent, painful, and devoid of essential reality, a monk, estranged from craving desires, aloof from evil dispositions, should enter and abide in the happiness, the joy, the bliss of the four Sublime Abodes. And what are the four?

"(1) With mind unlimited, purified, and full of loving-friendliness, a monk pervades the four quarters with loving-friendliness, and so also with mind unlimited, purified, and full of (2) compassion, (3) altruistic joy, and (4) equanimity. And not only the four quarters, but also the whole world—above, below, around, and everywhere—does the diligent monk continue to pervade with loving-friendliness, compassion, altruistic joy, and equanimity with mind unlimited and purified."

Thus spoke the Tathāgata; and the monks, glad at heart, rejoiced at the words of Lord Buddha and began to discuss among themselves the meaning of the discourse. But Maudgalyāyana, having become drowsy from the heat of noontide, sat yawning under a tree.

Buddha noticed that Maudgalyāyana's eyelids were drooping with sleepiness.

"O Maudgalyāyana, idleness is not the same as Āryan silence!" he declared. And continuing in verse, the Master said:

Rise up and sit alert!
What is the use of thy sleeping?
What sleep is there for the ailing,
Pierced by the arrow of pain?

Rise up and sit alert!
Exert thyself! Strive for calm!
Let not Death find thee asleep
And lure thee into his realm!

Dusty is drowsy indolence,
With dust bestrewn in its wake:

Diligently, with higher knowledge,
Draw out the arrow of pain!

• BUDDHA'S EXPLANATION • OF DEPENDENT ORIGINATION

Śākyamuni Buddha resided in the splendid Jetavana Monastery in Anāthapiṇḍada's Park near the river Aciravatī for a number of years, during which he preached the Dharma to his monks and to the folk of Śrāvastī.

On a certain occasion the Perfect One called the monks together to instruct them in the Law of Dependent Origination.

"What is the Law of Causation, monks? Verily, it is this Chain of Twelve Links:

1. *In the beginning there is ignorance.*
2. *Ignorance conditions the predisposing mental formations.*
3. *The predisposing mental formations condition discriminative consciousness.*
4. *Discriminative consciousness conditions mind-and-body.*
5. *Mind-and-body conditions the six senses.*
6. *The six senses condition contact.*
7. *Contact conditions feeling.*
8. *Feeling conditions craving.*
9. *Craving conditions attachment.*
10. *Attachment conditions the process of becoming.*
11. *The process of becoming conditions rebirth.*
12. *Rebirth conditions decay and death, likewise sorrow, lamentation, pain, grief, and despair.*

The Past Life

"(1) Being ignorant in their previous life as to the significance of existence, O monks, sentient beings accumulate karma, both good and bad—karma of thought, speech, and deeds. (2) Thus ignorance conditions the predisposing mental formations, creating temperament and personality.

The Present Life

"(3) Thus each being, going to rebirth, is endowed with discriminative consciousness, conditioned by the predispositions. Here is created the subjective world into which the being is reborn. (4) The mind and corporeality in which the being manifests itself are conditioned by discriminative consciousness; (5) the six senses of sight, hearing, smell, taste, touch, and mentation are conditioned by mind and corporeality; (6) eye-contact, ear-contact, nose-contact, tongue-contact, body-contact, and mind-contact are conditioned by the six senses; (7) feelings arising from these sense-contacts are conditioned by the nature of these contacts; (8) craving for visible forms, for sounds, for odors, for tastes, for bodily sensations, and for states of mind are conditioned by the feelings; (9) attachment to sights, sounds, odors, tastes, bodily sensations, and states of mind are conditioned by craving; (10) and the process of becoming is conditioned by attachment.

The Future Life

"(11) The being eventually dies and goes to another birth, his rebirth conditioned by the process of becoming. (12) Having been born again, he experiences the course of life again—decay and death, likewise sorrow, lamentation, pain, grief, and despair, all conditioned by rebirth.

"Now what do you think, monks? From the utter fading out and ending of ignorance comes also the ending of the predisposing mental formations, and so on down through the chain until, finally, decay and death, sorrow, lamentation, pain, grief, and despair are ended.

"Such is the arising of all this mass of pain, O monks: such is its utter extinction.

"If, monks, there is greedy longing for the pleasures of sense, if there is delight in them and craving for them, the state of consciousness established by that craving increases; wherever established consciousness increases, there is an arising of mind-and-body; wherever there is an arising of mind-and-body, there is a growth of the aggregates; wherever there is a growth of the aggregates, there is in the future a coming into renewed existence; wherever there is in the future a coming into renewed existence, there are in the future birth, decay, and death; and wherever there are in the future birth, decay, and death, O monks, there will be found sorrow, passion, and despair, I say.

"Now, the ordinary worldling is both enamored and repelled by sights, sounds, odors, tastes, bodily feelings, and mental states, and he lives in ignorance of cessation and release. When all mankind is like this worldling, ignorant, frustrated by pleasures, eluded by happiness and peace of mind, crushed by the burden of anguish and turmoil, doomed to death and reincarnation endlessly—then, O monks, a Tathāgata arises in the world, an Arhat, a Supreme Buddha perfect in morality and wisdom, a Sugata, a World-Knower, a Charioteer unsurpassed of men to be tamed, Teacher of gods and men, an Awakened Perfect One who, having arisen, preaches the eternal and never-changing Dharma. And then the worldling who perceives his worldliness and ignorance hears an exposition of the Dharma, forsakes the world, and enters upon the Āryan self-training. Then what happens?

"He, become master of the Āryan virtues, master of the Āryan control of the faculties, and master of the Āryan self-possessed mindfulness, lives apart from the common crowd. Rejecting worldly greed and despair, he puts away the taint of malevolence and abides in the thought of harmlessness. With kindly thought for every living thing he cleanses his heart of the taint of malevolence.

"Casting away sloth and torpor he abides free from them, conscious of inner illumination. Abandoning anxiety and apprehension, he abides immovable, inwardly serene. He abandons wavering; and, having overpassed it, *he abides free from torturing doubts, no more a disputer of the 'how' and 'why' of things.*

"Thus abandoning the five Hindrances (sensual hankering, malice, sloth and torpor, restlessness and worry, and skeptical doubt), wearing down by means of knowledge whatever impurities remain, aloof from evil things, he enters upon the Absorptions of meditation.

"Then, when he sees a form with the eye, he is no longer enraptured by enticing forms. He is not repelled by repulsive forms, but dwells with mindfulness established. Truly infinite is his sphere of thought. He knows that release of heart by wisdom, in conformity with reality, and by which all painful, unprofitable things come wholly and totally to an end.

"He rejects satisfaction and dissatisfaction. Whatever feeling he feels, be it pleasant, painful, or neutral, he does not welcome it, does not lay hold of it, does not cling fast to it. Thereby ceases the lure. By the cessation of the lure ceases attachment, the craving for existences, the craving for annihilation, and also birth, decay and death, and likewise sorrow, lamentation, pain, grief, and despair. With the destruction of the ten Defilements, the five Lower Fetters, the five Higher Fetters, the five Hindrances, the three Bases of False Belief, the five Ties, and the four Poisons comes the destruction of this whole mass of pain.

"Now, the monk in whom the Poisons are destroyed—who is a perfect Saint, an Arhat, emancipated by true insight—is incapable of perpetrating nine things. He is incapable (1) of deliberately depriving a living being of life, (2) of theft, (3) of sexual impurity, (4) of falsehood, (5) of laying up treasure for indulgence in worldly pleasures, (6) of partiality, (7) of hate, (8) of stupidity, and (9) of fear."

• NANDA AND THE NYMPHS •

On a certain occasion when the Perfect One was staying at the Jetavana Monastery, the monk Nanda, Buddha's half brother, son of King Śuddhodana and Lady Prajāpatī, voiced his discontent to a large number of monks, saying: "Brothers, I follow the religious life without zest: I can endure it no longer. Giving up the training I will go back to my bride in Kapilavastu and live the lower life of the world."

Now one of the monks who heard Nanda's confession went to the

Perfect One and repeated to him what Nanda had said. And the Master then summoned Nanda.

"Is it true as they say, Nanda," asked Buddha, "that you spoke to a large number of monks, telling them that you can no longer endure the religious life, and that you wish to return to the lower life of the world?"

"It is true, Lord."

"But how is it, Nanda, that you have lost your zest for the religious life?"

"When I left home, Lord, my bride, a Śākyan girl, the fairest in the land, looked back at me with hair half-combed and said, 'May you soon come back and take me in your arms again!' As I am always thinking of that, remembering how she looked and spoke, I have no zest for the religious life; and I long to return to the lower life of the world."

Without saying a word, the Perfect One stood up and took Nanda by the arm. By exercising great psychic power, Buddha created for himself and for Nanda mind-formed bodies. And just as a strong man might stretch out his bent arm or bend it when stretched out, even so did the Perfect One and the monk Nanda appear among the gods of the Heaven of the Thirty-Three Palaces.

Now at that time as many as five hundred pink-footed celestial nymphs were attending Śakra, the chief of the gods of that world.

Then the Perfect One said to Nanda, "Do you see these five hundred pink-footed celestial nymphs?"

"They are gorgeous, Master!"

"Now what do you think, Nanda? Which are the more lovely, more worth looking at, more alluring, the Śākyan girl, fairest in the land, or these five hundred celestial nymphs?"

"O Master! Just as if she were a mutilated monkey with ears and nose cut off, even so, Lord, the Śākyan girl, if set beside these celestial nymphs, is not worth a sixteenth part of them, she cannot be compared with them! Why, these five hundred nymphs are far more lovely, far more worth looking at, far more alluring!"

"Cheer up, Nanda, cheer up!" exclaimed the Master. "I guarantee that you shall win these five hundred pink-footed celestial nymphs!"

"If, Lord, the Perfect One guarantees that I shall win these pink-footed nymphs, then I shall indeed take the greatest pleasure in living the religious life!"

Thereupon Śākyamuni, taking Nanda by the arm, vanished with him from that heaven of sensual delight and reappeared in Jeta Grove. And so Nanda, forgetting his betrothed, the Śākyan girl, fairest in the land, resumed the life religious in his burning desire to possess the pink-footed celestial nymphs.

But the gentle and guileless Ānanda, cousin of the Tathāgata, feared for Nanda's welfare. He therefore went to Nanda and said: "Wrongly based, O Nanda, is your feverish desire to win the delights of heaven. Sojourn in heaven is only temporary, for the gods, like humankind and all other sensate beings, inevitably die when their span of years or their merit is exhausted. And a god, when he falls from heavenly realms, wails in deep distress: 'Alas, the delightful grove of Citraratha! Alas, no more the heavenly lake! Alas, the charming river of paradise, no longer! Oh, how dear they were to me!' "

And Ānanda continued, saying, "Just think how bitter to people here the anguish when they are about to leave this world: how much greater must be the pain of those pleasure-loving deities when comes their time to die! Just as the death of human beings is presaged by disagreeable symptoms, so also there are signs which indicate the imminent demise of a god. For instance, the god's clothing begins to collect dust, his radiance begins to fade, his magnificent garlands wither, sweat breaks out on his limbs, and his heavenly station fails to bring him delight.

"If, Nanda, you compare the happiness which the gods have enjoyed, tasting sensuous pleasures in celestial realms, with the suffering which fall from heaven brings, then the suffering is by far the greater of the two. Recognize that heaven is only temporary, that it bestows no real freedom, holds out no security, is not to be trusted, and gives no lasting satisfaction. Better by far is the striving for Emancipation, forasmuch as the inhabitants of heaven, even with all their power, come to an end. No intelligent man, Nanda, would set his heart on winning a brief stay among them."

But Nanda, infatuated by the enticing beauty of the heavenly nymphs, was not convinced: he continued his exercises in the hope of winning rebirth among them. And then the rumor began to be whispered among the monks:

"They say that Nanda, the Perfect One's half brother, leads the religious life in the hope of getting a bevy of celestial nymphs. They say that the Exalted One has assured him of getting five hundred pink-footed nymphs."

Thereafter all the monks who had been Nanda's comrades taunted him, calling him a hireling and a menial.

"Surely Nanda is a hireling, one easily bought with a price, for he leads the religious life for the sake of nymphs which the Perfect One has guaranteed that he will get."

Now the monk Nanda, being continually called "hireling" and "menial," grew worried and humiliated. Feeling the contempt with which his comrades regarded him, he lived in solitude apart from the other monks; and he perfected himself energetically. And in no long time he attained in this very world, realizing for himself by full knowledge, that supreme goal of the religious life, Nirvāṇa. Rebirth had been stopped, and he knew: the holy life had been lived, done was all that had to be done. Thus the venerable Nanda became another of the Arhats, *those Holy Ones for whom there is no more of becoming in the sphere of conditioned existence.*

And it came to pass one night, just before dawn, that a certain goddess, lighting up the whole of the Jeta Grove with surpassing radiance, came to see Lord Buddha, who then was sitting in meditation. Having come to the Perfect One, she stood respectfully at one side and said: "The venerable Nanda, Lord, by making an end of the Poisons, has won release from the Poisons, heart emancipated, mind emancipated."

The knowledge that this was true also arose in the Tathāgata. Then at the end of that night the venerable Nanda came to the Blessed One and said: "As to the Perfect One's promise that I should get five hundred pink-footed celestial nymphs, Lord, I release the Perfect One from that promise."

"Grasping your thought with my own, Nanda, I am aware that you have won Nirvāṇa. However, a goddess has also informed me that you are released from the Poisons of lust, existence-infatuation, false view, and ignorance. When, therefore, you ceased to cling to the things of the world, heart emancipated and mind emancipated—at the very moment you were released, Nanda, I was released from my promise."

Thereupon the Perfect One, inspired by Nanda's victory, uttered the following verse:

By neither pain nor pleasure stirred is he
Who has passed beyond lust's miry bog,
Crushing down the thorn of cruel desire,
And come at last to illusion's end.

Now Ānanda, amazed at Nanda's victory and amazed by the Tathāgata's power to visit a heaven of gods, was filled with wonder for many days. On this account he approached the Master, greeted him with respectful salutation, and sat down at one side.

"Does the Perfect One," he asked, "really know how to reach the worlds of heaven by supernormal power, by means of a mind-formed body?"

"I do indeed know, Ānanda."

"A strange thing it is, Lord! A marvel it is, Lord, that the Perfect One has this knowledge!"

"Yes, Ānanda. Strange indeed are the Tathāgatas and endowed with strange powers. Marvelous indeed are the Tathāgatas and endowed with marvelous powers. Whenever, Ānanda, the Tathāgata concentrates body in mind and concentrates mind in body, and enters into an awareness of ease and buoyancy and abides in it—at such times, Ānanda, the body of the Tathāgata is more buoyant, softer, more pliant, and more radiant.

"Now, Ānanda, by such concentration of body in mind and mind in body, the Tathāgata's mind-formed body with but little effort rises from the earth into the sky, and in divers ways enjoys supernormal power, as, for instance, being one he becomes multiform, and so forth; and he has power of the body even up to the world of Brahmā."

• SICKNESS AND DEATH OF ANĀTHAPIṆḌADA •

One day the wealthy householder Anāthapiṇḍada sent word to the Jetavana Monastery that he was severely ill; and he asked that Śāriputra come and preach to him.

The venerable Śāriputra accordingly set out for the house of Anāthapiṇḍada, taking Ānanda as his attendant. And having arrived, the two monks went into Anāthapiṇḍada's chamber and sat down upon seats which had been made ready.

"Well, householder," asked Śāriputra, "are you bearing up? Are you enduring? Do your pains abate and not increase?"

"No, reverend sir," answered Anāthapiṇḍada, "I am not bearing up, and severe pains assail me. The exceedingly great burning in my body is just as though I were being roasted over a pit of glowing charcoal."

"Then, householder, you must train your mind and put it under control by analyzing your bodily feelings and dissociating yourself from them. Your body is not the true essence of your being, and neither pleasure nor pain is experienced by your real self. Concentrate, householder, to abolish pain."

But Anāthapiṇḍada soon burst into tears; and Ānanda, thinking that the sick layman was unable to control his faculties, asked: "Is it because your mind is clinging to something, householder, that you are giving way?"

Anāthapiṇḍada smiled through his tears.

"No, reverend Ānanda, not that! I am holding on! I am not giving way! I have abolished pain by putting my mind under control! Wonderful, marvelous is your instruction, reverend Śāriputra!"

"Such instruction as this, householder, is not usually revealed to dwellers in the household life," replied Śāriputra. "It is to those who have gone forth from home to homelessness that instruction on mental concentration is revealed."

"Then, reverend Śāriputra, let it be revealed to laymen as well as to monks!" pleaded Anāthapiṇḍada with fervent emotion. "Many are those who are perishing through not hearing the Dharma!"

The wise and gentle Śāriputra then gave the wealthy householder further instruction; and when the heart of Anāthapiṇḍada had been made perfectly calm, happy, and confident, Śāriputra and Ānanda returned to the monastery in Prince Jeta's grove which Anāthapiṇḍada had built for Lord Buddha and the Saṅgha.

Not many days afterward, Anāthapiṇḍada, filled with happiness and free from pain, passed away and was reborn in a heaven among gods known as the Unworried Ones. Thus become, the god Anāthapiṇḍada revisited Earth in a mind-formed body, illuminating the whole Jetavana with wondrous radiance one night just before dawn. He went into the presence of Buddha and uttered joyous stanzas in praise of the proficiency of Śāriputra as a teacher of Dharma. And before he vanished from sight, Anāthapiṇḍada also said:

Blessed is this Jeta Grove,
Haunted by the Band of Saints,
Wherein the Dharma's Sovereign dwells:
A cause for joy to me is this!

• YAŚOJA AND THE FIVE HUNDRED MONKS •

When Śākyamuni was about forty years old, about five years after his Enlightenment, as many as five hundred monks headed by the ascetic Yaśoja, whose father was headman of five hundred fisher families, had come to the Jetavana at Śrāvastī to see the Perfect One.

The new arrivals, however, were very boisterous and noisy in greeting the resident monks and in making arrangements about bed and lodging and places to keep their bowls and robes.

On hearing the commotion, Buddha called to Ānanda.

"Ānanda, what is all this noise and hubbub? Methinks it sounds just like fishermen catching fish!"

"It is these five hundred monks headed by Yaśoja, Master. These new arrivals who have come hither to see the Lord are causing all this din."

"Ānanda, I want you to go and in my name say to those monks, 'The Teacher summons your reverences.' "

"Yes, Lord," replied Ānanda, and went and did as the Perfect One had asked. And when the noisy monks had come, the Perfect One said to them: "Monks, what is the meaning of this great noise and hubbub? Methinks it sounds just like fishermen catching fish!"

Yaśoja explained that his followers, just arrived, had been greeting the resident monks and making arrangements for their stay.

"Go away, monks!" said Buddha. "I dismiss you! You do not deserve to dwell with me!"

"Very well, reverend sir," replied Yaśoja who, together with his monks, saluted the Perfect One respectfully by walking around him three times, keeping him to their right.

Then Yaśoja and his disciples, after putting their lodgings in order, departed to the country of the Vṛjis far to the east. And after collecting alms, they went to the river Vargumudā close by the city of Vaiśālī, the Vṛji capital.

"Reverend sirs," said Yaśoja to his monks, "we have been dismissed by Gautama for our own good and profit, out of compassion for us, because he took pity on us. Come, now, reverend sirs, let us live in a way which would please Gautama, a way which Gautama would approve of."

Those monks accordingly lived apart from ordinary men—energetic, enthusiastic, self-perfected—and, as a result, they attained during the brief interval of the rainy season a comprehension of the Three Characteristics of conditioned existence, namely, Transience, Suffering, and Impersonality.

Now the Tathāgata, having stayed at Śrāvastī as long as he wished, set out on his rounds for Vaiśālī. And having arrived at that city, Buddha and the monks who had accompanied him took up residence in the Kūṭāgārasālā (the Hall with the Peaked Roof) in Mahāvana (Great Grove).

The Exalted One had not been long in Vaiśālī when he grasped with his thought the thoughts of those five hundred monks living on the banks of the Vargumudā.

"Ānanda," said Buddha, "this quarter seems to me illuminated. All radiant, Ānanda, this quarter seems to me. Methinks it will be pleasant for me to go to that place where, on the bank of the river Vargumudā, those monks headed by Yaśoja are dwelling. You might, therefore, take a message to those monks, saying, 'The Teacher calls for your reverences. The Teacher is anxious to see your reverences.' "

Late that evening, after Ānanda had transmitted the Tathāgata's message, Yaśoja and all of his monks entered the Hall with the Peaked Roof and stood before Buddha. But Śākyamuni was at that time seated, rapt in "immovable concentration;" and he gave no sign of greeting to the monks.

Yaśoja's monks, however, perceived the state in which Śākyamuni was then abiding; and they, too, sat down in immovable concentration.

And Ānanda, when the first watch of the night was drawing to its close, rose from his seat and, throwing his outer robe over one shoulder and joining the palms of his hands in respect, drew near to the Tathāgata.

"Lord, the night is fleeting; and the newly arrived monks have been seated for a long time. Will the Perfect One exchange greetings with them?"

But Śākyamuni remained silent. Then, as the second watch was almost over, Ānanda again rose from his seat and repeated his words. Still the Tathāgata was silent.

And as the last watch drew to its close, dawn being at hand, Ānanda got up from his seat for the third time and drew near to the Tathāgata.

"Lord, the night is far spent and wears a face of gladness, with dawn lighting up the sky. The newly arrived monks have been seated all night long! Let the Perfect One now exchange greetings with them!"

Buddha then withdrew from that state of concentration and said to Ānanda: "If you were better acquainted with meditation, Ānanda, it would not have occurred to you to keep on asking me to greet these monks. Both I and these five hundred monks, Ānanda, have all of us been sitting in immovable concentration."

Yaśoja and his five hundred monks remained in Great Grove and became ordained disciples of the Perfect One. And Buddha gave instructive discourses to the monks from time to time, plunging deep into the ocean of the Dharma.

• "RARE IS HUMAN BIRTH!" •

"Rare is human birth, O monks!" declared the Omniscient One on a certain occasion.

"Just as only a small part of India consists of delightful parks and gardens, of farms and pools of water, O monks, the larger part consisting of mountains, of rivers barring passage, of places beset with stumps and brambles, of rough and rocky ground—even so, monks, few are those beings that are born on land: more numerous are they that are born in the waters.

"Similarly, monks, few are those beings that are born among mankind: more numerous are they that are born outside the human race as nonhuman beings, animals, and ghosts.

"Again, monks, of those who decease from the human state, few are they who attain rebirth in the human race: more numerous are they who are reborn in a state of woe, among the animals, and in the world of ghosts.

"Suppose, monks, that a man should throw into the great ocean a yoke with one hole, and that a one-eyed turtle should pop up to the surface only once at the end of every century. Now what do you think, monks? Would that one-eyed turtle be very likely to push his neck often through that yoke?"

The monks replied: "He might do so, Lord, once in a while after the lapse of countless ages."

"Well, monks," continued the Tathāgata, "sooner, I declare, would that one-eyed turtle, popping up to the surface of the ocean only once every hundred years, push his neck through that yoke, than a fool who has once gone to the Downfall become a man. And why?

"Because, O monks, in living the life of an immoral man there is no clean living, no tranquility of spirit, no doing of kindly deeds, no acquiring of merit. Instead, cannibalism and the feeding on helpless animals prevails. Why?

"It is all owing to a failure to comprehend the Four Āryan Truths, namely, Suffering, the Cause of Suffering, the Cessation of Suffering, and the Path that leads to the Cessation of Suffering. Wherefore, O monks, strive, put forth energy, exert yourselves!"

As soon as the Perfect One had finished speaking, a certain novitiate monk came forward with a question.

"I have today eaten meat from my almsbowl, Master. Have I thereby committed an offense?"

"In your case, monk," replied Buddha, "you are guiltless of offense. For fish and meat are permissible if you have not seen, heard, or suspected that it was killed especially for you. But if a monk should make use of human flesh, a grave offense is involved. A monk should not eat the flesh of monkeys, elephants, horses, dogs, snakes, lions, tigers, leopards, cats, or bears, not even in times of famine.

"The layman who hunts and kills animals for sport, O monks, is no follower of mine. With such a one you are to have no words, and before such a one you are to turn your almsbowls upside down, not accepting offerings of food from bloodstained hands."

IX

THE LAST VISIT TO KAPILAVASTU

• ŚUDDHODANA'S DEATH; • THE ANGER-EATING DEMON

While Buddha was residing in the Kūṭāgārasālā in Mahāvana at Vaiśālī, in the fifth year after the Enlightenment, King Śuddhodana became mortally ill. And so the Tathāgata hastened to his father's bedside in the royal palace at Kapilavastu, taking with him Nanda, Ānanda, Śāriputra, Maudgalyāyana, and a number of other monks.

Hearing his illustrious son preach on the impermanence of all conditioned things, Śuddhodana Gautama, a lay disciple, attained Nirvāṇa and enjoyed the ineffable bliss of Nirvāṇa for a full week before he died and passed utterly away into the hypercosmic infinitude of Parinirvāṇa beyond the sphere of finite existence.

While King Śuddhodana's funeral was in progress, Buddha remained at Nigrodhārāma, the monastery in Banyan Park. And it was there that the Tathāgata explained that lay disciples may attain Nirvāṇa, even though the uttermost Goal is far more difficult for laymen than for monks.

"If a layman is able to say in truth that he has abandoned all attachment to family and friends, to this world and to the worlds of heaven, then I declare that there is no difference between such a lay disciple and the monk whose mind is free from the Poisons (lust, existence-infatuation, false view, and ignorance); that is to say, *there is no difference between freedom and the state of being free.*"

Now when the funeral was over, the Śākyan mourners began plotting a war against their Kolyan neighbors, for the Śākyas were warriors and discontented with peace. A certain irrigation embankment on that part of the river Rohiṇī which formed the boundary between the two countries was chosen by the Śākyan chieftains as an excuse for war.

"There is danger of famine in our eastern province," argued the warlords. "The Kolyas are endangering our national security by building a dike which prevents the flow of water into our paddy fields. Let us therefore dictate an ultimatum to the Kolyas."

The ultimatum was duly delivered; and the Kolyas subsequently sent a legation of nobles to Kapilavastu.

"Sirs," the Kolyas explained, "the dike is necessary to conserve water. Of what use is the irrigation system if the fields are washed out by floods during the rains?"

"Your scheme is unwise, and we do not approve of it," replied the Śākyas, who straightway made preparations for battle, thinking, "We shall preserve peace by waging war."

"Shame on you, sirs!" exclaimed the Kolyas, who maintained their right to construct the embankment. "If war is what you are looking for, we shall give you a taste of Kolyan valor!"

And so both sides went forth to do battle; and the banks of the Rohiṇī were lined with many hundreds of women and children weeping for their loved ones who might be killed in the bloody affray.

When Buddha saw the two armies prepared to redden the waters of the Rohiṇī with the blood of their men, he went up and spoke to the leaders in a voice that all could hear.

"Do you, sirs, consider that battle is a fitting memorial to my father the king, a monarch devoted to peace? Tell me, O princes, is earth of any intrinsic value, of any enduring worth?"

"No, Ascetic," replied the leaders, "but the water—"

"Is water, then, of intrinsic and everlasting value, not merely here and now, but beyond this world?"

"No, Ascetic, it is not. But the exigency of the times calls for the sacrifice of blood."

"And the blood of men, is that of any intrinsic value?"

"Its value is beyond price!"

"Then is it reasonable," asked the Perfect One, "to stake that which is priceless against that which has no intrinsic value?"

The nobles perceived the wisdom of this reasoning and abandoned their dispute, albeit reluctantly. And knowing their hearts to be hard and devoid of compassion, Buddha instructed them with a parable.

"Once upon a time a certain sickly-looking and decrepit demon took his seat on the throne of Śakra, governor of the gods. And the gods of the Heaven of the Thirty-Three Palaces, angered and annoyed by the impudent demon, spoke indignantly, saying, 'Oh, what a scandal, oh, what a horror! Just look at this wretched demon who has seated himself on the throne of Śakra!' Now, the more the gods were angered, annoyed, and spoke with indignation, in the same proportion did the demon grow handsomer, better-looking, and more pleasing.

"Then the gods of that heaven-world approached Śakra, governor of those gods; and having drawn near to him, they said: " 'Sir, a certain sickly-looking and decrepit demon has come here and seated himself on your throne. And all the gods of the Heaven of the Thirty-Three Palaces, sir, are angered, annoyed, and speak with indignation against the impudence of that miserable demon. But the more angry they become, in the same proportion does the demon grow handsomer, better-looking, and more pleasing. Now surely, sir, it must be a demon that feeds on anger!'

"Then Śakra drew near to where the anger-eating demon was; and having drawn near, he threw his cloak over his shoulder, placed his right knee upon the ground, stretched out his joined palms to the demon, and thrice announced himself in this manner: " 'Sir, your obedient servant, Śakra, governor of the gods! Sir, your obedient servant, Śakra, governor of the gods! Sir, your obedient servant, Śakra, governor of the gods!'

"And the more that Śakra humbly proclaimed his own name, the more sickly-looking and decrepit became the demon; and straightway the anger-eating demon disappeared.

"Then Śakra resumed his seat on his throne and took advantage of the occasion to induce in the gods a more fitting frame of mind by uttering this verse:

'My mind's not easily cast down,
Nor easily does it swerve aside.
Not for long can I be angry,
For anger finds no place in me.
I never say harsh, angry words,
And never boast about my fame.
I strive to keep myself subdued
In interest of my future weal.'

And as the Sugata returned to Banyan Park, he said to Ānanda: "Governments and royal rule, Ānanda, are nuisances like robbers, pestilence, famine, mosquitoes, gnats, and so forth. It is a wise man indeed who has learned to endure them with fortitude."

• BUDDHA AND THE JAINAS •

Buddha remained at Kapilavastu, staying in the monastery in Banyan Park, intending to go forth on his rounds at the end of the rainy season when some robes which certain monks were making for him were finished.

One day a Jaina layman named Siṃha went to Buddha to ask the Perfect One if he taught a doctrine of nonaction, as did the Nirgranṭha leader Vardhamāna Jñātaputra. Declared the Enlightened One: "There is a way, Siṃha, in which one might correctly say of me that the Ascetic Gautama teaches the principle of nonaction; but there is also a way in which one might correctly say of me that the Ascetic Gautama teaches the principle of action. How is this?

"I proclaim the non-doing of evil conduct of body, speech, and thought. I proclaim the non-doing of various kinds of wicked things.

"But, Siṃha, I also proclaim the doing of good conduct of body, speech, and thought. I proclaim the doing of various kinds of good things."

Now, shortly afterwards, while the Tathāgata was still at Kapilavastu, the Nirgranṭha Jñātaputra died at Pāpā in the country of the Mallas. And from the moment he died, the Jainas became split and divided, and quarrels and disputes broke out among them. They argued and attacked one another's opinions with such fanatical violence that all the people were disgusted.

It happened that Cunda the novice, a Buddhist monk, had been in Pāpā at the time of Jñātaputra's death. And after the rains had come to an end, Cunda left Pāpā and came to Kapilavastu and told the matter to Śākyamuni.

"Killing seems to be the way of the followers of Jñātaputra," said Cunda. "Even the white-robed lay disciples were disgusted with his monks."

"So it is, Cunda, in the case of an imperfect religion," declared Buddha. "In this case, Cunda, there is a teacher not fully Enlightened, and a doctrine and discipline badly expounded, badly set forth, not leading to Nirvāṇa, not tending to serenity, and set forth by one not fully Enlightened, with support destroyed and without resource.

"In that doctrine and way of life the devotee has neither reached a position which accords with that doctrine, nor right conduct, nor does he walk in accordance with that doctrine, but becomes a hypocrite, a sanctimonious fraud.

"In this respect, Cunda, the teacher is at fault and his false teaching is at fault, but the devotee is not to be judged harshly. But if anyone should say to such a devotee, 'Come, friend, live up to the tenets of your religion as your teacher taught you'—then both he who gives such advice and he who takes it produce much demerit for themselves. And why? Because that doctrine and discipline are badly expounded, badly set forth, do not lead to Nirvāṇa, do not tend to serenity, and are set forth by one not fully Enlightened, with support destroyed and without resource."

• KṚṢĀ GAUTAMĪ AND THE MUSTARD SEED •

One day, when the rainy season had ended, Kṛṣā Gautamī, the wife of a rich man, was plunged deep into grief by the loss of her only son, a baby boy who had died just when he was old enough to run about.

Kṛṣā Gautamī was the woman who had uttered a joyous verse at the time when she observed from her balcony Prince Siddhārtha Gautama riding through the streets of Kapilavastu, the resolve to renounce the world newly established in his mind.

In her grief Kṛṣā Gautamī carried the dead child to all her neighbors in Kapilavastu, asking them for medicine. Seeing her, the people shook their heads sadly out of pity.

"Poor woman! She has lost her senses from grief. The boy is beyond the help of medicine."

Unable to accept the fact of her son's death, Kṛṣā then wandered through the streets of the city beseeching for help everyone she met.

"Please, sir," she said to a certain man, "give me medicine that will cure my boy!"

The stranger looked at the child's eyes and saw that the boy was dead.

"Alas, I have no medicine for your child," he said, "but I know of a physician who can give what you require."

"Pray tell me, sir, where I can find this physician."

"Go, dear woman, to Śākyamuni, the Buddha, just now residing in Banyan Park."

Kṛṣā went in haste to the Nigrodhārāma; and she was brought by the monks to Buddha.

"Reverend Lord," she cried, "give me the medicine that will cure my boy!"

Lord Buddha, Ocean of Infinite Compassion, looked upon the grief-stricken mother with pity.

"You have done well to come here for medicine, Kṛṣā Gautamī. Go into the city and get a handful of mustard seed." And then the Perfect One added: "The mustard seed must be taken from a house where no one has lost a child, husband, parent, or friend."

"Yes, Lord!" exclaimed Kṛṣā, greatly cheered. "I shall procure the mustard seed at once!"

Poor Kṛṣā Gautamī then went from house to house with her request; and the people pitied her, saying: "Here is the mustard seed: please take all you want of it."

Then Kṛṣā would ask: "Did a son or daughter, father or mother, die in your family?"

"Alas! The living are few, but the dead are many. Do not remind us of our deepest grief!"

And there was no house but that some relative, some dear one, had died in it.

Weary and with hope gone, Kṛṣā Gautamī sat down by the wayside, sorrowfully watching the lights of the city as they flickered up and were extinguished again. And at last the deep shadows of night plunged the world into darkness.

Considering the fate of human beings, that their lives flicker up and are extinguished again, the bereft mother suddenly realized that Buddha in his compassion had sent her forth to learn the truth.

"How selfish am I in my grief!" she thought. *"Death is universal; yet even in this valley of death there is a Path that leads to Deathlessness him who has surrendered all thought of self!"*

Putting away the selfishness of her affection for her child, Kṛṣā Gautamī went to the edge of a forest and tenderly laid the dead body in a drift of wildflowers.

"Little son," she said, taking the child by the hand, "I thought that death had happened to you alone; but it is not to you alone, it is common to all people."

There she left him; and when dawn brightened the eastern sky, she returned to the Perfect One.

"Kṛṣā Gautamī," said the Tathāgata, "did you get a handful of mustard seed from a house in which no one has ever lost kith or kin?"

"That, Lord, is now past and gone," she said. "Grant me support."

"Dear girl, the life of mortals in this world is troubled and brief and inseparable from suffering," declared Buddha, "for there is not any means, nor will there ever be, by which those that have been born can avoid dying. All living beings are of such a nature that they must die whether they reach old age or not.

"As early-ripening fruits are in danger of falling, so mortals when born are always in danger of dying. Just as the earthen vessels made by the potter end in shards, so is the life of mortals. Both young and old, both those who are foolish and those who are wise—all fall into the power of death, all are subject to death.

"Of those who depart from this life, overcome by death, a father cannot save his son, nor relatives their kinsfolk. While relatives are looking on and lamenting, one by one the mortals are carried off like oxen to the slaughter. People die, and their fate after death will be according to their deeds. Such are the terms of the world.

"Not from weeping nor from grieving will anyone obtain peace of mind. On the contrary, his pain will be all the greater, and he will ruin his health. He will make himself sick and pale; but dead bodies cannot be restored by his lamentation.

"Now that you have heard the Tathāgata, Kṛṣā, reject grief, do not allow it to enter your mind. Seeing one dead, know for sure: 'I shall never see him again in this existence.' And just as the fire of a burning house is quenched, so does the contemplative wise person scatter grief's power, expertly, swiftly, even as the wind scatters cotton seed.

"He who seeks peace should pull out the arrow of lamentations, useless longings, and the self-made pangs of grief. He who has removed this unwholesome arrow and has calmed himself will obtain peace of mind. Verily, he who has conquered grief will always be free from grief—sane and immune—confident, happy, and close to Nirvāṇa, I say."

Then Kṛṣā Gautamī won the stage of Entering-the-Stream, and shortly afterwards she became an Arhat. She was the first woman to have attained Nirvāṇa under the dispensation of Śākyamuni Buddha.

• PRAJĀPATĪ, THE FIRST NUN •

Now, it came to pass that Lady Prajāpatī (aunt and foster mother of the Exalted One) heard from Kṛṣā Gautamī's own lips of the bliss of Nirvāṇa. Thereupon Prajāpatī, already a lay disciple of Buddha, went with longing for the Highest Attainment to Nigrodha Park where Śākyamuni was.

"It would be for my welfare, O Lord," said Prajāpatī, "if the Perfect One would reveal to me a teaching, hearing which from the lips of the Perfect One I might dwell alone, solitary, zealous, enthusiastic, and firm in purpose."

"Well, my dear Gautamid aunt," replied Buddha, "I will teach you about teachings in general. There are bad religions in the world; and those you ought to avoid. How can you tell a bad religion?

"Of whatever teachings you are able to assure yourself, 'These doctrines conduce to passion, to bondage, to wealth and fame, to covetousness, to discontent, to company, to sluggishness, to delight in harming'—of such teachings you may affirm with certainty: 'This is not the Dharma; this is not the discipline of the Āryas; this is not the Master's teaching.'

"But of whatever teachings you can assure yourself, 'These doctrines conduce to dispassion, to detachment, to material poverty, to frugality, to contentedness, to solitude, to energy, to delight in harmlessness'—of such teachings you may affirm with certainty: 'This is the Dharma; this is the discipline of the Āryas; this is the Master's teaching.' "

Prajāpatī Gautamī was pleased with this useful lesson; and not many days afterward she returned to the Tathāgata with another request.

"It would be good, Lord," she said, "if the Perfect One would permit women to go forth from the household life to the homeless state under the Dharma and discipline declared by the Tathāgata."

Three times did Lady Prajāpatī make this petition, and three times Buddha refused her, saying: "Enough, O Gautamid! Do not desire that women be permitted to go forth from the household life to the homeless state under the Dharma and discipline declared by the Tathāgata!"

Then Prajāpatī Gautamī at the thought "the Perfect One does not permit women to join the Saṅgha" became sad and sorrowful. With tears moistening her eyes, she saluted the Tathāgata by walking around him rightwise. And then she went away.

The autumnal cool season had come, the robes which the monks had made were finished, and the Perfect One, having stayed at Kapilavastu as long as he wished, set out on his rounds toward Vaiśālī, chief city of the Vṛjis and Licchavis.

Having arrived there, he resumed residence in the Hall with the Peaked Roof in Great Grove. And in the meantime Prajāpatī Gautamī had cut off her hair, put on yellow robes, and set out from Kapilavastu with a large company of women who wished to renounce the world. Among them was Princess Yaśodharā, Buddha's wife.

Journeying by stages, the Śākyan women came at last to Vaiśālī and went to Mahāvana and stood outside the entrance porch of the Kūṭāgārasālā.

Now, the monk Ānanda saw Lady Prajāpatī standing there at the head of the women, her feet swollen and covered with dust, her countenance sad, and her eyes filled with tears.

"Why are you standing there outside the porch, O Gautamid?" he asked her.

"O reverend Ānanda, it is because the Perfect One does not allow women to go forth from the household life to the homeless one under the Dharma and discipline declared by him!"

"How do you know this, O Gautamid? Have you presented your request to him?"

"Yes, my lord Ānanda," replied Prajāpatī sorrowfully, "I asked him while he was staying at Kapilavastu; and he refused permission."

"In that case, O Gautamid, remain where you are for a little while, and I shall ask the Perfect One if he will permit the going-forth of women."

Thereupon Ānanda went inside the monastery and approached the Tathāgata. Three times Ānanda presented his request that women be allowed ordination, and three times Buddha refused him, saying: "Enough, Ānanda! Do not desire the going-forth of women under the Dharma and discipline proclaimed by me!"

Then Ānanda thought, "It is clear that the Master refuses to permit women to join the Saṅgha. What if I now ask him in a different way?" So Ānanda said to the Perfect One: "Lord, are women capable, after going forth from the household life to the homeless one—are they capable of realizing the fruit of Stream-Entering?"

"Women are capable of doing so, Ānanda," replied the Tathāgata.

"Lord, are women capable of realizing the fruit of Once-Returning?"

"Yes, Ānanda."

"Of Never-Returning?"

"Yes, Ānanda."

"Of Arhatship?"

"Yes, Ānanda, women are capable of realizing the fruit of Arhatship."

"Then, Lord, if women are capable of attaining the fruits of the four supramundane paths, consider how great a benefactress Prajāpatī Gautamī has been. She is the sister of the mother of the Perfect One; and as his nurse and foster mother she gave him milk, feeding him from her own breast when his mother died. It would be a good thing, Lord, if women were allowed to go forth from the household to the homeless life under the Dharma and discipline declared by the Perfect One."

The Tathāgata considered Ānanda's words and then replied, saying: "If, Ānanda, Prajāpatī Gautamī will accept eight strict rules, let that be reckoned to her as full ordination.

"(1) A nun, even if of a hundred years' standing, shall first salute a monk, shall rise up before him, shall entreat him with folded hands and make obeisance, even if that monk has only that day been ordained. (2) A nun shall not spend a rainy season in a district where there are no monks. (3) A nun shall look to the Order of Monks to be advised of the new and full moon days and the coming of a monk to preach the sermon. (4) At the end of the rainy season retreat, a nun shall invite criticism in the presence of the assemblies of monks and nuns regarding offenses seen, heard, and suspected.

"(5) A nun guilty of serious offense shall go on probation for a year. (6) When a nun has spent two years in the practice of the precepts, she shall ask for full ordination. (7) A nun shall neither rebuke nor scold a monk on any pretext. (8) Nuns may not reprove monks, but monks may reprove nuns.

"These rules are to be honored, respected, revered, and worshiped, and are not to be transgressed as long as life shall last. If, Ānanda, Prajāpatī Gautamī will accept these eight strict rules, let that be reckoned to her as full ordination."

Ānanda went out at once to Prajāpatī and repeated to her the eight strict rules which he had received from Buddha.

A murmur of joy arose from the company of women who had accompanied Lady Prajāpatī from Kapilavastu; and all gladly accepted the eight rules for nuns.

Many of the women, including Prajāpatī and Yaśodharā, quickly attained Nirvāṇa, just as Kṛṣā Gautamī had done even while still a laywoman. True happiness was theirs at last—happiness which time could not destroy nor gods or devils take away.

Then Ānanda returned to the Perfect One, bowed respectfully, and said: "Prajāpatī Gautamī has accepted the eight strict rules. The sister of the mother of the Perfect One has become ordained."

"If, Ānanda," Buddha replied, "women had not been allowed to go forth from the household life to the homeless one under the Dharma and discipline proclaimed by the Tathāgata, the religious life would have lasted a long time, the good life would have lasted a thousand years. But as women have now gone forth, Ānanda, the religious life will not last long, the good life will last only five hundred years.

"Just as families in which there are many women and few men are easily molested by robbers and pot-thieves, even so in that congregation in which women have received ordination the religious life does not long endure. When mildew blight afflicts a flourishing rice field, or red rust afflicts a flourishing cane field, neither field endures for long. So it is with the religious life in a Saṅgha which has admitted women.

"Just as a man, Ānanda, might with foresight build a dike for a great reservoir to prevent the water from flowing out, so have I with foresight proclaimed these eight strict rules not to be transgressed as long as life shall last."

And then, addressing the monks who had gathered around him, Śākyamuni said: "In Himālaya, king of mountain ranges, O monks, there are tracts of level country, delightful places frequented by both monkeys and human beings. In such places, monks, hunters set traps of pitch in the monkeys' tracks to catch them.

"Now, those monkeys who are free from folly and greed, on seeing a pitch-trap, keep far away from it. But a foolish, greedy monkey is unable to resist the temptation. What happens?

"First of all, that monkey handles the pitch with one paw. And his paw sticks fast. Then, thinking to set himself free, he grasps it with the other paw, but that also sticks fast. To free both paws he gets first one foot, and then the other, in the pitch. And to free both paws and both feet, he lays hold of them with his muzzle, and that sticks fast, too.

"So, monks, that monkey, thus caught in five ways, lies down and howls, a prey for the hunter who comes and roasts him for eating there and then.

"It is exactly the same way, monks, with one who roams in wrong pastures. Do not, therefore, roam out of bounds; for Māra seizes his chance, Māra seizes his opportunity. Now, what is a monk's wrong pasture and range? Verily, it is the five-stranded cord of sensual pleasure, namely, objects sensed by the eye, ear, nose, tongue, and body—objects desirable, charming, bewitching, and pleasure-producing.

"Roam in pastures that are your own, O monks, keep to your ancestral range; for, so roaming, Māra gets no chance, no opportunity, to overcome a man. And what is a monk's own pasture? It is the four Fundamentals of Attentiveness, namely, contemplation of body, feelings, mind, and thoughts, seeing all as they really are.

"A monk, for example, duly realizes that this body, doomed to decay and death, is composed of flesh and blood, bone and sinew, hair and nails, liver and lights—a vile skin-bag filled with urine and dung and various kinds of stench, nine-holed, and trickling here and there.

"And thus he abides, likewise reflecting on feelings, mind, and ideas, seeing all in conformity with reality. That, O monks, is a monk's own pasture, his own ancestral range."

X

THE SECOND SIX YEARS OF TEACHING

• THE DELUSIONS OF BRAHMĀ •

After staying at Vaiśālī for a time, the Tathāgata continued his journeys, making his rounds from place to place and turning the Wheel of Dharma with the wish: "Oh, that all beings might be inclined to perfect Enlightenment! Oh, that everyone might tread the Path to Release and make an escape from misfortune!"

Now it came to pass that Buddha stayed for a time among the Mallas at Anupiyā, one of their towns. There he went to the pleasance where Bhārgava the Wanderer was dwelling.

"Welcome to the Perfect One!" said Bhārgava when he saw the Tathāgata approaching. "Let my Lord the Perfect One come near. It has been a long time since the Perfect One has come this way. May it please you, Lord, to be seated: here is a seat made ready."

Śākyamuni sat down; and Bhārgava, taking a low stool, sat down beside him for a friendly chat.

"Bhārgava," said the Tathāgata, "there are certain recluses and brahmins who declare it as their traditional belief that the beginning of things was the doing of a creator-god, of Brahmā. When I asked them who created the creator-god, they became confused and asked it of me as a counterquestion. And I answered them this way: "Universes endlessly evolve and dissolve, and have done so since beginningless time. When, sooner or later, this world-system begins to reevolve, the world of the Brahma gods appears, but it is uninhabited. Life then begins to evolve, and some being or other, either because his span of years has passed or because his merit is exhausted, deceases from the immaterial realm and comes to life in the world of the Brahmās. And there he lives, made of mind, feeding on rapture, radiating light from himself, traversing space, and continuing in beauty. Thus does he remain for a long, long time.

"Now there arises in him, from his living there so long alone, a dissatisfaction and a craving.

" 'Oh, how I wish that other beings might come to keep me company in this place!'

"And just then, either because their years or their merit has become exhausted, other beings fall from the higher state and appear in the heaven of the Brahmā gods as the companions of Brahmā; and in all essential respects they lead a life like his.

"When this happens, the being who was first reborn gets this idea: 'I am Brahmā, Great Brahmā, the Vanquisher, the Unvanquished, the All-Seeing, the Disposer, the Almighty, the Creator, the Chief, the Assigner, the Great I AM, the Father of all that are and are to be. By me are these beings created. And why is that so? A while ago I thought, "Oh, how I wish that other beings might come into existence!" Such was the aspiration of my mind, and lo! these beings really did come!'

"And, Bhārgava, those beings who arose after him adopt this line of reasoning: 'This worthy being must be Brahmā, Mahābrahmā, the Vanquisher, the Unvanquished, the All-Seeing, the Disposer, the Almighty, the Creator, the Chief, the Assigner, the Great I AM, the Father of all that are and are to be. By this Brahmā have we, good sirs, been created. And why is that so? Because he, as we see, was here before us, but we arose after him.'

"When this takes place, the being who first arose becomes longer-lived, handsomer, and more powerful; but those who appeared after him become shorter-lived, less handsome, and less powerful. And it happens from time to time that one or another of those beings, on deceasing from that state, comes to the state of a human being on earth.

"Thus come, he might enter the religious life and perfect himself just enough to recall his former abode, but not what went before. And so he thinks: 'That Worshipful Brahmā, that Great Brahmā, the Vanquisher, the Unvanquished, the All-Seeing, the Disposer, the Almighty, the Creator, the Chief, the Assigner, the Great I AM, the Father of all that are and are to be—he by whom we were created, he is permanent, constant, eternal, unchanging, and he will remain so for ever and ever. But we who were created by Brahmā, we have come into the world all impermanent, unstable, short-lived, and destined to return to dust according to the Creator's will.'

"Now, Bhārgava, the belief in an almighty creator-god is a delusion of the ignorant. For if the world had been made by a creator-god, there could be no such thing as sorrow or calamity, neither doing right nor doing wrong. For all deeds, pure and impure, good and evil, must come from the creator.

"If there were a creator, then all living beings should meekly submit, patient beneath their maker's power. In such a case, however, would it be of any use to practice virtue? It would be quite the same whether one do good or evil—there would be no reward for doing good. Since the deeds themselves must have been contrived by the creator, then all would be the same.

"And if it be said that there is another cause beside Brahmā as creator, then the god is not almighty. Thus you see, Bhārgava, *the theory of a creator-god is useless: it is filled with contradictions.*

"Now I, Bhārgava, have attained the highest Wisdom. Not only am I acquainted with Knowledge: I know all that is to be known. And what is more, I do not misapply that Knowledge. As I do not misapply it, I have seen Nirvāṇa, realizing which a Tathāgata is infallible and ineffable.

"As I have declared my Knowledge time and again in divers ways, certain recluses and brahmins have accused me falsely of uttering groundless, empty lies, saying, 'The Ascetic Gautama is all wrong, and so are his monks.'

"They say, for instance, that I teach that he who has attained that stage of salvation called the Beautiful regards the universe in its entirety as ugly. What I really said was, 'Whenever one has attained that stage of salvation called the Beautiful, he knows in truth what beauty is.' "

"But it is they, Lord," declared Bhārgava, "who are all wrong! I am delighted with the words of the Perfect One, and I have faith in the Perfect One. Perhaps the Perfect One can train even me to attain that stage of salvation called the Beautiful!"

"It would be hard for you, Bhārgava, holding other views, of different persuasion, and having other inclinations, different aims, and trained in a different system—it would be hard for you to attain that stage of salvation called the Beautiful and cast off all fetters both human and divine. Nevertheless, O Bhārgava, guard carefully that faith which you have in me!"

• BUDDHA CHALLENGES • GOD AND THE DEVIL

Now when the god Brahmā heard it rumored that Buddha declared him to be deluded, he appeared to the Perfect One in a blaze of light and said: "It will not be well for you, O Ascetic, it will be harm and ill to you to teach that I, Brahmā, Great Brahmā, am doomed to death and decay. Even as I am eternal, persistent, everlasting, indissoluble, immutable, not subject to passing away and rebirth—even as I am the Highest, not to be surpassed—so also is my world eternal, persistent, everlasting, indissoluble, immutable, free from passing away and reappearance—and, further, so also is rebirth into my heaven the highest liberation."

"Not so, Mahābrahmā," replied Buddha. "Neither you nor your

world is as you say: a higher liberation than rebirth into your heaven exists, I declare."

At that moment Māra, the Evil One, appeared to Buddha, but remained invisible to Brahmā.

"Beware of him, O Ascetic!" exclaimed the Evil One. "Beware, O Sugata! He is Brahmā, Great Brahmā, the Vanquisher, the Unvanquished, the All-Seeing, the Disposer, the Almighty, the Creator, the Chief, the Assigner, the Great I AM, the Father of all that are and are to be! Long before you there were ascetics who were the enemies of craving, who were the foes of Brahmā; and these, at the dissolution of the body at death, fell into wretched states of existence. Therefore I advise you, O Ascetic, to accept what Brahmā says. Do not contradict the word of Great Brahmā!"

Then Brahmā spoke again to Buddha, saying: "Speak if you will, O Ascetic; but whatever you say, my world is truly free from decay and death, it is truly permanent, it is truly the highest liberation. If you take Earth as your basis, O Ascetic, if you take the elements as your basis, if you take the gods, if you take me as your basis, O Ascetic, you must obey me, you must yield to me."

The Perfect One did not reply to Brahmā, however, but turned to Māra and said: "Well do I know you, O Evil One: abandon your hope that I do not recognize you! You are Māra the Malign; and this Brahmā here, these angels and heavenly hosts of Brahmā,—they are all in your hand, they are all in your power. You, O Evil One, certainly think, 'Gautama must also be in my hand, Gautama must also be in my power!' I, however, am not in your hand, I am not in your power, for by me you are seen!

"Now, then, O Brahmā, your Brahma-world is not free from death and decay, not permanent, not the highest liberation. For if it were, there would be no passing-beyond, no Nirvāṇa. But I, having attained Nirvāṇa, have gone beyond limitation, beyond the sphere of existence and nonexistence. *I, O Brahmā, have become extinct.*

"The earth and the elements," continued Buddha, "the gods and you, O Brahmā, have I recognized as impermanent, painful, and essentially unreal. And having known all things, I have renounced and rejected all things, detaching myself from them. And in this, O Brahmā, not only am I your equal in knowledge, not only am I not less than you, but I am far greater than you."

At these words of the Perfect One, many thousands of gods and angels raised a great shout, declaring Buddha to be "God of Gods," superior to all gods, the envy of all gods. And Māra, perceiving that his plot was defeated, tried in vain to dissuade the Perfect One from teaching the Doctrine of Truth.

• BRAHMĀ'S DISENCHANTMENT •

It came to pass that a certain monk, desiring to know where the basis of corporeality ceases to exist, entered a state of mental absorption whereby he ascended, in a mind-formed body, to the various worlds of the gods.

First he went to the Heaven of the Four Celestial Kings, then to the Heaven of the Thirty-Three Palaces, then to the Heaven of the Yāma-Gods, and so on, each time asking the gods of each heaven-world the following question: "My friends, where does the basis of all corporeality utterly cease?"

And in each heaven the gods replied: "We, O monk, do not know where the basis of all corporeality utterly ceases. But there are other gods, higher and more glorious than we, who might know the answer to your question."

So it went until, finally, the monk had elevated his consciousness to the level of the three Brahma-worlds. And to the hosts of gods in those worlds he posed the same question.

"Good friends, perhaps you can tell me where the basis of corporeality utterly ceases."

"Alas, monk, we do not know," answered the Brahma gods. "There is, however, Great Brahmā, the Omniscient, the Almighty, the Father of all that are and are to be. He, far more glorious and excellent than we, is surely able to tell you what you wish to know."

"But where, my friends, is this Mahābrahmā at the present moment?"

"We do not know, O monk, where Brahmā is, or in what direction

Brahmā may be found. But when certain signs are seen, notably a radiance, an effulgence, Brahmā himself appears."

The monk waited patiently; and in no long time a radiance appeared, an effulgence appeared, and forthwith Brahmā himself appeared.

"My friend," said the monk to Great Brahmā, "where does the basis of corporeality utterly cease?"

"I, O monk, am Brahmā, Great Brahmā, the Vanquisher, the Unvanquished, the All-Seeing, the Disposer, the Almighty, the Creator, the Chief, the Assigner, the Great I AM, the Father of all that are and are to be."

"Friend," said the monk, "I did not ask you, 'Are you Brahmā, Great Brahmā,' and so forth. What I asked you is this: 'Where does the basis of corporeality utterly cease?"

"I, O monk, am Brahmā, Great Brahmā, the Vanquisher, the Unvanquished, the All-Seeing—"

"But friend," protested the monk, "I heard all that at first! What I want to know is where the basis of corporeality utterly ceases!"

Then Mahābrahmā took the monk by the arm and led him to one side out of earshot of the hosts of gods.

"O monk," said Brahmā, "these gods and angels of my heaven believe that I see all things, know all things, have penetrated all things. For this reason I did not answer you in their presence. I, O monk, do not know where the basis of corporeality utterly ceases. Therefore it was a sin and a crime that you left the Perfect One and went elsewhere in quest of an answer to this question. Turn back, O monk; and having approached the Buddha, ask him this question; and as he shall explain it to you, so believe."

The monk arose from the state of mental concentration that had taken him to the worlds of the gods and went at once to the Tathāgata. And having respectfully greeted the Perfect One, the monk asked: "Where, Lord, does the basis of corporeality utterly cease?"

"I perceive, O monk, that you have searched even as far as the world of Mahābrahmā without having found the answer to your question," replied Buddha. "And when you failed, you returned to me. Well, monk, you phrased your question incorrectly. What you should have asked is this: 'Where does the

basis of corporeality find no footing?' And the answer is: 'In Transcendental Consciousness does the basis of corporeality find no footing.' And where the basis of corporeality finds no footing, there do mind and body and all the qualities associated therewith—long and short, fine and coarse, good and bad—utterly cease."

Thus spoke the Utterly Awakened One.

• MIRACULOUS DISPLAYS FORBIDDEN •

The sun was flashing forth with autumnal splendor when Buddha returned to Rājagṛha. Now, soon after he had taken up lodgings in the Veṇuvana Monastery in the Squirrels' Feeding Ground (Kalandakanivāpa), a wealthy merchant of Rājagṛha, in order to find out if Arhats really exist, and at the same time advertise his wares at the expense of religion, had set up a tall bamboo pole at the top of which was tied a sandalwood bowl.

"This bowl," declared the merchant, "will be given to any ascetic or brahmin who is sufficiently perfected and versed in psychic attainments to rise up in the air and take it down from the top of the pole."

The sandalwood bowl was such a desirable one, sweet-scented and beautifully decorated with intricate carvings, that, one after another, the leaders of the six heretical sects attempted to get it down from the pole; but all of them were unable to do so.

Several disciples of Buddha were gathered there to watch the feat, among them Piṇḍola Bhāradvāja and Maudgalyāyana.

"Would it not be well, venerable Piṇḍola," said Maudgalyāyana, "if a disciple of the Perfect One should bring down the bowl and thereby demonstrate the power of the Dharma?"

"Yes, it might be well, venerable Maudgalyāyana," replied Piṇḍola.

And thereupon Piṇḍola Bhāradvāja concentrated his thought: the bowl vanished from the top of the pole and reappeared in Piṇḍola's hands.

On seeing this feat accomplished, the crowd cheered enthusiastically. And Buddha, just then approaching, asked Ānanda concerning the cause of the commotion.

"Lord, the venerable Piṇḍola Bhāradvāja has fetched down from that tall bamboo pole a sandalwood bowl belonging to the great merchant. That is why the people are making so much noise."

The Tathāgata then went up to Piṇḍola and rebuked him, saying: "It is not proper, Bhāradvāja, it is not becoming, it is not fitting, it is not worthy of a religious man, it is not allowable, it is not to be done! How can you, for the sake of a miserable wooden bowl, exhibit to the common people a condition of Arhats, a wonder of psychic power? Even as a vulgar woman exhibits herself undressed to the common people for the sake of a miserable pittance, so did you exhibit to the common people a condition of Arhats, a wonder of psychic power, for the sake of a miserable wooden bowl!"

Having thus rebuked Piṇḍola, the Perfect One then addressed the other monks.

"A condition of Arhats, O monks, a wonder of psychic power, is not to be exhibited to the common people. Whoever exhibits them is guilty of wrongdoing. Break this wooden bowl; and having reduced it to fragments, give the pieces to the monks as perfume for ointment."

Then a certain lay follower from Nālandā, Kevatta by name, ran forward and approached Śākyamuni in entreaty.

"May it please the Lord," he said, "to allow his disciples to perform a miracle of magic power at Nālandā in order that the people of Nālandā be converted to the Dharma."

Nālandā was a town not far from Rājagṛha.

"O Kevatta," declared Buddha, "I despise, loathe, abhor, and reject miracles of magic power and divination! My disciples and I gain adherents only by the miracle of instruction."

Kevatta's request was not entirely denied, however, for in due time the Tathāgata and a group of monks went to Nālandā and taught the inhabitants of that town so that they became converted to the Religion of the Buddhas.

• PARABLE OF THE PRODIGAL SON •

Once when Lord Buddha was staying on Mount Gṛdhrakūṭa (Vulture Peak), he told his disciples that the attainment of Nirvāṇa means the attainment of perfect Buddhahood and an eternal spiritual Life so full and rich that thought is unable to grasp its significance. The disciples were amazed and thrilled to hear that the omniscience of Buddhahood, no less, is the glorious destiny of all sincere followers of the Path.

"Therefore try to understand the mystery of the Buddhas, the holy Masters of the world," advised Śākyamuni. "Forsake all doubt and uncertainty: verily you shall become Buddhas: rejoice!"

When those venerable disciples, Subhūti, Kātyāyana, Mahā-Kāśyapa, and Maudgalyāyana, heard this wonderful Law unheard of before, undreamt of before, they were struck with wonder, amazement, and rapture. They instantly rose up from their seats, went up to the place where Buddha was sitting, knelt before him, and addressed him in this strain: "And just now, O Lord, we hear from the Lord that all disciples are Bodhisattvas who are destined to supreme perfect Enlightenment. We are astonished and amazed, and deem it a great gain that today, on a sudden, we have heard from the Lord a voice such as we have never heard before. We have acquired a magnificent jewel, O Lord, an incomparable jewel! We had not sought, nor searched, nor expected so magnificent a jewel! It has become clear to us, O Lord; it has become clear to us, O Sugata!"

And the venerable Mahā-Kāśyapa spoke further, saying: "We are struck with wonder and rapture on hearing the thrilling voice of the Master speaking such unexpected words. Why, in an instant of time we shall have acquired a great treasure of precious jewels such as we were not thinking of, nor expecting! We are delighted and amazed, O Lord!

"It is just as if, Lord, a certain young man, led astray by low companions, left his father and wandered away to a distant country. The father, grieved by the loss of his son, went everywhere looking for him, but found no trace of him anywhere. And in the course of his search, the father came to a great city where he built a house and acquired much wealth by engaging in business. And the father often thought, 'Alas, it has been many years since my son ran away. I can never be happy until I find my son to enjoy all this wealth!'

"Meanwhile, the prodigal son had squandered his meager possessions and wandered from village to village, poor and miserable, begging food and clothing, and vitiated by scabs and itch.

"In the course of time the unfortunate boy came to the city where his father was living, and unwittingly went to his father's mansion to beg food and raiment. And the rich man happened to be sitting in the courtyard at that time, surrounded by trustees who were counting money and writing bills.

"The son, blinded by all that wealth and magnificence, failed to recognize his father, and thought: 'What am I doing here? This man must be a king or a rich householder. It would not be wise for me to risk getting caught to do forced labor! It would be better for me to ask the way to the street of the poor and make haste to leave this place.'

"But the rich father recognized his son and ordered servants to bring him back. The poor son was no sooner seized, however, than he fainted away at the thought: 'Surely these are executioners: what good will food or clothing do me now?'

"On seeing the young man's terror, the father considered: 'This my poor son does not recognize me. He cannot understand my magnificence nor believe that I am his father. It is better that I keep the truth from him for a time and let him think that I am a stranger who offers him employment.'

" 'You are free to go wherever you wish,' said the rich man, 'but consider, sir, that I will give you food and clothing, and pay you double wages to clean up the manure pile over there.'

"The son accepted the position, removed the pile of filth, cleansed the place where it had been, and took up his abode in a hovel near the mansion. His father observed him meanwhile through the windows, thinking, 'Here is my son engaged in a low occupation. As soon as he gets used to that, I shall give him a higher position in my service; and he may at last be able to grasp the fact that I am really his father.'

"So it happened; and, little by little, as the son advanced in the service of the rich man, his confidence increased. And one day the rich man thought: 'My son has arrived at the consciousness of being noble. It is time to reveal the truth to him.'

"Summoning his son and all of his friends, associates, and fellow citizens, the rich man declared: 'This man here, good sirs, is my very own son whom I lost a long time ago. He is the owner of all my property:

to him I bequeath it all and entirely: let him do with it what he wants: from this day forward all of it is his. Ah, my dear son, do you not now recognize your father who desires your welfare above all else?'

"Immediately recognizing his father, the son burst into tears and exclaimed, 'O my dear father, I committed an offense against you by running away from home many years ago, and yet you have repaid my foolishness with kindness! Verily, I am unworthy to receive so magnificent an inheritance!'

"But the man's father handed over all his wealth to his son with loving heart; and the son, amazed and filled with rapture, considered: 'Without searching or asking for it, even without expecting it, I have acquired a great treasure of precious things!'

"In like manner has the Tathāgata, who knows our low disposition, acknowledged us as his true sons, heirs of all that is possessed by the father. We have been prompted by the Lord to clear up the rubbish heap of the mental and moral defilements; and as we did the Lord's bidding we did not suspect, or even imagine, that the Nirvāṇa we had earned was the incomparable treasure of perfect Buddhahood!"

When Mahā-Kāśyapa had finished speaking, Śākyamuni said: "With my Buddha-eye of Insight, monks, I see that Kāśyapa shall become a Buddha at a future epoch, after having paid his respects to the Tathāgatas of many worlds in all the directions of space. Indeed, Kāśyapa shall become a matchless spiritual Buddha of unsurpassed glory, Lord of a magnificent field of worlds, an eternal Pure Land of holy delight.

"Just like Akṣobhya Buddha of the world Abhiratī in the eastern quarter of space, attended by the Mahāsattva-Bodhisattvas Samantabhadra and Mañjuśrī—just like Śaśiketu Buddha of the world Ratnasambhava in the southern quarter of space, attended by the Mahāsattva-Bodhisattvas Kṣitigarbha and Ratnapāṇi—just like Amitābha Buddha of the world Sukhāvatī in the western quarter of space, attended by the Mahāsattva-Bodhisattvas Avalokiteśvara and Mahāsthāmaprāpta—just like Amoghasiddhi Buddha of the world Vimalāvatī in the northern quarter of space, attended by the Mahāsattva-Bodhisattvas Sarvanīvaraṇaviṣkambhi and Viśvapāṇi—just like Siṃha Buddha of the world Akutobhayāvatī in the nadir, attended by the Mahāsattva-Bodhisattvas

Bhaiṣajyarāja and Vajragarbha—just like Nakṣatrarāja Buddha of the world Raśmiprabhāsa in the zenith, attended by the Mahāsattva-Bodhisattvas Prajñāpāramitā and Ākāśagarbha—this mighty Kāśyapa shall become an inexhaustible wellspring of merit for uncountable millions of beings."

• THE "LION'S ROAR" OF ŚĀRIPUTRA •

At one time when Śākyamuni Buddha was residing in the mango grove on the outskirts of Nālandā, the venerable Śāriputra came to the place where the Perfect One was, saluted him, and sat down at one side.

"Lord," said Śāriputra, "I have such great faith in the Perfect One that methinks there never has been, nor will there be, nor is there now, any other who is greater and wiser than the Perfect One, that is to say, as regards the highest Enlightenment!"

"Grand and bold, Śāriputra, are the words you have uttered—a veritable lion's roar," replied Buddha. "Of course, then, you have known all the Buddhas of past and future, comprehending their Mind with your mind, knowing their Wisdom and the Emancipation which they attained?"

"No, Lord."

"But at least, then, you know that I am an Arhat, a Buddha. Do you comprehend my Mind with your mind?"

"No, Lord."

"Well, Śāriputra, it would seem that you have no knowledge concerning Buddhas past, present, or future. How is it, then, that your words are so grand and bold? Why have you roared this all-inclusive lion's roar?"

"It happened one day," declared Śāriputra, "that I had come to the Perfect One to listen to an exposition of the Dharma. Now, while the Perfect One was teaching me the Dharma, I, understanding the Dharma, perfected one certain facet of the Dharma, namely, faith in the Master. And I confessed in my heart: 'The Perfect One is supremely Enlightened: well taught by him is the Dharma: blessed is the Saṅgha!'

"Moreover, Lord, all the Buddhas, whether of past, present, or future, have banished all corruptions of the mind by Wisdom, with hearts well established in the four Fundamentals of Attentiveness (analytical contemplation of the true nature of body, feelings, mind, and ideas), and thoroughly exercised in the seven Limbs of Wisdom (attentive recollection of what has been done and spoken in the past, investigation of the Dharma, energy activated by investigation, joyous enthusiasm arising from energy, tranquility arising from enthusiasm, concentration of mind arising from tranquility, equanimity arising from concentrated mind).

"Then, too, Lord, the skillful way in which the Perfect One teaches the Dharma is unsurpassed, showing how a disciple by destruction of the Poisons (lust, existence-infatuation, false view, ignorance) may know and realize for himself even in this very life sane emancipation of mind, and so attaining may abide therein immune. All this the Perfect One understands; and beyond what he understands there is nothing left to understand. Nor is there any other who is greater and wiser than the Perfect One, that is to say, as regards the highest Enlightenment."

When Śāriputra had spoken thus, the venerable Udāyin addressed the Tathāgata, saying: "It is wonderful and marvelous, Lord, to see how self-contained, serene, and aloof the Perfect One is, when he who is so mighty and powerful will not advertise his own merit! If any teachers of other religions were to discern in themselves even one such Buddha quality—why, they would wave a flag because of it!"

Thereupon Buddha declared: "Take note of this, Udāyin, that what you say is true. And you, Śāriputra, should often discourse on this matter to both monks and nuns, and to both lay brothers and lay sisters. Whatever foolish ones there may be who feel doubt and misgiving concerning the Tathāgata, when they have heard such a discourse, doubts and misgivings will be banished from their minds.

"Well, Śāriputra, let such a discourse occur to you now. My back is aching: I will stretch it."

• FARMER BHĀRADVĀJA •

Once upon a time the Master, wandering from town to town, came to the brahmin village of Ekanāla in Magadhan country and decided to stay there for a time.

It was planting time; and the brahmin farmer Bhāradvāja had five hundred plows in yoke.

Now, early one morning Śākyamuni took bowl and outer robe and approached the farmer at work. It was the hour for distributing food to the hired help; and Buddha drew near and stood at one side to beg alms-food. And the farmer Bhāradvāja, when he saw Buddha standing there for alms, said: "Ascetic, I plow and plant; and when I have plowed and planted, I eat! You, Ascetic, also ought to plow and plant, for having done so, you will have earned your food."

"Brahmin," replied the Tathāgata, "I, too, plow and plant; and when I have plowed and planted, I eat."

"But we do not see the Ascetic Gautama's yoke and plow, nor his plowshare, nor his goad, nor his oxen. The Ascetic Gautama speaks nonsense!"

To this the Perfect One replied in meter, saying:

Faith is the seed, austerity the rain,
Wisdom is my yoke and plow.
My pole is modesty, my mind, the strap,
Mindfulness my plowshare and goad.
Guarded in action, guarded in speech,
Restrained in food and drink,
Truth's my hoe to clear the weeds,
Tenderness is my deliverance.
Exertion is my team in yoke
That draws me to Security and Peace.
And on it goes, no turning back,
To where there is no suffering.
Just so this plowing is plowed, from which

Comes Immortality's deathless fruit.
And whosoever plows this plowing,
Set free is he from every ill.

Then the farmer Bhāradvāja, taking a large copper bowl filled with rice gruel, offered food to Buddha, saying: "Let the reverend Gautama eat this rice gruel! A plowman indeed is the Perfect One, since he plows a plowing for Fruit free from decay!"

"Not for me is food earned by chanting hymns," replied Śākyamuni. "Such fare is not for Tathāgatas, O brahmin, for Buddhas reject food obtained by hymn-singing and practicing religion for pay! No, Bhāradvāja, other food must be offered to a recluse wholly consummate, free from the Poisons, untroubled, calm."

"Then, reverend Gautama, to whom shall I give this rice gruel?"

"Brahmin, I see no one in the world with its gods and men by whom that rice gruel, if eaten, could be digested, except by the Tathāgata or by one of his disciples. Therefore, brahmin, throw that rice gruel away."

Bhāradvāja reluctantly poured the rice gruel into a nearby puddle of water. And the rice gruel, thrown into the water, seethed and hissed and sent forth steam and smoke. So astonished was Bhāradvāja, so alarmed was Bhāradvāja, that his hair stood on end.

"Amazing, reverend Gautama!" he exclaimed, falling with his head at Buddha's feet. "Truly, Lord, the reverend Gautama is unsurpassed in the world! Lo! I go to the reverend Gautama for refuge, to the Dharma and to the Saṅgha for refuge! I wish to become a follower of the reverend Gautama: grant me ordination this very day!"

And so the farmer Bhāradvāja was given full ordination at Śākyamuni's hands. And in no long time the venerable Bhāradvāja attained the supreme goal of the holy life, Nirvāṇa, for the sake of which men and women of good family rightly go forth from the household life to homelessness.

• DISCOURSES TO HOUSEHOLDERS •

Śākyamuni Buddha preached many sermons to lay disciples and householders in the course of his career. And once upon a time a certain householder approached the Perfect One and declared that he, aspiring to live the religious life, had renounced all worldly practices.

"What you, O householder, call 'worldly practice' is one thing," said the Master, "but what is meant by 'worldly practice' in the Āryan discipline is another thing.

"These eight Precepts in the Āryan discipline conduce to the renunciation of worldly practices: (1) Through making no onslaught on living beings, harming is renounced, (2) through taking only what is voluntarily given, pilfering is renounced, (3) through speaking truthfully, deceit is renounced, (4) through gracious speech, malicious speech is renounced, (5) through the absence of coveting, greed is renounced, (6) through the absence of invective, angry blame is renounced, (7) through the absence of vindictiveness, wrathful rage is renounced, and (8) through humility, self-conceit is renounced.

"When I say that through making no onslaught on living beings harming is renounced, I mean that an Āryan disciple considers the matter this way:

" 'I am attaining the renunciation of those fetters because of which I was one who made onslaught on living beings. Verily, if I were to harm living beings, conscience would upbraid me; intelligent persons, having found me out, would censure me; and at the dissolution of my body at death, I should arise in a world of woe. But those painful mind-and-body aggregates which would arise because of onslaught on living beings come not to be when onslaught on living beings is renounced.'

"And in like manner the Āryan disciple reasons concerning the other seven rules.

"O householder, it is like a hungry dog, weak from starvation, who might find his way into a slaughter-yard. Suppose the butcher flings that dog a bare bone with only a trace of blood on it. Do you think that the dog's hunger would be allayed by such a bare bone?

"In the same way, householder, an Āryan disciple reflects, 'Sensual pleasure has been likened by the Master to a bare bone, of great suffering, of great tribulation, which is only the beginning of a long series of sufferings,' and having by higher insight penetrated the truth of the matter, and *having laid aside that indifference which is based upon diversity, he develops only that indifference which is based upon unity, and in which all hankering after worldly things is brought to an end.*"

• THE ŚIṂŚAPĀ LEAVES •

In the ninth year after the Enlightenment, the Tathāgata went with a large company of monks to the great and flourishing city of Kauśāmbī, located on the bank of the river Jumnā about a hundred miles west of Vārāṇasī. Kauśāmbī was the capital of the Vatsas, ruled at that time by King Udena.

Arriving at that city, the Perfect One took up residence in a grove of śiṃśapā trees. And one day the monk Māluṅkyāputra sat apart from his fellows, thinking: "There are certain things that the Perfect One has left unexplained, certain views that the Perfect One has not expounded. I am not pleased by his failure to explain them. I, myself, will therefore approach the Perfect One and say to him: 'If the Perfect One will explain the truth of these things to me, then I will follow the religious life under the Perfect One. But if the Perfect One refuses to explain them to me, then I will give up the training and go back to the lower life of the world.' "

So Māluṅkyāputra, rising from his solitude in the late afternoon, entered the śiṃśapā grove and drew near to the Perfect One, seating himself at one side.

"There are these views, Lord, the truth or falsity of which the Perfect One has not declared, namely, 'Eternal is the world, temporary is the world; finite is the world, infinite is the world.' Or again, 'Life and body are the same, life is one thing and body is another.' Or again, 'An Arhat is beyond death, an Arhat is not beyond death, an Arhat both is and is not beyond death, an Arhat neither is nor is not beyond death.'

"If the Perfect One will declare these things to me," continued Māluṅkyāputra, "I will continue in the holy life; but if he does not, I will give it up and return to the lower life of the world. Now, if the Perfect One knows that the world is eternal, let him declare it to be so. If he knows that the world is temporary, let him so declare it. And so also with regard to the other views that I have mentioned. But if the Perfect One does not know which opinions are true and which are false, then why doesn't he admit his ignorance in so many words?"

"Now, Māluṅkyāputra," replied Buddha, "did I say to you, 'Come, Māluṅkyāputra, follow the religious life under me and I will declare to you, "Eternal is the world" or "Temporary is the world,' " and so forth?"

"No, Lord, you did not."

"And did you, Māluṅkyāputra, say to me, 'Lord, I will follow the religious life under the Perfect One, and the Perfect One will declare to me, "Eternal is the world" or "Temporary is the world,' " and so forth?"

"No, Lord, I did not."

"That being the case, foolish man, who are you to find fault? He who asks the questions you have asked, Māluṅkyāputra, would surely come to the end of his days before those questions of his would be answered by the Tathāgata!

"Pay close attention, Māluṅkyāputra. Suppose a man were pierced by an arrow well steeped in poison, and his relatives were to summon a physician, a surgeon. Then suppose the man says: " 'I will not have this arrow pulled out until I know something about the man who shot the arrow, both his name and his clan, whether he be tall or short or of middle stature, whether he be a black man or swarthy or fair, whether he be of such and such a village or suburb or town.

" 'I will not have this arrow pulled out until I know something about the bow, by whom it was made, and whether it be a longbow or cross-bow. I will not have this arrow pulled out until I am told something about the bowstring that drove the arrow, whether it was made of creeper, reed, tendon, or of hemp or sap-tree . . . till I know of the arrow by which I have been pierced, whether it be a reed shaft or fashioned from a sapling . . . till I know of the feathers of it . . .' and so on and so on.

"Well, Māluṅkyāputra, that man would die, but still the matter would not be found out by him. Just so, Māluṅkyāputra, he who should ask the ontological questions you have asked would come to the end of his days before those questions of his would be answered by the Tathāgata!

"Now, Māluṅkyāputra, to say that the existence of the religious life should depend on those two opposing views, namely, that the world is eternal or temporary, that life and body are or are not the same thing, and so forth—that is not the Way. But I am one who declares that, whether the world be eternal or temporary, whether life and body be the same or not, and so on, nevertheless there is birth, there is decay, there is death, there are sorrow, grief, woe, lamentation, and despair; and it is the destruction of these things that I do explain.

"Therefore, Māluṅkyāputra, bear in mind that what I have declared is declared, and what I have not declared is not declared. Bear that in mind. And what have I not declared? That the world is eternal or temporal, and the other views you have mentioned. And why have I not declared those things?

"Because, Māluṅkyāputra, those things are not concerned with welfare, because they are not principles of the religious life, because they do not conduce to cessation, to serenity, to the Wisdom Supreme, to Nirvāṇa. That is why I have not explained those things. And what have I declared?

"I have declared, 'This is Suffering, this is the Cause of Suffering, this is the Cessation of Suffering, this is the Path leading to the Cessation of Suffering.' I have explained these things because they are concerned with welfare, because they are principles of the religious life, because they conduce to cessation, to serenity, to the Wisdom Supreme, to Nirvāṇa."

Thus spoke the Exalted One; and the monk Māluṅkyāputra was satisfied with what the Exalted One said.

The next day the Tathāgata took up a handful of śiṃśapā leaves and said to the monks who were present in the grove: "Now what do you think, O monks? Which are the more, these few śiṃśapā leaves that I hold in my hand, or those that are in this entire śiṃśapā grove?"

"Few in number, Lord, are those śiṃśapā leaves that are in the hand of the Perfect One; far greater in number are those in this entire śiṃśapā grove."

"Just so, monks, those things which I know by my superknowledge, but have not revealed, are greater by far in number than those things which I have revealed. And why, monks, have I not revealed them?

"Because, O monks, they do not conduce to welfare, to cessation, to calm, to Nirvāṇa. That is why I have not revealed them. But what have I revealed? Suffering and the extinction of suffering. Therefore, monks, exert yourselves diligently to realize Pain, Pain's Origin, Pain's Ending, and the Path to Pain's Ending. Build yourselves a Raft of Dharma for crossing the current of life and death to Yonder Shore of Immortality."

• FLAMES OF WRATH •

News of Śākyamuni's unsurpassed mental and moral perfection spread rapidly throughout the district of the Vatsas; and when it reached the ears of a brahmin named Māgandiya, that brahmin decided then and there that only Buddha would make a suitable husband for his daughter, Magandiyā.

And so Māgandiya brought black-haired Magandiyā, tall and of flawless complexion, to the śiṃśapā grove at Kauśāmbī and offered her to the Perfect One.

"Here, Great Ascetic, is a gem of womanhood, a flower of the brahmin caste much sought after by kings, even by Udena, the Kauśāmbī king. Take note of her beauty, the loveliness of her form, the purity of her complexion. Alluring and well versed in the delicate and feminine arts, my daughter will be a pleasing wife to you."

The Perfect One was filled with disgust by this proposal. Looking beneath the haughty and coldly beautiful exterior of the brahmin woman with his superhuman eye of Insight, he perceived raging fires of self-will, conceit, and cruel passion.

At last the Perfect One spoke to Māgandiya, saying: "When I saw Craving, Discontent, and Greed, the daughters of Māra, I experienced no desire for amorous pleasures. Why, then, have you brought to me this skin-bag filled with urine and dung? I should not care to touch her even with my foot!"

Magandiyā stiffened under the impact of this rejection, and hot anger flared up in her eyes.

"If you would not have so desirable a gem as this," said her father in disappointment, "a woman longed for by kings, pray tell me what theory, what rule and rite, what way of life is yours!"

"Māgandiya," replied Buddha, "for such as I the dogmas concocted from theories and vain imaginings are eschewed as maggot-infested rubbish. I have looked into all the theories that clutter the minds of deluded men, and pondering them, I have accepted none. *But seeking Truth I have discovered peace of mind.*"

"But, Ascetic, you are only telling me that you do not accept orthodox views," retorted Māgandiya. "Can you convince me that you have really attained peace of mind?"

"Māgandiya, purification does not result from dogmas, creeds, or theology, nor from rules and sacramental rites. So rejecting these, by not accepting them, having no faith in them, the man devoted to the quest for peace of mind does not cling to craving desires. The craving of a thoughtless man grows like a creeper—he runs from life to life like a monkey searching for mangoes. As a tree, even though it has been cut down, grows up again so long as the root is safe and strong, just so does pain return again and again so long as craving remains unkilled."

"Well, Ascetic, if you think that purification does not come from dogmas, creeds, or theology, or from rules and sacramental rites, methinks your Doctrine is just mere foolishness; for many people believe that purification comes from faith in dogmas."

"But, Māgandiya, your questioning arises from your dependence on mere opinions," declared the Tathāgata, "and through blind faith in opinions you fall into error. Perceiving not the slightest ray of Truth, you therefore see all as foolishness. Consider, Māgandiya! Why should a brahmin say of one view, 'that is the truth,' while contending of another, 'that is a lie'? But the silent sage who leaves home for the homeless state, remote from the pleasures of sense, abiding unspotted by the world, does not delight in disputation.

"There are no enfettering bonds for him who is loosed from conjecture,"

continued Śākyamuni, "there is no shadow of error in those whom Truth has set free. But the slaves of dogmas and theories, arguing and wrangling, are seldom at peace with the world."

Thereupon the brahmin Māgandiya and his daughter, Magandiyā, went away. And Magandiyā nursed a grudge against the Perfect One for spurning her.

Shortly thereafter, Magandiyā became a consort of King Udena. And when she found out that Queen Sāmāvatī had been converted to Buddhism by the Exalted One, and the five hundred women of the king's seraglio with her, Magandiyā's fierce hatred incited her to plot the death of the queen.

One night when Sāmāvatī and the five hundred women were assembled in the royal conservatory playing musical instruments and singing, Magandiyā bolted the doors securely and set the palace on fire.

The sweet voices of the women and the melodious tones of flute and clarinet were suddenly drowned out by the deafening roar of flames which licked the walls like hungry demons. Magandiyā ran out laughing hysterically into the courtyard as the roaring of the flames and the screams of the trapped women rent the air.

"Burn, wretched fools!" she shrieked. "No more will Śākyamuni's monks receive your gifts! Oh, that Śākyamuni might burn with you!"

The palace was still in flames hours later, lighting the night sky with a ruddy glow that could be seen for many *yojanas* around. Blazing beams and rafters fell crashing into the white-hot debris, sending great clouds of sparks up into the sky to vanish like temporary stars in the blackness of the night. And King Udena sat not far from the conflagration, groaning with inconsolable anguish.

The next day a large number of monks came to the Perfect One and said: "Last night, Lord, the palace of King Udena caught fire, and the five hundred women of the king's seraglio, the chief of them being Sāmāvatī, came to their end in the royal conservatory. What, Lord, is the destiny, what the future lot, of those female lay disciples of the Perfect One?"

"O monks, among those female lay disciples, some are Stream-

Entrants who have with faith entered upon the Āryan Eightfold Path prescribed by me to destroy the suffering of beings. Some are Once-Returners, that is to say, they will sometime return once to this or to a similar world from heaven before attaining the Immortal State. And some are Never-Returners, that is to say, they will not return to this world, but will attain Nirvāṇa from a heaven-world. Not without rich reward, monks, are all those female lay disciples who have met their end."

• THE ETERNAL LAW OF LOVE •

It came to pass, while Buddha was dwelling at Kauśāmbī, that a certain monk had violated a rule of the discipline obligatory for all members of the Saṅgha. But because that monk had refused to admit that he had committed an offense, he had been expelled from the Brotherhood. Now, some of the monks maintained that he ought not to have been treated so severely, for the Master taught that an action is not morally wrong unless the doer thereof commits the evil deed with conscious intent.

Thereupon a great dissension arose, with monks, nuns, and even lay disciples arguing heatedly among themselves. Taking their quarrel to Buddha, some declared, "That monk received his just desserts," while others exclaimed, "No, Lord, that monk did not realize what he was doing, and cannot even now see that what he did was wrong."

Then Śākyamuni thought, "Here I am worried by monks, nuns, and lay disciples. I live in discomfort, not at ease. What if I were to live alone, remote from the crowd?" So the Perfect One set his bed and room in order, and without informing his attendant or notifying the monks, he started out alone and unattended on the road to Pārileya, thinking:

The deer untethered roams the wild
Wherever he pleases in search of food.
Seeing liberty and freedom, I will
Wander alone like a rhinoceros.

Everywhere free and at odds with none,
And well content with what I find,
Enduring dangers without dismay, I'll
Wander alone like a rhinoceros.

And when the Tathāgata reached the village of Pārileya, he took up his abode at the foot of a lovely śāla tree in a certain glade of Guarded Forest, where he was attended by a certain bull elephant.

Buddha and the elephant lived together happily for three months, at the end of which time the monks, repentant, came to the Perfect One and sought and received his forgiveness for their noisy squabbling.

"O monks," declared the Tathāgata, "there are two who store up great demerit for themselves. Which are the two? He who does not ask forgiveness after committing a wrong, and he who dose not forgive after the wrong has been confessed and forgiveness implored.

"Now, monks," continued the Master, "pay close attention, and I will teach you.

"Our innermost nature is the result of what we have thought, directed by our thoughts, made up of our thoughts. If a man speaks or acts with an evil thought, pain follows him as the wheel follows the beast of burden. But if a man speaks or acts with a pure thought, happiness follows him like one's ever-accompanying shadow.

" 'He abused me! he beat me! he defeated me! he robbed me!' Hatred will never cease in those who harbor such thoughts. But hatred will quickly pass away from them who do not harbor such thoughts. Not through hatred is hatred conquered at any time or in any place: hatred is conquered by love. This is an eternal law."

The contentious monks became ashamed of themselves when they heard these words.

"When men speak evil of you, O monks," said Śākyamuni, "you must train yourselves thus: 'Our heart shall be undisturbed, no evil word will we send forth, but remain compassionate of others' welfare, of kindly heart without resentment: and him who speaks evil of us will we suffuse with thoughts charged with love, and so abide. And making that our standpoint, we will suffuse the whole world with loving thoughts, far-reaching, wide-spreading, boundless, free from spite, free from ill-will, and so abide.'

"Moreover, monks, though robbers who are highwaymen should cut you up in pieces limb by limb with a two-handed saw, yet if the mind of any one of you should take offense thereat, such a one is no follower of my Teaching.

"And bear in mind again and yet again this parable of the saw which I have taught you. Do you not see, O monks, that every syllable of it, both small and great, must mold your conduct?"

"We do, Lord."

"Therefore, monks, bear in mind this parable of the saw which I have just taught you, for it shall conduce to your profit and welfare for many a long day.

"Whatever is to be done by one who is expert in seeking out what is good, having attained that tranquil state of Nirvāṇa, let him be able and upright, conscientious, gentle of speech and mild, not having vain conceit, contented, easily satisfied, having few wants, carefree, with faculties of sense composed, discreet and not arrogant, and not greedy after gifts. And let him not do anything mean and small in spirit for which the Āryas might censure him.

"Let him wish, 'May all beings be happy and secure! Oh, may they all be free from worry! Whatever living beings there are, feeble or strong, big or little, tall or short, visible or invisible, those living close at hand or far away, whether they be born or unborn—oh, may every living thing be full of bliss!'

"Let no one deceive another or hold another in contempt or scorn. Let no one in anger or resentment wish another's harm. As a mother at the risk of her life watches over her child, her only child, so also let everyone cultivate a boundless love toward all beings. And let a man cultivate good will toward all the world, a boundless love, above and below and across, unobstructed, free from meanness, free from enmity.

"To those in need, O monks, give without restraint; and in the giving of yourselves, give even your life if necessary. And in doing these things one should not use any measure or thought of self, thinking, 'this is what I would have them do unto me.'

"Develop the power of loving-friendliness, O monks. When I was living on the mountain slope, monks, I drew to myself lions and tigers by the power of loving-friendliness. Surrounded by lions and tigers, by panthers and buffaloes, by antelopes, stags, and boars, I lived in the forest. No living being is terrified of me; and neither am I afraid of any living being. The power of love is my support."

Lord Buddha then prepared to return to Kauśāmbī with the monks; and on the way back, the repentant monks, filled with joy by the words of the Perfect One, sang a song of happiness.

We live happily indeed,
Not hating those who hate us!
Among those who hate us
Let us dwell free from hatred!

We live happily indeed,
Free from ailments among the ailing!
Among men who are ailing
Let us dwell free from ailments!

We live happily indeed,
Free from greed among the greedy!
Among men who are greedy
Let us dwell free from greed!

We live happily indeed,
We, who call nothing our own!
Feeders on rapture are we,
Just like the Irradiant Gods!

• THE VALUE OF DOUBT •

Once when Buddha was journeying with a company of monks in Kośala country north of Kauśāmbī, he reached Kesaputra, a village of Kālāma noblemen. And the Kālāmas, when they heard the rumor that the Ascetic Gautama had arrived in Kesaputra, went to meet him; and when they had approached him, they said: "Lord, there are some recluses and brahmins here in our village who extol and praise their own views, but spitefully disparage and tear apart the views of others. In fact, Lord, recluses and brahmins come continually to Kesaputra and do this. And as we listen to them, doubt and wavering arise in us as to which of those people are telling the truth and which are telling lies. We do not know whom to believe!"

"Your doubts are well founded, O Kālāmas," answered the Enlightened One. "Well-founded indeed is your wavering; for your wavering arises about a matter that is open to doubt.

"Mark my words well, O Kālāmas. Do not believe anything on the basis of mere hearsay, thinking that it must be true because you have heard it for a long time. Do not believe traditions merely because they are old and have been handed down through many generations. Do not believe anything on account of mere rumors which people bandy about without using their powers of reasoning. Do not believe anything just because it accords with the testimony of your scriptures. Do not believe anything on the basis of supposition or mere inference. Do not believe anything because presumption is in its favor. Do not believe anything just because it agrees with your preconceived notions. Do not believe anything on the mere authority of your teachers and priests—just because they may be pleasing speakers or have charming personalities or claim the respect of the people.

"Whenever you know for yourselves, 'These teachings are not good, they are full of faults, they are condemned by the Āryas, they, when followed out and put into practice, conduce to strife, ruin, and sorrow'—then, Kālāmas, do indeed reject them.

"But whenever you know for yourselves, after thorough investigation, 'These teachings are good, they are free from faults, they are praised by the Āryas, they, when followed out and put into practice, conduce to the welfare and happiness of ourselves and of other beings as well'—then, Kālāmas, accept them as true, live up to them, act according to them.

"As the wise test gold by cutting it and examining the streak made by rubbing it across a piece of touchstone, *so should you accept my words only after examining them according to your own experience and reason, and not merely out of regard for me.*"

Thus spoke the Supremely Awakened One; and the Kālāmas of Kesaputra, on hearing this advice, became followers of Śākyamuni and lived in accordance with the Dharma.

• THE FOUR RELIGIOUS ABODES •

Buddha continued his journey eastward and finally reached Aṣyapura, a township of the Aṅgas, where he stayed for a while.

Now, there were brahmin priests nearby who were sacrificing horses, sheep, goats, cows, and other creatures with great cruelty on a blood-smeared altar decorated with obscene and horrifying images of gods.

"Let no one deceive you, monks," said Buddha. " 'Purify your hearts and cease to kill'—that is True Religion. To abandon covetousness and lust, to become free from evil passions, and to cast away all hatred and ill will—that is the right sacrifice and the true practice-realization. Only those sacrifices which are free from butchery are approached by Arhats and by those who have entered on the Way which leads to Arhatship."

And the Master continued, saying: "People call you 'ascetics,' O monks; and you, if you are asked who you are, should acknowledge that you are ascetics. As you are really ascetics, and so profess, you must train yourselves this way: " 'The proper path of an ascetic is the Path that we profess. Accordingly, our ascetic life is true, and our profession real; and by doing those things on account of which we enjoy robes, bowl, bed, and medicine, they will be of great fruit and great blessing. And thus our leaving the world will not be barren of result, but will bring forth blessings and merit.'

"Having purified himself from bad and evil qualities, the true ascetic considers himself released from those qualities. As he thus reflects, exultation arises; as he exults, joy arises; with his mind filled with joy, his body is calmed; when his body is calmed, he experiences happiness; and being happy, his mind is concentrated. He then enters the four Religious Abodes.

1. "With thoughts accompanied by LOVING-FRIENDLINESS, he abides pervading one quarter with loving-friendliness, likewise the second, the third, and the fourth—above, below, and everywhere. He abides pervading the entire world with mind charged with loving-friendliness, with an abundantly great and immeasurable freedom from hatred and malice.

2. "With thoughts accompanied by COMPASSION, he abides pervading one quarter with compassion, likewise the second, the third, and the fourth—above, below, and everywhere. He abides pervading the entire world with mind charged with compassion, with an abundantly great and immeasurable freedom from hatred and malice.

3. "With thoughts accompanied by ALTRUISTIC JOY, he abides pervading one quarter with altruistic joy, likewise the second, the third, and the fourth—above, below, and everywhere. He abides pervading the entire world with mind charged with altruistic joy, with an abundantly great and immeasurable freedom from hatred and malice.

4. "With thoughts accompanied by EQUANIMITY, he abides pervading one quarter with equanimity, likewise the second, the third, and the fourth—above, below, and everywhere. He abides pervading the entire world with mind charged with equanimity, with an abundantly great and immeasurable freedom from hatred and malice."

And concluding his discourse with the observation that all castes, all races, are equal as regards the life of a true ascetic, a genuine Ārya, the Tathāgata set out with a few monks for Cālika Hill while most of the monks returned directly to Śrāvastī, far to the west, to be rejoined later by Śākyamuni.

These things took place toward the end of the twelfth year after the supreme Enlightenment under the Bodhi tree at Buddhagayā. Buddha was forty-seven years old at this time.

XI

THE THIRD SIX YEARS OF TEACHING

• MEGHIYA'S DEFECTION •

In the thirteenth year after his Enlightenment, the Tathāgata took with him Meghiya, then his personal attendant, and went to Cālika Hill near the village of Jantu, there to dwell for a time with a small number of monks.

Now, one day the venerable Meghiya went up to Buddha, and after greeting the Perfect One with a salutation of respect, he said: "I should like very much, Lord, to enter Jantu village in quest of alms."

"Do whatever you think it time for, Meghiya," replied Buddha.

So Meghiya, taking bowl and robe, entered Jantu and collected alms-food in his bowl. And after eating his meal, he went to the river Kimikālā and took his exercise by walking up and down the riverbank. Now, while he was thus stretching his legs, he happened to glimpse a delightfully lovely mango grove; and at the sight of it he thought: "Truly lovely and delightful is this mango grove! What a wonderful place for a clansman to strive in for concentration! If I can talk the Perfect One into giving me leave, I will come here and strive!"

The venerable Meghiya went straightway to the Exalted One, told him about the grove, and requested permission to retire to it.

"Wait a little while, Meghiya," said Śākyamuni. "I am alone till some other monk arrives."

"But, Lord," Meghiya protested, "the Perfect One has nothing further to be done, has nothing more to add to what he has done. But for me, Lord, there is more yet to be done, there is more to be added to what I have done. If the Perfect One grants me leave, I will go to that mango grove to strive for concentration."

Śākyamuni again told Meghiya to wait until another monk should arrive; but Meghiya made his request even a third time. Then Buddha said: "Well, Meghiya, what can I say when you talk of striving for concentration? Do what you think it time for."

Meghiya then took leave of the Perfect One and went away to that mango grove. And having arrived there, he sat down at the foot of a certain tree to meditate.

Now during the time that Meghiya remained in the grove, there continually came to him three evil, unprofitable modes of thought—thoughts lustful, thoughts malicious, and thoughts harmful. Then at eventide he arose from his solitude and returned to Buddha.

"While I remained in that mango grove, Lord, there came to me continually three evil, unprofitable modes of thought. Verily, it is strange that I, who went forth from home to homelessness, should be thus assailed!"

"Meghiya, when the heart's release is immature, five things conduce to its maturity," declared the Tathāgata. And what are the five?

1. "As regards the first thing, Meghiya, a monk has a lovely intimacy, a lovely friendship, a lovely comradeship.

2. "Then again, Meghiya, a monk is virtuous; he abides restrained by

the restraint of the precepts; he is perfect in the practice of right behavior; and seeing danger in trifling faults, he undertakes and trains himself in the ways of the discipline.

3. "Then again, Meghiya, as regards talk that is serious and suitable for opening up the heart, and which conduces to passionlessness, to comprehension, to perfect Insight, to Nirvāṇa—that is to say, talk about wanting little, about contentment, about solitude, about avoiding society, about putting forth energy—talk about virtue, concentration of mind, and the attainment of Wisdom and Release—with talk such as this the monk gains pleasure without pain, and in full measure.

4. "Then again, Meghiya, a monk abides resolute in energy for the abandoning of unprofitable things, for the acquiring of worthwhile things; he is firm and strong in effort, not laying aside the burden in things worthwhile.

5. "Then again, Meghiya, a monk possesses perception, is endowed with the insight that goes on to discern the coming-to-be and the passing-away of all things; and with the Āryan penetration he goes on to penetrate the utter ending of all anguish.

"Moreover, Meghiya, by the monk who is established in these five conditions, four other things are to be made to increase, namely, (1) the idea of the unlovely is to be made to increase for the abandoning of lust, (2) amity is to be made to increase for the abandoning of malice, (3) attentiveness in breathing exercises is to be made to increase for the suppression of wandering thought, and (4) *the consciousness of impermanence is to be made to increase for the uprooting of egocentric pride.*"

• A NIGHT IN THE POTTER'S SHED •

Continuing his travels westward, the Tathāgata reached Rājagṛha, capital of the Magadhas, residence of Śrenika Bimbisāra, the Magadhan king. And forasmuch as it was sundown when he arrived, Buddha decided not to go at once to the Sītavana (Cool Grove), but to spend the night in a temporary lodging. He therefore drew near to the dwelling of Bhārgava the potter.

"If it be agreeable to you," said the Master to Bhārgava, "I will pass the night in your shed."

"I have no objection, sir," said Bhārgava, "but there is a wandering recluse here who has just begun to pass his first rainy season in my shed. If he consents, by all means stay as long as you please."

Now, this particular wandering ascetic, Vidyākara by name, had gone forth from the household life to the homeless state through faith in the Perfect One.

"If it be agreeable to you, brother," said the Perfect One to Vidyākara, "I will spend one night in the shed."

"Stay as long as you please, friend," replied Vidyākara. "Methinks the shed is big enough!"

Then the Tathāgata spread a heap of straw at one side and sat down upon it cross-legged, holding his body straight and setting mindfulness before him as his aim. Vidyākara did likewise; and thus they sat in meditation far into the night.

After a while this thought occurred to Śākyamuni: "I wonder whether this clansman is well disposed. Suppose I question him."

"Having faith in whom, brother," asked Buddha, "did you go a-wandering from home to homelessness? Who is your teacher? Whose doctrine do you approve of?"

"Friend," replied Vidyākara, "there is a Recluse called Gautama, of the Śākyan clan, one who went forth as a wanderer from the land of the Śākyas. About this Gautama, whom I accept as Lord, such is the good rumor that is noised abroad: 'The Perfect One is he, Arhat, Supremely Enlightened Buddha, perfect in knowledge and practice, Sugata, Knower of all worlds, Charioteer of men who would be tamed, Teacher of gods and men, the Tathāgata!' Having faith in that Perfect One, I went forth as a homeless brother. That Perfect One is my teacher. The Doctrine of that Perfect One is the one that I approve of."

"But where is that Perfect One now dwelling, brother, that Arhat who is a Supremely Enlightened Buddha?"

"In the northern country to the west, friend, there is a town called Śrāvastī. That is where the Perfect One is now dwelling."

"Have you ever met him, brother? Would you know him if you were to see him?"

"No, friend," said Vidyākara, "I have never seen that Perfect One. If I should see him I should not be able to recognize him."

Then thought the Perfect One: "So this clansman went forth as a homeless brother through faith in me! What if I now teach him the Dharma?"

"I will teach you a teaching, brother," said Buddha. "Listen carefully and apply your mind to what I say."

"Very good, friend," answered Vidyākara.

Lord Buddha then expounded at length the sixfold nature of man; and when he had finished, he admonished Vidyākara, saying: "Bear in mind this sixfold analysis of mine, brother."

Vidyākara was astonished and overjoyed.

"I have found the Master!" he exclaimed. "I have found the Sugata! The Supreme Buddha have I found!"

He then sprang up from his seat, threw his robe over one shoulder, and bowing his head at Buddha's feet, he prostrated himself before the Perfect One, saying: "Mine is the fault, Lord, mine the offense! Such was my folly, my blindness, my stupidity, that I thoughtlessly used the word 'friend' in speaking to the Perfect One! Let the Perfect One accept this acknowledgment of my offense as such for my restraint in the future!"

"No fault is yours, brother, in thus addressing me, not knowing that I am he whom you accept as your teacher. But commendable indeed is the spirit shown by your confession; for herein, brother, lies growth in the Āryan discipline, that, *when one has seen his fault as a fault, he should confess it as such and practice self-restraint in future time.*"

"O Lord, may I receive full ordination from the Perfect One?"

"But, brother, have you got your necessary robes and begging bowl?"

"No, Lord, my outfit is not complete."

"But, brother, the Tathāgatas do not confer full orders upon those whose requisites are not complete."

Whereupon Vidyākara was delighted with the words of the Exalted

One, and gave thanks. And as the day was breaking, Vidyākara went forth from the potter's shed in search of robes and bowl.

Now while Vidyākara was going about the streets of Rājagṛha on his quest, a stray cow gored him so severely that he died.

And having learned of the matter, a number of monks went to the Master and said: "Lord, the clansman named Vidyākara, who was given brief instruction by the Perfect One, has been killed. What is his lot? What is his after-death state?"

"A sage, O monks, is Vidyākara the clansman. He walked according to the ordinances of the Dharma; *and he did not vex me with questions having nothing to do with Dharma.* Vidyākara, by destroying the Fetters which bind to the lower world, has come to be by apparitional birth in a heaven of the Pure Abodes. He is destined to win Nirvāṇa, his lot is not to return to a world such as this."

• EXCESS OF ZEAL •

Remaining in Rājagṛha, but taking up residence in the Sītavana Monastery, the Tathāgata ordained with full orders a certain rich man's son by the name of Soṇa Kolivisa. And Soṇa, anxious to attain Nirvāṇa quickly, resided in the Sītavana.

Now it came about that Soṇa lacerated his feet through excessive zeal in walking up and down while striving; and the place where he walked was bedaubed with blood like a butcher's shambles. And finally Soṇa reasoned to himself as follows: "Here I am, one of those disciples of the Perfect One who dwell in earnest zeal; yet, strive as I will, my heart is not released from the Poisons. Now, great possessions await me at home. I can employ my wealth for doing good deeds. Suppose I were to return to the lower life of the world and employ my wealth for doing good deeds."

When Buddha saw the place where Soṇa was accustomed to walk up and down, he asked the monks: "Whose is this walk, monks, all bedaubed with blood like a butcher's shambles?"

"Lord," they replied, "the venerable Soṇa, through zealousness in walking up and down, has cut his feet on stones, so that his walking place is in this state."

Then Buddha went to the lodging of Soṇa.

"Is it not true, Soṇa, that, as you have been walking up and down with excessive zeal, you have become discouraged because you have failed to attain the heart's release from the Poisons? Is it not true, Soṇa, that you have actually considered returning to the lower life of the world?"

"It is true, Lord," said Soṇa, head lowered in shame.

"Tell me, Soṇa. Formerly, when you lived at home, were you not skilled in playing the lute?"

"Yes, Lord."

"Well, Soṇa, when your lute strings were too tight, did your lute give out sounds of correct pitch? Was the instrument fit for playing?"

"No, Lord, the lute was then not fit for playing, for the taut strings gave forth sounds too high in pitch."

"What happened, Soṇa, when the strings were slack?"

"In that case, Lord, they gave forth tones too low and sluggish."

"Now tell me, Soṇa. When your lute strings were neither overly taut nor overly slack, but adjusted to the proper tension, did your lute then give out sounds of correct pitch? Was the instrument then fit for playing?"

"It was, Lord, just as the Perfect One says."

"Exactly so," declared Śākyamuni, "excess of zeal makes one's mind weary; and, on account of mental fatigue, one's thoughts become irritable and uncertain. And lack of zeal makes one liable to sluggishness, which is equally bad. Therefore, Soṇa, persist in evenness of zeal, master your faculties, and make that your mark. Thus advancing little by little, mastering one step before taking another, happiness will come to you, and with happiness, Nirvāṇa."

Thereupon Soṇa persisted in evenness of zeal, mastered his faculties, and made that his mark. Anxiety of mind was abandoned, and happiness took its place. With the arising of happiness came perfect realization of the Deathless, and Soṇa knew for sure: *"Destroyed is rebirth, lived is the life religious, done is what had to be done. There is no more of life for me on terms like these."*

• VAKULA'S INFATUATION •

Now while Buddha was still residing near Rājagṛha, a young brahmin named Vakula, a native of Śrāvastī, chanced to hear the Dharma preached.

When Vakula first set eyes on the Perfect One, taking note of the handsomeness and perfection of the Tathāgata's visible body, he became strongly infatuated. Never sated with the sight of the Perfect One, he followed the Master everywhere in order to be near him.

One day Vakula thought, "There is no chance here in my lodging for me to see him constantly"—so he joined the Saṅgha and did nothing but contemplate the Perfect One. And Śākyamuni, perceiving that Vakula had become infatuated with him, waited patiently for the maturity of the monk's insight. But on a certain occasion, when Vakula was alone with him, he said: "What is it to you, Vakula, this vile body of mine that you see?"

"So good-looking is the Perfect One," replied Vakula, "that I never get enough of seeing the Perfect One."

"He who sees the Dharma, Vakula, is he who sees me. For, seeing the Dharma, I am seen; and, seeing me, the Dharma is seen."

At these words Vakula stopped gazing at Śākyamuni, but he nevertheless was unable to tear himself away from the Perfect One's presence.

Buddha then thought, "This monk will never reach Enlightenment unless I do something to shock him out of his infatuation."

"Vakula!" said Buddha. "It is now the last day of the rainy season. For your own good I must ask you to go away."

Thus bidden, Vakula had no choice but to depart. And as he walked out of the monastery, it seemed to him as though the world had come to an end. "What is life to me if I cannot see him any more?" Dejected and brokenhearted, Vakula proceeded to Mount Gṛdhrakūṭa (Vulture Peak) and climbed to a place of precipices. But the Perfect One knew instantly that Vakula was intent upon killing himself.

"This monk," thought Buddha, "finding no comfort away from me, will destroy the conditions for winning the topmost fruits."

Thereupon the Perfect One, making haste to follow Vakula, succeeded in overtaking the monk on the hill.

"Vakula!" he called. And then:

Now let the monk with ecstasy,
Happy in the Religion of the Buddhas,
Go on up to the holy, happy Path
Where things composite excite him nevermore.

And Buddha stretched forth his hand, saying: "Come, monk!"

Filled with joy and rapture at the thought, "I see the Ten-Powered One; and it is my good luck to hear him say 'Come!' " Vakula recovered his reason. Pondering the Master's verse, and then transcending his rapture, Vakula then and there realized Arhatship together with a full grasp of the Dharma, both in the spirit and in the letter.

• PŪRṆA, APOSTLE OF LOVE •

When the Enlightened One had stayed at Rājagṛha as long as he wished, he set out on the road to Kośalan country, and in due time reached the chief city of Śrāvastī. There he stayed at the Jetavana Monastery in the park of Anāthapiṇḍada.

Now, a certain monk by the name of Pūrṇa heard that the Perfect One was staying at Śrāvastī, so he packed up his belongings and started out for that city. And having come to where Buddha was, he was instructed, aroused, inspired, and gladdened by a religious discourse from the lips of the Master.

The Tathāgata taught Pūrṇa how feelings ought to be analyzed by a mindful monk and how pleasure and pain ought to be regarded and borne. And when the discourse had ended, Pūrṇa expressed a desire to go out into the world as a missionary and preach the Dharma to others in order that they might be saved from misery and despair.

"Where, Pūrṇa, do you wish to go?" asked Buddha.

"I would dwell in the district of the Śroṇāparāntakas, O Lord," replied Pūrṇa.

"But, Pūrṇa, the Śroṇāparāntakas are hot-tempered people, they are violent, cruel, reviling, furious, and abusive! If the Śroṇāparāntakas meet you with insulting and angry words, and curse and abuse you in their fury, what will you think?"

"If they do so, Lord, I shall think that they are surely good and kind men—they who address me with insulting words, they who are angry and curse me, but who do not strike me with their fists nor throw rocks at me."

"But suppose they do strike you with their fists or throw rocks at you? What will you think?"

"I shall think that they are kind and good men," answered Pūrṇa, "since they do not attack me with clubs and swords."

"And if they attack you with clubs and swords?"

"I shall think that they are kind and good, since they do not kill me."

"And if they kill you?"

"Then, Lord, if they kill me, I shall certainly think that they are kind and good, since they deliver me with so little trouble from this vile body."

"Very good, Pūrṇa, very good!" declared Buddha. "Equipped with such perfect patience and love, you may fix your abode in the country of those violent men. Go, Pūrṇa, yourself released, release others; yourself arrived at the Other Shore, conduct others across the ocean of life and death; yourself having attained Nirvāṇa, cause others to win Nirvāṇa."

So Pūrṇa, at the end of that night, dressed himself early and went into Śrāvastī for alms. And after mealtime, he returned to the Jetavana Monastery, took up his sleeping mat, and departed for the district of the Śroṇāparāntakas.

Having arrived at one of their villages, he went about with bowl and robe begging alms-food. Now a certain hunter, seeing him, thought: "Hah! This is an unlucky day for that bowl-carrying fool with shaven head! It will be fun to kill him!"

Thus thinking, the hunter loaded his bow with a stone-tipped shaft and drew the bowstring back to his ear.

Pūrṇa chanced to turn about at that very moment; and when he saw the hunter aiming at him, he opened his outer robe.

"Good fellow, I have entered your country for a purpose hard to fulfil," said Pūrṇa. "Strike here!"

So astonished was that hunter that he lowered his bow.

"Death holds no terror for this wanderer," he thought. "Why should I kill so patient and guileless a man?"

With this thought in his mind, the hunter became kindly disposed; and Pūrṇa then taught him the essentials of the Dharma and established him in the Three Refuges—the "Triple Gem" of Buddha, Dharma, Saṅgha.

But this was only the beginning of the venerable Pūrṇa's success among the Śroṇāparāntaka folk. In three months' time he had converted more than a thousand men and women to Buddhism, overcoming them by kindness, conquering them by harmlessness, capturing them with love.

• THE STORY OF VIŚĀKHĀ •

Among the many persons converted by Buddha during his first mission to Rājagṛha (when he fulfilled his promise to King Bimbisāra) was a little girl named Viśākhā, daughter of a rich man.

It came to pass that Viśākhā's father moved with all his household to Sāketa, a city of Kośala, then ruled by King Prasenajit. And when Viśākhā reached sixteen years of age, she was married to a young man of Śrāvastī named Pūrṇavardhana, son of a treasurer named Mṛgāra.

Viśākhā's wedding party lasted four months; and among the many presents she received at the end of that time was a magnificent stole made entirely of precious metals skillfully set with flawless precious stones. The stole was known far and wide as the great creeper parure.

Viśākhā's parure was worth a king's ransom, for the materials were valued at ninety million pieces of money, and the workmanship at a hundred thousand pieces of money. But what was the deed done in a previous existence which caused Viśākhā to obtain such a parure? Well, they say that in the time of Kāśyapa Buddha she gave cloth for robes to twenty thousand monks, also thread and needles and dyeing materials, all her own property; and the parure was the result of that liberality.

Now Mṛgāra, Viśākhā's father-in-law, had for a long time been favorably disposed toward the sect of the naked ascetics. For this reason he neglected to invite Lord Buddha to the celebration of his son's wedding, even though Śākyamuni was dwelling close by in the Jetavana Monastery near Śrāvastī. Instead, he honored the naked ascetics by preparing a feast for them.

While the naked ascetics were dining, Mṛgāra sent for Viśākhā, saying: "Let my daughter-in-law come and worship the 'Arhats.' "

Being a devout Buddhist, Viśākhā was filled with delight when she heard the word "Arhat;" but when she had come into the dining hall and had seen the naked ascetics, she became embarrassed and disgusted.

"These shameless persons cannot be Arhats!" she said aloud. "O father-in-law, why did you summon me before these men who let themselves be seen naked by women and children?"

Thereupon the naked ascetics reproached Mṛgāra for his daughter-in-law's words.

"Why, O householder, did you not find someone else for a daughter-in-law? Verily, you have taken into your house an incorrigible troublemaker, a disciple of the Recluse Gautama! Make haste and throw her out of the house!"

Thought Mṛgāra to himself: "It is out of the question for me to throw her out just because these men tell me to do so. She comes from too powerful a family." So he dismissed the naked ascetics, saying: "Your reverences, young people sometimes speak without thinking. Pray hold your peace."

Then he seated himself upon a costly cushion and began to eat sweet rice pudding from a golden bowl. And at that very moment a Buddhist monk came and stood in the doorway for alms-food. Viśākhā was standing and fanning Mṛgāra; and when she saw the monk she thought, "It would not be fitting for me to announce him to my father-in-law." So she moved off in such a manner as to call Mṛgāra's attention to the monk.

Now Mṛgāra, although he saw the monk, pretended that he did not see him, and kept on eating with his head bent down, foolish, unconverted man that he was.

"Pass on, reverend sir," said Viśākhā when she perceived Mṛgāra's pretense, "my father-in-law is eating stale fare."

Mṛgāra, although he had borne with the talk of the naked ascetics, removed his hand from the bowl when Viśākhā said "he is eating stale fare" and exclaimed: "Take this pudding away and turn the girl out of the house! The impertinence of her, accusing me of eating unclean food, and in a time of festivity at that!"

But all the servants in the house belonged to Viśākhā. Who was there to seize her? There was no one who dared so much as open his mouth.

"Father," said Viśākhā, "I'll not leave so easily as you seem to think! I am not a common woman, picked up at some river bathing place; and daughters whose parents are still living are not turned out so easily. Summon householders of good character and let them establish my guilt or innocence!"

"As you say," replied Mṛgāra, who forthwith caused eight householders of good character to be summoned. And when they had arrived, he said to them: "This young girl, when I was eating rice pudding from a golden bowl, said that I was eating unclean food. Imagine saying such a thing, and in a time of festivity, too! Find her guilty and throw her out of my house!"

"Dear girl, is it so, as he says?"

"That is not the way I would tell it," answered Viśākhā. "A certain Buddhist monk on his begging rounds came and stood in the doorway; and my father-in-law, who was eating sweet rice pudding, paid no attention to him. Then I thought, 'My father-in-law is not acquiring any merit in this existence, but is consuming old, stale merit.' So I said, 'Pass on, reverend sir, my father-in-law is eating stale fare.' Now, how am I at fault?"

"You are not at fault," answered the householders. "You have spoken justly. Why, Mṛgāra, are you angry with her?"

"Sirs, I grant that there is no fault," said Mṛgāra.

"Then, if she is guiltless, why did you attempt without cause to turn her out of the house?"

"Good sirs," interjected Viśākhā, "although at first it was not fitting that I should leave at the order of my father-in-law, yet now that you have found me guiltless, it is a good time for me to go."

So saying, she gave orders to her male and female servants to get ready the carriages and to make other necessary preparations.

"Dear girl, I spoke in ignorance," protested Mṛgāra, speaking partly to be heard by the householders. "Please forgive me."

"Good sir, I forgive you all there is to forgive," declared Viśākhā. "Nevertheless, it remains a fact that I am a daughter in a family that has faith in the Religion of the Buddhas; and to see something of the monks is necessary to us. If I am allowed to wait on the monks at my pleasure, I will stay."

"Dear girl, wait on your monks as much as you please."

Viśākhā accordingly sent an invitation to the Perfect One and received him at her house the next day. And the naked ascetics, when they heard that Buddha was coming to the house of Mṛgāra, went also, and seated themselves outside the house on all four sides.

"All the arrangements for the reception are ready," said Viśākhā to Mṛgāra. "Let my father-in-law come and attend upon the Tathāgata."

But as Mṛgāra was about to go, the naked ascetics restrained him, saying: "O householder, do not go near the Ascetic Gautama!"

So after hesitating for a moment, he turned to Viśākhā and said, "Let my daughter-in-law wait on Gautama herself."

Viśākhā turned away. And after she had waited on the Perfect One and on the monks who had accompanied him, the meal then being finished, she sent a message to Mṛgāra.

"Let my father-in-law come and hear the sermon."

Now, Mṛgāra was really very anxious to hear the Dharma preached, so to the naked ascetics he said: "I suppose it would not do at all if I refused to listen to Gautama's discourse."

"Well then," said the naked ascetics when they saw that he was bent on going, "you may listen to Gautama's discourse if you will sit behind a curtain."

They went ahead of Mṛgāra and hung up a curtain; and on a seat behind the curtain Mṛgāra sat attentively to hear Lord Buddha's sermon.

Perceiving what had occurred, Śākyamuni thought, "Sit behind a curtain if you will, or behind a wall, or behind the highest mountain, or even at the end of the world. I am Buddha; and I can make you hear my voice even if you had been born without ears." And he began to teach Dharma in "graduated discourse," beginning with the simpler topics and leading on to more profound truths.

(Now, when a Supreme Buddha teaches Dharma, those in front and those behind, and those beyond a hundred or a thousand worlds, exclaim: "The Master is looking at me! The Master is teaching the Doctrine to me!" To each one it seems as if Lord Buddha were beholding and teaching him alone.)

As he sat behind the curtain, Mṛgāra turned over and over in his mind the teaching of the Tathāgata, became established in the thousandfold-ornamented fruit of conversion, and acquired an immovable and unquestioning faith in the Three Refuges.

Stepping out from behind the curtain, Mṛgāra approached his daughter-in-law and touched her arm affectionately, saying: "My dear Viśākhā! From this day forward you are my mother!"

Thus Mṛgāra gave Viśākhā the position of mother; and henceforth she was always called "Mṛgāra's mother." For like a loving mother guiding her son into paths that are good and lead to health and happiness, the pure and gracious Viśākhā guided Mṛgāra into the Path of Dharma which leads to the extinction of suffering and the attainment of Nirvāṇa.

Then Mṛgāra bowed reverently at the feet of the Happy One and exclaimed: "O World-Honored One! A great benefactress to me is my daughter-in-law! Thanks to my daughter-in-law, I am released from all danger of rebirth in a lower state of existence. Truly, it was for my gain and welfare that my daughter-in-law came to my house!"

Now on a certain holiday in Śrāvastī, the people went to the Jetavana to listen to an exposition of the Dharma. And Viśākhā, wearing the great creeper parure, likewise proceeded to the monastery. Before she entered, however, she removed the parure, so as not to appear ostentatious, and made of it a bundle which she gave into the keeping of a servant girl.

At the close of the sermon, Viśākhā rose from her seat, worshiped the Perfect One, and went forth from his presence. But the servant girl forgot all about the parure and left it behind in the monastery.

Now, it was the custom of the blessed Ānanda, when the congregation had departed, to pick up and put away anything that had been forgotten. And so that day he noticed the great creeper parure, and announced his discovery to the Tathāgata.

"Lord, Viśākhā has gone, forgetting her parure."

"Lay it aside, Ānanda."

Ānanda lifted it up and hung it on the side of the staircase.

Viśākhā had not gone far from the monastery when she remembered the parure.

"Dear girl," she said to the servant maid, "give me the parure. I wish to put it on."

"Oh, mistress!" cried the maid. "I forgot to bring it from the monastery!"

"Go, then," said Viśākhā, "and bring it here. But if the reverend Ānanda has found it and laid it somewhere for safekeeping, do not take it. I will make a present of it to the monks."

When Ānanda saw the servant girl, he said to her: "Why have you returned, dear girl?"

"I went away forgetting my mistress' parure."

"It is safe," said Ānanda. "I have hung it up by the staircase. Go and get it if you wish."

"My lord," said the girl, "an article which has been touched by your hand is not to be reclaimed by my mistress."

And so she returned to Viśākhā empty-handed.

"Dear girl," explained Viśākhā, "never will I wear an article which Śākyamuni's chief disciples have touched. I will make the Saṅgha a present of the parure. Nevertheless, it would be troublesome for the monks to take care of it, as none among them may deal in merchandise or handle money. What if I sell it and give the monks suitable things? Go fetch it, dear."

After the servant girl had brought back the parure, Viśākhā did not put it on, but sent for some jewelers to appraise its value.

"It is worth ninety million," they said, "to which a hundred thousand should be added for the workmanship."

"Then take the parure to a buyer," said Viśākhā. "I wish to sell it."

"That would be futile, dear lady. There is no one who is able to take it at such a price; and a woman worthy of wearing such a parure is difficult to find."

So Viśākhā bought back her own parure by paying the price herself; and placing ninety million and one hundred thousand pieces of money in a cart, she had the sum taken to the monastery.

"O Light of the World!" she said as she made obeisance to Buddha. "The reverend Ānanda has touched my parure with his hand; and from the time he has touched it, it is impossible for me to wear it again. For to do so would be the same as using for some common purpose a holy, consecrated article. I have endeavored to sell it, thinking that with the money obtained I would give things suitable for the monks. But when I saw that there was no one able to buy it, I made up the price myself. Lord, which donation shall I give?"

"Dear, kind Viśākhā," said the Perfect One, "a dwelling place for the monks in East Park (Pūrvārāma) would be fitting."

And so Viśākhā, with joyous mind, purchased a site in the Pūrvārāma and constructed a spacious and well-appointed monastery containing a thousand rooms for the monks, a large and beautiful council hall on the first floor, and above it a splended suite of rooms to serve as Śākyamuni's private apartment.

On the day when the furnishing of the monastery was completed, when the shadows of eventide were lengthening, Viśākhā walked with her children around and around the new monastery, meanwhile singing sweetly.

And Lord Buddha, sitting in his perfumed apartment, listened to Viśākhā's joyous song.

"O monks," said the Perfect One, "just as a skillful florist, when he gets a large heap of flowers, will go on and on making all manner of garlands, even so does the mind of Viśākhā incline to go on and on doing all manner of gracious deeds."

• EIGHT WONDERS OF THE MIGHTY OCEAN •

Although the Enlightened One never wholly gave up his journeying to the various towns of northeastern and north-central India, he came more and more, with advancing years, to make Śrāvastī in Kośalan country his permanent residence, dwelling alternately at the Jetavana (Prince Jeta's Grove) in Anāthapiṇḍada's Park and at the Pūrvārāma (East Park), which had been donated by Viśākhā, known as "Mṛgāra's mother."

Now on one occasion, when the Perfect One was staying at the Pūrvārāma, the storied monastery donated by Mṛgāra's mother, he was seated amidst a large number of monks, for it was a moon-day when preaching services are conducted and confessions made by the monks.

Instead of preaching, however, Buddha sat in silence.

Then the blessed Ānanda, when the night was fleeting, when the first watch was waning, rose from his seat and approached the Perfect One with folded hands, saying: "The congregation of monks has long been seated, Lord. Let the Perfect One recite the regulations for the monks."

At these words the Tathāgata remained silent.

In the middle watch of the night Ānanda again made his request, and so also in the third watch.

"Lord, the night is far spent. The last watch is waning. Dawn being at hand, the night wears a face of gladness. The congregation of monks has long been seated. Let the Perfect One now recite the regulations for the monks."

"Ānanda," said Buddha, "the assembly is not wholly pure!"

Thereupon the venerable Maudgalyāyana, chief of those who possess supernormal powers, grasped Buddha's thought with his thought and focused his attention upon that entire assembly of monks. And Maudgalyāyana perceived which person was immoral, impure, of perverted nature—suspicious in behavior, a doer of covert deeds, one who was no recluse although claiming to be one, no follower of the religious life although claiming to be such, one rotten within, one full of lusts, a rubbish heap of filth—sitting there in the congregation of monks.

On perceiving that person Maudgalyāyana rose up from his seat and went over to him and said: "Get up, sir! You are seen by the Perfect One! You are not allowed to associate with the monks!"

But that person made no move, nor did he utter a word. Then a second and yet a third time did Maudgalyāyana repeat his words, but that person made no reply.

Then the venerable Maudgalyāyana seized that person by the arm and marched him outside the porch door and drew the bolt across. This done, Maudgalyāyana went up to the Perfect One and said: "Lord, that person has been ejected by me. The assembly is wholly pure. Let the Perfect One now recite the regulations for the monks."

"It is a strange thing, Maudgalyāyana," declared the Perfect One, "it is a wondrous thing, Maudgalyāyana, how that deluded person should wait until he was thrown out!"

Then the Master admonished the monks, saying: "From this time forth, monks, I shall not observe the four quarters of the moon (sabbath days). I shall not recite the regulations for the monks. Henceforth observe the moon-days yourselves, recite the regulations yourselves. It is out of place, monks, it is not fitting, that the Tathāgata should observe the moon-days or recite the regulations when the congregation is not wholly pure.

"O monks," continued the Tathāgata, "there are eight strange and wondrous things about the mighty ocean, beholding which again and again the asuras delight in the mighty ocean. What are the eight? Listen, monks, and I will tell you.

1. "O monks, the mighty ocean deepens and slopes gradually down, hollow after hollow, not plunging by a sudden precipice. This is the first strange and wondrous thing, seeing which again and again the asuras delight in the mighty ocean.

"Likewise, monks, in this Dharma and discipline the training is gradual, progress is gradual, step by step; and there is no sudden penetration to Insight. This is the first strange and wondrous thing, seeing which again and again monks delight in this Dharma and discipline.

2. "Then again, O monks, the mighty ocean is established by the forces of nature and does not transgress its bounds. This is the second

strange and wondrous thing, seeing which again and again the asuras delight in the mighty ocean.

"Likewise, monks, the charge which I have enjoined on my disciples is not transgressed by them, even at the cost of life. This is the second strange and wondrous thing, seeing which again and again monks delight in this Dharma and discipline.

3. "Then again, O monks, the mighty ocean has no part nor lot with a dead body; for whatever dead body is put into the mighty ocean, straightway it washes it ashore, casts it up on the shore. This is the third strange and wondrous thing, seeing which again and again the asuras delight in the mighty ocean.

"Likewise, monks, whatever person is immoral, impure, of perverted nature—suspicious in behavior, a doer of covert deeds, one who is no recluse although claiming to be one, no follower of the religious life although claiming to be such, one rotten within, one full of lusts, a rubbish heap of filth—with such the Saṅgha has no part nor lot, but straightway throws him out. Even though seated amid the monks of the Saṅgha, yet he is far from the Saṅgha, and far is the Saṅgha from him. This is the third strange and wondrous thing, seeing which again and again monks delight in this Dharma and discipline.

4. "Then again, O monks, Gaṅgā, Jumnā, Aciravatī, Śarabhū, Mahī, and all the other great rivers abandon their former names and lineage on reaching the mighty ocean, and henceforth go by the name of just 'mighty ocean.' This is the fourth strange and wondrous thing, seeing which again and again the asuras delight in the mighty ocean.

"Likewise, monks, the four castes, on going forth from house to homelessness in the Dharma and discipline proclaimed by the Tathāgata, abandon their former names and lineage and go by the name of just 'sons of Śākyamuni.' This is the fourth strange and wondrous thing, seeing which again and again monks delight in this Dharma and discipline.

5. "Then again, O monks, whatever streams flow into the mighty ocean, and whatever rain from the sky falls into it, yet there is no diminution nor overflowing seen in the mighty ocean. This is the fifth

strange and wondrous thing, seeing which again and again the asuras delight in the mighty ocean.

"Likewise, monks, even though many monks pass away with that utter passing-away which leaves no condition for rebirth, yet there is no diminution nor increase to be seen in the Infinite Ocean of Parinirvāṇa. This is the fifth strange and wondrous thing, seeing which again and again monks delight in this Dharma and discipline.

6. "Then again, O monks, the mighty ocean is of one flavor, the flavor of salt. This is the sixth strange and wondrous thing, seeing which again and again the asuras delight in the mighty ocean.

"Likewise, monks, the Dharma has but one flavor, the flavor of Emancipation. This is the sixth strange and wondrous thing, seeing which again and again monks delight in this Dharma and discipline.

7. "Then again, O monks, the mighty ocean has many gems of various sorts—the pearl, diamond, lapis lazuli, sapphire, crystal, coral, ruby, emerald, silver, gold. This is the seventh strange and wondrous thing, seeing which again and again the asuras delight in the mighty ocean.

"Likewise, monks, in the Dharma is many a gem—the four Fundamentals of Attentiveness, the five Controlling Faculties, the five Powers, the seven Limbs of Wisdom, the Āryan Eightfold Path, and so on. This is the seventh strange and wondrous thing, seeing which again and again monks delight in this Dharma and discipline.

8. "Then again, O monks, the mighty ocean is the abode of mighty creatures—leviathans, sharks, whales, sea monsters, sea sprites, sea serpents, mermaids. And some of these creatures are very large. This is the eighth strange and wondrous thing, seeing which again and again the asuras delight in the mighty ocean.

"Likewise, monks, the Dharma is the abode of mighty beings—the Stream-Entrant, he who fares on by realizing the fruits of Stream-entering, the Once-Returner, he who fares on by realizing the fruits of once-returning, the Never-Returner, he who fares on by realizing the fruits of never-returning, the Arhat, and he who fares on by realizing the fruits of Arhatship. This is the eighth strange and wondrous thing, seeing which again and again monks delight in this Dharma and discipline."

• LORD BUDDHA AS TEACHER •

One day a brahmin accountant came to the Master at East Park, saluted him with courteous greeting, and said: "As I approached this storied monastery, reverend Gautama, I got a gradual view of it. Now, reverend Gautama, just as in a course of archery the training of the archers is a progressive one, so also with us brahmins our theological training is gradual, the approach is step by step. Is it possible, reverend Gautama, for this Dharma and discipline of yours to be likewise taught progressively?"

"It is so, brahmin," replied Buddha. "Take the case of a clever horse trainer. He takes a thoroughbred in hand, gives him his first lesson with bit and bridle, and then proceeds with a further step. In exactly the same way, brahmin, the Tathāgata takes in hand a man to be trained and gives him his first lesson, thus: 'Come, brother! Be kind and harmless. Live self-restrained by the restraint of the Precepts. Become versed in the practice of good conduct. Seeing danger in trifling faults, undertake the training and become a pupil in the moralities.'

"As soon as he has mastered all that," Śākyamuni continued, "the Tathāgata gives him his second lesson, thus: 'Come, brother! Seeing an object with the eye, do not become captivated by its general appearance or by its details. Persist in overcoming that wretched dejection caused by craving, caused by an uncontrolled sense of sight—those evil states which would overwhelm one like a flood. Guard the sense of sight, win control over the sense of sight. And do the same with the other faculties of sense. When you hear a sound with the ear, smell an odor with the nose, taste a flavor with the tongue, or with body touch a tangible thing, or when with mind you are conscious of a thing, do not become captivated by objects of sense.'

"As soon as he has mastered all that, the Tathāgata gives him a further lesson, thus: 'Come, brother! Use moderation in eating. Do not eat thoughtlessly, do not eat for the enjoyment of it, or as a luxury, or for making your body beautiful, but eat to keep yourself alive and in good health, free from sickness, and for strength and energy to pursue the holy life with this thought, "I check my former feeling. I will allow no new feeling to arise, that maintenance and comfort may be mine.' "

"Then, brahmin, when he has won restraint in food, the Tathāgata gives him a further lesson, thus: 'Come, brother! Abide alert. By day and by night, when walking, sitting, or lying down—in everything you do—be attentive and self-possessed, and cleanse your heart from things which may hinder you.'

"Then, brahmin, when he is devoted to alertness, the Tathāgata gives him a further lesson, thus: 'Come, brother! Be possessed of mindfulness and self-control. In going forth or going back, have yourself under control. In looking forward or looking behind, in bending or relaxing, in wearing robes or carrying bowl and robe, in eating, chewing, tasting, in relieving yourself, in walking, standing, sitting, lying, in sleeping or waking, in speaking or keeping silence, have yourself under control.'

"Then, brahmin, when he is possessed of mindfulness and self-control, the Tathāgata gives him a further lesson, thus: 'Come, brother! Seek out a secluded lodging, the root of a tree in a grove, a mountain, a cave or mountain grotto, a cemetery, a forest retreat, a heap of straw in the open air.' And he does so. And when he has eaten his food he sits down cross-legged, and keeping his body straight, he proceeds to practice meditation in order to attain the Absorptions.

"Now, brahmin, for all monks who are pupils, who have not yet attained mastery of Mind, who abide aspiring for the unsurpassed security of Nirvāṇa, such is the method of my course of training.

"But as to those monks who are Arhats, who have destroyed the Poisons of lust, existence-infatuation, false view, and ignorance, who have lived the holy life, done their task, laid down the burden, won Salvation, utterly destroyed the Unwholesome Roots of greed, hatred, and delusion, and are released by perfect Insight—for such as those these things are conducive to comfort in the present life and to mindful self-control as well."

On hearing these words of the Perfect One, the brahmin accountant said: "But tell me, reverend Gautama, do the disciples of the worthy Gautama, thus advised and trained by him—do all of them win the Absolute Perfection which is Nirvāṇa, or do some fail to attain it?"

"Some of my disciples," said Buddha, "thus advised and trained by me, do indeed attain it. But others do not."

The brahmin's countenance brightened with interest.

"But what is the reason, reverend Gautama? Here we have Nirvāṇa. Here we have the Path to Nirvāṇa. Here we have the worthy Gautama as instructor. What is the reason, I ask, why some disciples thus advised and trained do attain, while others do not?"

"That, brahmin, is a question that I will not answer just at this point. But answer me this, so far as you are willing. Are you familiar with the road to Rājagṛha?"

"Yes, indeed, reverend Gautama. I am thoroughly familiar with the road to Rājagṛha."

"Then answer me this, brahmin. Suppose a man should come, anxious to go to Rājagṛha. He comes up to you and says, 'Sir, I wish to go to Rājagṛha. Tell me how I can get there.' Then suppose you say to him, 'All right, my good man, this is the way for you to go. Take this road and you will come to Sāketa. Keep on going and you will come to Pāṭaliputra. Then go a bit farther and you will see the delightful hills, the delightful park, the delightful grove, the delightful lotus pond of Rājagṛha.'

"Thus instructed by you," continued the Perfect One, "thus advised by you, he takes the wrong road and goes off toward the west. Then a second man comes up to you with the same request, and you give him the same directions. But the second man follows your instructions and arrives in Rājagṛha safe and sound.

"Now, brahmin, why does one man fail and the other succeed? Here we have Rājagṛha, here we have the road to Rājagṛha, and here we have you as instructor. But after all your advice and instruction, one man took the wrong road and went west, while the other man reached Rājagṛha safely."

"Is that any concern of mine, reverend Gautama?" asked the brahmin. "I am just the revealer of the way."

"Well, brahmin," replied Śākyamuni, "here we have Nirvāṇa, here we have the Way to Nirvāṇa, and here am I as instructor. Yet some of my disciples, thus advised and trained by me, do attain Nirvāṇa while others do not. The Tathāgata is one who reveals the Path; and those who set out in confidence on the Path that I proclaim shall surely attain the Goal."

• "INFINITE IS THIS ROUND!" •

"O monks!" said the Enlightened One to the yellow-robed assembly in the Jetavana Monastery one morning.

"Yes, Lord," replied the monks.

"Suppose, monks, that there was a man who wished to live for a hundred years, and that someone were to say to that man: 'Listen, good man, do you realize that you have left yourself undefended against the involvements of existence in this round of rebirth? You will be wounded morning, noon, and night with a hundred spears. Being thus wounded three times a day with a hundred spears day after day even for a hundred years—well, good man, you will certainly come to realize at the end of your hundred years the Four Āryan Truths, which up till now have never entered your head.'

"Now, monks, an intelligent man, being told all this, would not lose a moment to investigate the Four Āryan Truths. And why?

"Infinite, O monks, is this round of rebirth; and the first beginning of blows with spears, swords, and axes has no determining point in time. This being so, monks, still I do not say that a realization of the Four Āryan Truths is painful and grievous. Rather, I say that such a realization is pleasant and happy. Now, what are the Four Āryan Truths?

"The Āryan Truth about Suffering, the Āryan Truth about the Cause of Suffering, the Āryan Truth about the Cessation of Suffering, and the Āryan Truth about the Path leading to the Cessation of Suffering.

"Without beginning is the past, O monks; without end is the future. Indeterminate is the beginning of this round of birth and death and rebirth. Those beings hindered by ignorance and fettered by craving, thereby running through the current of existence, have had no beginning. Without the destruction of their ignorance and craving, those

beings hindered by ignorance and fettered by craving, thereby running through the current of existence, *will have no end of pain.*

"Now what do you think? Which is the greater, the flood of tears shed by you on this long, long journey, forever running through the current of existence, weeping and wailing because conjoined with things painful, because separated from things beloved, or the water of the four mighty oceans?"

"As we understand the Dharma preached by the Perfect One," replied the monks, "greater is this flood of tears shed by us, Lord, than the water of the four mighty oceans."

"Exactly so!" declared Buddha. "Well do you understand the Dharma which I have preached to you! Verily, greater is the flood of tears shed by you than the water of the four mighty oceans. But how is this possible? *Beginningless is this round, without beginning are beings.*

"Not to be discovered, O monks, is any end of this round of birth and death and rebirth. Those beings hindered by ignorance and fettered by craving, thereby running through the current of existence, will have no end. There will come a time when the mighty oceans will dry up, vanish, and be no more. There will come a time when the mighty earth will be devoured by fire, perish, and be no more. And yet there will be no end of suffering. How is this possible? Endless is this round, without end are beings.

"For a long, long time have you undergone misfortune, undergone torment, undergone death and filled the graveyards full—long enough to be dissatisfied with all forms of becoming, long enough to turn away from them and free yourselves from them.

"Monks, the bones of a single person running on, faring on, even for a single eon would make a heap many millions of multimillions of times greater than Mount Vipula, were there a collector of those bones, and if the collection could be preserved."

Then a certain monk asked: "How long, Lord, is the eon?"

"Long indeed is the eon, brother," replied the Tathāgata. "It is not easy to reckon as so many years, so many centuries, so many millennia, so many hundred thousand years."

"But can an illustration be given, Lord?"

"An illustration can be given, monk. Suppose there were a mighty mountain four *yojanas* in length, breadth, and height, without crack or cranny, not hollowed out, one solid mass of rock, and that a man should come at the end of every century and rub that mountain just once with a silken cloth. Sooner, monk, would that mighty mountain be worn away by this method, sooner used up, than the eon."

And the monks, hearing this discourse of the Perfect One, were filled with wonder.

• DISCOURSES ON NIRVĀṆA •

Once upon a time the monk Rādha went to the Perfect One at Śrāvastī for instruction. Seated at one side, the venerable Rādha said: " 'A being! A being!' they say, Lord. Tell me, Lord, to what extent can one be called a being?"

"That desire, Rādha," declared Śākyamuni, "that lust, that lure, that craving which is concerned with body—ensnared by it, fast ensnared by it, one is called a being.

"That desire," continued the Tathāgata, "that lust, that lure, that craving which is concerned with feeling, or with perception, or with the predisposing mental formations, or with discriminative consciousness—ensnared by it, fast ensnared by it, one is called a being.

"Consider boys or girls playing with little sand castles, Rādha. So long as they are not rid of desire, not rid of affection, not rid of feverish longing and craving for those little sand castles, exactly so long do they delight in them, are amused by them, set store by them, are jealous of them.

"But, Rādha, as soon as those boys or girls are rid of desire, rid of affection, rid of feverish longing and craving for those little sand castles, straightway with hand and foot they scatter them, break them up, knock them down, cease to play with them.

"In exactly the same way, Rādha, scatter your body, your feeling, your perception, your predispositions, your discriminative consciousness, break them up, knock them down, cease to play with them, apply yourself to the destruction of craving for them. *Verily, Rādha, the extinction of craving is Nirvāṇa."*

Then the venerable Rādha said: " 'Māra! Māra!' they say, Lord. Tell me, Lord, to what extent does Māra exist?"

"Where a body is," replied the Perfect One, "there is Māra or things of the nature of Māra, or at any rate what is perishing. Therefore, Rādha, regard the body as Māra. Consider it to be of the nature of Māra. Regard it as perishing, as a corpse, as an arrow, as pain, as a source of pain. They who regard it in this way regard it rightly. And the same may be said of feeling, perception, the predispositions, and discriminative consciousness."

"But 'rightly regarding,' Lord," asked Rādha, "for what purpose?"

"Rightly regarding, Rādha, for the sake of disgust."

"But disgust, Lord—what is the purpose of that?"

"Disgust, Rādha, is to bring about passionlessness."

"And the purpose of passionlessness?"

"Passionlessness, Rādha, has Release as its purpose."

"But Release, Lord—what is it for?"

"Release, Rādha, means Nirvāṇa."

"But Nirvāṇa, Lord—what is the aim of that?"

"This, Rādha, is a question that goes too far. You can grasp no limit to this question. Rooted in Nirvāṇa is the religious life. Nirvāṇa is its Goal. Nirvāṇa is its End."

Now, some time afterwards the Perfect One was teaching and establishing the monks with a discourse according to Dharma that was centered on Nirvāṇa. And those monks, paying close attention, taking it all in, were listening to Buddha's words with ready ears.

"O monks," said Śākyamuni, "the man who does not understand and comprehend the universe, who has not detached his mind from it, who has not abandoned the universe, can make no progress in extinguishing pain. But he who does understand and comprehend the universe, who has detached his mind from it, who has abandoned the universe—it is he who makes progress in extinguishing pain.

Who, knowing the universe in every part,
For all its forms has no desire,
By comprehension of the universe,
He makes escape from universal pain.

Then continued the Perfect One, saying: "O monks, there exists a condition in which the four great elements are not, in which boundless space is not, in which infinite consciousness is not, in which nothingness is not, in which neither-perception-nor-nonperception is not. There is neither this world nor a world beyond, nor both together; nor do sun and moon exist there. There, monks, I declare there is no being born and no dying, there is no falling and no arising. It is not something fixed, yet it does not change; it is, in fact, not based on anything which can be grasped with the mind. *Verily, monks, it is Nirvāṇa, the End of turmoil.*

"There is, O monks, an Unborn, an Unbecome, a Not-made, an Incomposite. If this were not so, monks, there could not be any escape from that which is born, become, made, composite. But since the phenomenal world—this saṃsāra—has qualities converse to those of Nirvāṇa, such an escape is possible."

A certain monk of the assembly then rose from his seat, made obeisance to Buddha, and said: "Lord, the venerable Tiṣya speaks thus to a number of the monks: 'Truly, brothers, my body has become as though drugged. The four quarters have become dim to my eyes, and the teachings are no longer clear to me. Sloth and torpor have taken hold of my heart. Joyless to me is the religious life; and I waver in the teachings.' "

"Where is Tiṣya just now?" asked the Exalted One.

"Outside the porch, Lord, wearing a dejected look."

"Summon brother Tiṣya in my name to come hither, saying, 'The Master wishes to have a word with you.' "

Tiṣya was called into the assembly hall; and the Perfect One asked him if what had been said about him were true.

"It is true, Lord," replied Tiṣya with downcast countenance.

"Now, Tiṣya," said Buddha, "I want your opinion on a certain matter.

In a body that is not rid of passion, not rid of desire, of feverish craving, do there arise states of change and instability? Do sorrow and grief, woe, lamentation, and despair arise?"

"Yes, Lord, they do."

"Well said, Tiṣya! And is it the same with feeling, perception, the predispositions, and discriminative consciousness?"

"Yes, Lord, it is."

"Well said, Tiṣya! Now tell me what you think. When body, feeling, and so forth are rid of passion, desire, and feverish craving, do sorrow, grief, woe, lamentation, and despair arise?"

"Surely not, Lord."

"Well said, Tiṣya! Now what do you think? Is body permanent or impermanent?"

"Impermanent, Lord."

"And feeling, perception, the predisposing formations, and discriminative consciousness—are they permanent or impermanent?"

"Impermanent, Lord."

"Now then, Tiṣya, he who understands this is repelled by body, repelled by feeling, perception, the predispositions, and by discriminative consciousness. Being repelled by them, he does not crave them; by not craving them, he is set free. And in this freedom comes the insight that this sphere of freedom is happiness and bliss, and that the sphere of craving is sorrow, grief, woe, lamentation, and despair. Thus he realizes: 'Rebirth is destroyed, lived is the holy life, done is my task, and there is no more life for me on this world's terms.'

"Suppose now, Tiṣya, that there are two men, one unskilled and the other skilled in traveling. And the one who is unskilled asks the way of the other who is familiar with that way. And the second replies, 'Yes, good man, this is the way. Go on a bit and you will come to a place where the road divides. Leave the left-hand path and take the right-hand path. Continue on that path and you will come to a thick forest. Keep on going and you will come to a great marshy swamp. Go on a bit farther and you will see a steep precipice. Continuing, you will at last come to a delightful stretch of level ground.'

"This is a parable, Tiṣya; and this is what it means. By 'the man who is unskilled in traveling' is meant the common people. By 'the man who is skilled in traveling' is meant a Tathāgata, an Arhat, a Buddha. By 'dividing of the road' is meant a state of wavering. 'The left-hand path' is a name for the false eightfold path, namely, the path of wrong view, wrong thought, and so forth. 'The right-hand path,' Tiṣya, is a name for this Āryan Eightfold Path, namely, Right View, Right Thought, Right Speech, Right Action, Right Livelihood, Right Effort, Right Attentiveness, Right Concentration. 'The thick forest' is a name for ignorance. 'The great marshy swamp' is a name for sensual desires. 'The steep precipice' is a name for vexation and despair. 'The delightful stretch of level ground,' Tiṣya, is a name for Nirvāṇa—the pure, permanent, everlasting happiness.

"Be of good cheer, Tiṣya, be of good cheer! I am the Tathāgata. I am here to teach you, to advise you, to offer you support. *Keep in mind, Tiṣya, that earnestness is the path of immortality, while thoughtlessness is the path of death. Those who are earnest do not die, but those who are thoughtless are as if dead already.*"

At that point a brahmin who was present in the congregation of monks arose and addressed the Master, saying: "Reverend Gautama, is that which you call Nirvāṇa a permanent state of being or is it not?"

"Nirvāṇa, brahmin, consists of the nonexistence of sorrow."

"There are four conditions in the world which are spoken of as nonexistent, O Gautama," said the brahmin. "The first is that which is not yet in existence, like the pitcher to be made out of clay. The second is that which, having existed, has been destroyed, as a broken pitcher. The third is that which consists of the absence of something different from itself, as we say that an ox does not exist as a horse. Lastly, that which is purely imaginary, as the hair of a turtle or the horns of a rabbit. Now if, by having rid ourselves of sorrow, we arrive at Nirvāṇa, then Nirvāṇa is the same as nothingness, and may be considered nonexistent. Yet if this be the case, how is it that you define Nirvāṇa as purity, permanence, and everlasting bliss?"

"But brahmin," said Śākyamuni, "have I not previously stated that in Nirvāṇa nothingness is not? Now, if I taught that Nirvāṇa were like the pitcher, not yet made out of clay, or like the nonexistence of a pitcher

that has been broken, or like the hair of a turtle or the horns of a rabbit—something purely imaginary—*then I, brahmin, would be a nihilist teaching eternal death, not timeless Immortality!*

"But Nirvāṇa, brahmin, may be compared to the nothingness defined as the absence of something different from itself. As you say, brahmin, although the ox has not the existence of the horse, you cannot say that the ox does not exist; and although the horse has not the existence of the ox, you cannot say that the horse does not exist. Nirvāṇa is like that. In the midst of sorrow there is no Nirvāṇa, and in Nirvāṇa there is no sorrow. Just as illusion exists in the phenomenal world, so in Nirvāṇa there is the nonexistence of illusion.

"Nirvāṇa is the realm of self-realization attained by Āryan Wisdom, which is free from the discrimination of eternality and extinction, free from differentiation between existence and nonexistence. When the Bodhisattvas face and perceive the happiness of perfect tranquilization, they are moved by a feeling of love and compassion inspired by their vows to save all beings, saying, 'So long as they do not attain Nirvāṇa, I will not attain it myself.' Thus they keep themselves away from Nirvāṇa. BUT THE FACT IS, THEY ARE ALREADY IN NIRVĀṆA; BECAUSE IN THEM THERE IS NO ARISING OF DISCRIMINATION BETWEEN SELF AND OTHERS."

Then another brahmin, one who had become a novice in the Saṅgha, questioned the Perfect One.

"Unaided and alone, O Śākyamuni," declared Upasīva the novice, "I am unable to cross the great flood of birth and death. Pray tell me, All-Seeing One, with what to lean upon may I find support and cross this flood?"

"Be mindful," replied Buddha, "and try to develop that state of mind wherein all is seen to be delusion—illusory and not truly existing. Supported by the conviction that 'no-thing is,' cross the flood. Put aside lusts, avoid doubts, and by night and day seek the destruction of craving."

"Will a person who does this, who is released in the highest degree from illusion's snares—will he abide in that crossing-over without backsliding?"

"That is so, Upasīva."

"Well now," asked Upasīva, "if he abide without departing from that state of mind and heart for a long term of years, and then should die, will the consciousness of that person be reborn?"

"There is mundane consciousness, Upasīva, the consciousness of discriminations," replied the Perfect One, "and the transcendental consciousness of Nirvāṇa. The Nirvāṇa-consciousness cannot be indicated: it is limitless, radiant, and shining everywhere. Mind-and-body ceases in the consciousness of Complete Nirvāṇa, leaving no trace at all. For as the flame blown out by the wind disappears and cannot be found, even so the Arhat when released from mind-and-body disappears and cannot be found."

"He who has disappeared—is he nonexistent, or does he continue to exist eternally, though free from the ills of life? This, O Sage, explain to me well, for this is a matter well known to you."

"There is no measuring of him who has disappeared, whereby one might know of him that he either is or is not. For when all the elements of finite existence are removed, all modes of description are also removed."

Addressing the congregation of monks, the Happy One, the Arhat, continued, saying: "There are, O monks, two 'Nirvāṇa-elements,' namely, the Nirvāṇa-element with the basis of sensate existence still remaining and the Nirvāṇa-element without the basis of sensate existence remaining.

"Which, monks, is the Nirvāṇa-element with the basis still remaining?

"Here, monks, a monk is an Arhat, one in whom the Poisons are destroyed, who has lived the holy life, done what was to be done, laid down the burden, achieved his own welfare, destroyed attachment to becoming, one who is free through knowing rightly, and has won the Goal. There remain to him just the five faculties; and through their being undemolished he suffers what is agreeable and what is disagreeable, he experiences pleasure and pain. It is his destruction of Greed, Anger, and Delusion, monks, that is called the Nirvāṇa-element with the basis still remaining.

"And which, monks, is the Nirvāṇa-element without the basis remaining?

"In this case, monks, a monk is an Arhat, one in whom the Poisons are destroyed, and so forth as before. But all his feelings, monks, do not experience either pleasure or pain: they have become cold. It is his utter passing-away that is called the Nirvāṇa-element without the basis remaining.

"O monks, possessed of two things in this very life a monk lives at ease, in perfect happiness, directed toward Nirvāṇa. What are the two things? Rapturous emotion on occasions for rapture and, being thrilled thereby, the making of strenuous effort.

One who has wisdom should be strongly thrilled
At thrilling times. A monk discreet and ardent
Should thoroughly examine things by wisdom.
Thus living filled with fervor, filled with peace,
And not elated, but given to calm,
He'll attain Extinction of the Poisons—NIRVĀṆA.

After this discourse had been given, a monk by the name of Yamaka grasped it wrongly, thinking that the Perfect One taught that Arhats are annihilated at their death. And Yamaka expressed his wrong view to several of the monks who, in turn, reported the matter to the venerable Śāriputra.

Then the venerable Śāriputra, having arisen from his meditation in the evening, went to Yamaka and exchanged courteous and pleasant greetings with him.

"Now, what is this, friend Yamaka," asked Śāriputra, "that I have heard about your view of the Arhat who has passed into Parinirvāṇa?"

"Thus do I understand the Dharma taught by the Perfect One," replied Yamaka, "that the Arhat, on the dissolution of his body at death, is annihilated, destroyed, and does not exist after death."

"Say not so, friend Yamaka!" exclaimed Śāriputra. "Do not slander the Perfect One, for it is not good to slander the Perfect One! The Perfect One would never say that a person who has attained Nirvāṇa, on the dissolution of his body at death, is annihilated, destroyed, and does not exist after death! Abandon this wicked heresy of yours, Yamaka!"

"But reverend Śāriputra, I must conclude, from the Perfect One's discourse, that Arhats do not exist after death."

"Now, Yamaka," said Śāriputra, "what do you think? Are body and the other aggregates of conditioned existence permanent or impermanent?"

"Impermanent."

"Well now, friend Yamaka, whatever body there is, whatever feeling, perception, predisposing mental formations, whatever discriminative consciousness—all should be correctly regarded with right view as, 'This is not mine, I am not this, this is not my self.' What do you think, friend Yamaka? Do you look upon a released person as body?"

"No, sir."

"Do you look upon him as feeling, perception, the predispositions, or discriminative consciousness?"

"No, sir."

"Do you look upon a released person as existing in body or in the other aggregates, or as different from body or the other aggregates?"

"Neither, sir."

"Then, friend Yamaka, a released person, an Arhat, is not knowable in truth and reality even in this life. And yet you pretend to understand the existence of an Arhat in this life by saying that his existence ceases at death!"

"Reverend Śāriputra, it was because of my ignorance that I held that former wicked view," confessed Yamaka.

Śāriputra and Yamaka were then joined by a wandering ascetic who lived on roseapples.

"O reverend Śāriputra," said the wandering ascetic, "they talk so much about Nirvāṇa. What is Nirvāṇa?"

"Whatever is the extinction of passion, of aversion, of confusion," replied Śāriputra, "this is called Nirvāṇa."

"But is there a way, a course, for the realization of this Nirvāṇa?"

"Yes, O wanderer. And what is it? It is the Āryan Eightfold Path, namely, Right View, Right Thought, Right Speech, Right Action, Right Livelihood, Right Effort, Right Attentiveness, and Right Concentration."

"Excellent, your reverence, is this Āryan Eightfold Way for the realization of Nirvāṇa. But there's no denying that diligence and fortitude are needed for following this Eightfold Way!"

Now, a dispute regarding the difference between an Arhat and a Buddha once arose among the monks. Some believed that a Buddha is higher than an Arhat, while others considered each to have attained the same Goal.

When word of this dispute came to the knowledge of Śākyamuni, he addressed the monks and said: "O monks! What is the distinction, what is the difference between a Tathāgata who, being fully Enlightened, is an Arhat, from a monk who is freed by Insight?"

"For us, Lord," replied the monks, "things are established in the Perfect One, and we have the Perfect One for our Guide and our Refuge. It would be a good thing, Lord, if the Perfect One were to make this matter clear to us. Hearing the Perfect One, the monks will bear it in mind."

"Then listen, monks, and pay close attention. I will speak."

"Yes, Lord."

"The Tathāgata, monks," declared Buddha, "is he who causes a Way to arise which had not arisen before, who brings about a Way not brought about before, who proclaims a Way not proclaimed before. He is a Knower of a Way, he understands a Way, he is skilled in a Way.

"And now, monks," concluded the Tathāgata, "his disciples are wayfarers who follow after him. That, O monks, is the distinction that differentiates the Tathāgata, an Arhat, from a fully Enlightened disciple, an Arhat. Both have attained Nirvāṇa; one leads while the other follows."

Thus said the Perfect One.

XII

SOJOURN AT ŚRĀVASTĪ

• ĀNANDA APPOINTED ATTENDANT •

During the twentieth year after the Enlightenment, Buddha journeyed often about the environs of Śrāvastī to preach the Doctrine of Release. On one of these occasions he was traveling on the Kośalan highway with the venerable Nāgasamāla as his personal attendant. And as the two went along, Nāgasamāla espied a side road; and on seeing it he said to the Master: "That is the road to take, O Lord. Let us go by that road."

"But this is the right road, Nāgasamāla," replied the Perfect One. "Let us go by this road."

And a second and yet a third time Nāgasamāla expressed his opinion, but Buddha was adamant.

"No, Nāgasamāla, the right road to take is this one. I will go by this road."

Vexation overcame Nāgasamāla; and he forthwith set the Blessed One's bowl and extra robe down upon the ground. And he left the Master and went away, saying: "Here, Lord, are your bowl and robe. I shall go where I please!"

Now it came to pass that as Nāgasamāla went along that side road, robbers fell upon him and beat and kicked him, broke his bowl, and tore his robes to tatters.

Then the venerable Nāgasamāla went back to the Tathāgata, and having approached him, exclaimed sorrowfully: "Master, as I journeyed along that road, robbers fell upon me—and see what has happened!"

Thereupon Buddha, considering the significance of the event, uttered the following stanza:

Traveling hither and yon the sage
Rubs shoulders with the blockhead.
But when he finds he's a rascal, he lets him go
As a milk-fed heron abandons water.

Reflecting upon this incident, and remembering the occasion when the venerable Meghiya abandoned him against his wishes, Buddha decided that the time had come for him to appoint a permanent attendant.

So when he had returned to Śrāvastī, he announced his intention to the monks. Śāriputra was the first to rise and offer himself, but the Perfect One declined, telling him that his work was preaching and teaching. Buddha also rejected Maudgalyāyana and others among the chief disciples.

Ānanda, meanwhile, sat silent, not venturing to offer himself until the Perfect One should speak.

"Well, Ānanda," said Buddha, "would you find it irksome to attend me, following me step by step wherever I go?"

"No, Lord," replied Ānanda, "I should not find it irksome; but I am unworthy of the honor of serving the Perfect One. I am still a pupil,

Lord: I have yet to attain Arhatship. Much remains for me to do. Verily, Lord, I am not worthy to serve the Perfect One as his personal attendant."

"Now, Ānanda, surely you, a pure-hearted Śākya, my own cousin, are worthy to attend me. In what way could I consider you unworthy? Reconsider, Ānanda."

Ānanda remained silent for a moment, then his face brightened as an idea occurred to him.

"Very well, Lord," he said. "Gladly will I act as the Perfect One's servitor, provided that the Perfect One is willing to agree to eight conditions."

"And what are the eight?"

"O Lord, that I may refuse four things, namely, that should the Perfect One be presented with a fine robe, it is not to be given to me; that I am not to partake of alms given to the Perfect One; that I am not to dwell in the Perfect One's magnificent perfumed chamber; that I am not to be included in invitations extended only to the Perfect One.

"And, O Lord, that I may accept four things, namely, that I may accompany the Perfect One whenever he receives an invitation that includes the monks; that I may present to the Perfect One persons who come from afar to see the Perfect One; that I may have access to the Perfect One at all times; that whatever teaching the Perfect One should give in my absence will be repeated to me afterwards from the Perfect One's own lips."

"Well said, Ānanda!" declared the Tathāgata. "Regard yourself, therefore, as my attendant from this day forward!"

The blessed Ānanda then replied to the Lord's acceptance of him with a felicitous stanza of resolution.

No matter where the Lord goes a-wandering,
There go I after him, step by step;
And when he makes known the Word of Truth,
I shall treasure the comforting knowledge in my heart.

• BUDDHA TAMES THE UNTAMED •

Now it came to pass that a furious robber known as Aṅgulimāla was terrorizing Śrāvastī. Even King Prasenajit of Kośala had heard of him and, in fact, was filled with dismay by the mere mention of the outlaw's name. For Aṅgulimāla ("Garland of Fingers"), continually eluding all attempts to capture him, mistreated his victims horribly.

One day as Buddha was going into the city of Śrāvastī for alms, Aṅgulimāla followed him. But the Perfect One, by the exercise of psychic power, caused the robber to stand motionless.

"I have heard somewhat about you, Aṅgulimāla," said the Perfect One. "Now tell me, Aṅgulimāla, why is it that you no longer dog my footsteps?"

"I do not know, O Recluse of mighty power! I cannot move! I cannot help standing still!"

"But, Aṅgulimāla, it is not you, but I, who stand still!"

"You walk, O Recluse; yet you say you are standing still!" said Aṅgulimāla with consternation. "And to me, who am standing still, you say that I am not so doing! Answer me, O mighty Sage! How is it that you are standing still and I am not?"

"I STAND STILL IN EVERY WAY," Buddha replied. "I have laid aside violence toward living beings. But you, Aṅgulimāla, are unrestrained toward living beings! Therefore I stand still and you do not stand still."

Aṅgulimāla realized that Buddha spoke the truth, and he saw himself for the first time as the cruel man that he was. Tears of remorse filled his eyes as he begged the Sugata to to permit him to become a follower, a monk in the Saṅgha. Buddha did not refuse his request.

Days later King Prasenajit came to visit Śākyamuni, as was his custom; and in the course of the conversation the king mentioned Aṅgulimāla's sudden and mysterious disappearance.

"Many are the fingerless hands in my realm, many are the fingers that Aṅgulimāla wears as a necklace! Oh, that Aṅgulimāla may never return to my kingdom! Oh, that I may never be so unlucky as to encounter such as he!"

"Unlucky, O king?" Buddha smiled as he directed Prasenajit's attention to one of the monks sitting nearby. "That monk, O king, is Aṅgulimāla."

King Prasenajit's astonished eyes searched Buddha's face for an explanation; and the Perfect One forthwith related the whole matter. Then, as if dazed, Prasenajit approached Aṅgulimāla and offered him robes and the other requisites of a monk.

"Enough, O king," replied Aṅgulimāla. "I have my three robes."

Prasenajit turned to Lord Buddha.

"Truly, Lord, the Perfect One is the Subduer Supreme, a mighty World-Conqueror! Verily, Lord, the Perfect One is a Trainer unsurpassed, a Tamer of the untamed!"

And thereupon King Prasenajit fell at Lord Buddha's feet and received the Light of the World.

At another time, when the Master was staying in the Jetavana Monastery in Anāthapiṇḍada's Park, an apparition, one Rohitaṣya, a son of the gods, came to the Perfect One toward dawn and illuminated the whole countryside with a wondrous radiance.

After making prostrations, Rohitaṣya addressed Buddha, saying: "Is there any place, O Lord, going to which one would find no birth, no growing old, no falling away to rise up elsewhere in rebirth? Can one, Lord, by going far away know the end, see the end, or reach the end of the cosmos?"

"No, friend," answered the Perfect One. "I declare that there is no place, going to which one would find no birth, no growing old, no falling away to rise up again elsewhere in rebirth. By going, no matter how far away one may go, I declare that one cannot know the end, see the end, or reach the end of the cosmos."

"Wonderful, O Lord!" exclaimed the god called Rohitaṣya. "A marvel it is, O Lord! How aptly spoken are the words uttered by the Perfect One!

"In days gone by," continued the apparition, "I was a sage called Rohitaṣya. A pupil of Bhodya was I; and I had cultivated the supernormal power of flying through space. I had the speed of an arrow. So mighty was my stride that it was just like the stretch between the Eastern and Western Oceans. To me, Lord, possessed of such speed and mighty stride, there came this desire: 'By faring far I will reach the end of the world.' And so, Lord, unfed by food or drink, without resting or sleeping, I journeyed on for nigh a hundred years. But I never reached it. I never came to the end. I died before I reached world's end."

"That was to be expected," said Buddha. "Nevertheless, friend, I do not say that without reaching world's end an end of woe cannot be made, for you can end it here and now. For, my friend, this very body with its sense-impressions and its thoughts and ideas—THIS SIX-FOOT BODY IS THE WORLD, THE BEGINNING OF THE WORLD, THE END OF THE WORLD, AND THE WAY THAT LEADS TO THE END OF THE WORLD."

Hearing this saying of the Master, Rohitaṣya, encouraged, disappeared on the spot, returning to his abode in a heavenly world.

Soon afterwards, Aṅgulimāla, the converted robber, had run into trouble. The people, hating him for his misdeeds, stoned him, wounding him severely and breaking his bowl. But the Perfect One said to him: "SURELY, ANGULIMĀLA, YOU MUST KNOW THAT THE LAW OF KARMA IS INEXORABLE. Your former evil action is just now bearing fruit; but be of good cheer, Aṅgulimāla! Had not misfortune struck you now, you might have been tortured in the hells for many eons."

• BUDDHA, THE COMPASSIONATE PHYSICIAN •

It once happened at Śrāvastī that a monk by the name of Tiṣya was suffering from dysentery and lay where he had fallen down in his own excrements. And the Perfect One was making his rounds of the monks' lodgings, with Ānanda in attendance, and came at last to the dwelling place of Tiṣya.

Now when the Perfect One saw the sick monk lying where he had fallen in his own excrements, he approached him and asked: "O monk, what is it that ails you?"

"I have dysentery, Lord," replied Tiṣya feebly.

"But is there anyone taking care of you?"

"No, Lord."

"Why is it, brother, that the monks do not take care of you?"

"I am useless to the monks, Lord. That is why they do not take care of me."

Buddha turned to Ānanda.

"Go, Ānanda, and fetch water. We shall wash this monk."

"Yes, Master," replied Ānanda. And when the water had been brought, Lord Buddha poured it out while Ānanda washed Tiṣya from head to foot. Then Buddha, taking him by the head, and Ānanda, taking him by the feet, together laid him on the bed.

The Perfect One then called the congregation of monks together and questioned them, saying: "Monks, is there a monk in your midst who is sick?"

"There is, Lord."

"And what ails that monk?"

"Lord, that monk has dysentery."

"But, monks, is there anyone taking care of him?"

"No, Lord."

"Why not? Why don't you monks take care of him?"

"That monk is repulsive, and filthy with his own excrements, Lord. That is why we don't take care of him."

"Monks, you have no mother and no father to take care of you. If you will not take care of each other, who else, I ask, will do so? O monks, he who would tend me, let him tend the sick. If a sick man among you have a teacher, let his teacher take care of him and await his recovery. If he have a tutor or a lodger, a disciple or a fellow pupil, such should take care of him and await his recovery. If no one take care of him, it shall be reckoned an offense."

Śākyamuni continued: "There are five characteristics, O monks, possessed of which a sick man is hard to nurse. (1) He will not take remedies, (2) he observes no moderation in taking them, (3) he does not take the prescribed drugs, (4) he does not disclose his symptoms to the nurse who desires his welfare, nor does he say whether his sickness wanes or waxes or stands still, and (5) he is impatient of his bodily feelings that arise—painful, sharp, burning, bitter, grievous, unpleasant, life-destroying.

"Such, monks, are the five characteristics possessed of which a sick man is hard to nurse. And the five characteristics which make him easy to nurse are the opposites of these.

"There are five characteristics, monks, possessed of which one is of no use as a nurse. (1) One is incapable of prescribing medicine, not knowing the proper remedies, what is good and what is bad, (2) one administers what is unfit and not what is fit, (3) one nurses the patient out of greed and not out of love, (4) one is squeamish about the removal of excrements, saliva, and vomit, and (5) one is incapable of teaching the patient from time to time with pious conversation, incapable of cheering him, of comforting him and encouraging him to endure.

"Such, monks, are the five characteristics possessed of which one is of no use as a nurse. And the five characteristics which make a good nurse are the opposites of these."

On another occasion the Tathāgata said: "O monks, it is as if some blind-born man, because he sees no sun, moon, planets, or stars, should say, 'There are no visible things at all!' But a great physician who knows all diseases takes compassion on the blind man and reflects thus: 'The disease of this man originates in the wicked deeds he committed in former lives. Surely it is impossible to cure this disease with the drugs in common use; but in Himālaya, king of mountains, there are wondrous herbs. These I shall obtain and administer to the blind man.'

"And the compassionate physician does so. Some of the herbs he chews with the teeth, others he triturates, others he boils, others he compounds in divers ways; and then he introduces them into a vein of the blind man's body by means of a needle.

"Owing to this treatment, the blind-born one recovers his eyesight; and at last, seeing all visible phenomena with his own eyes, he exclaims: 'Oh, how foolish I was that I denied the existence of visible things! It was from ignorance that I spoke as I did!'

"IN THE SAME WAY DO PEOPLE OF GREAT IGNORANCE, SPIRITUALLY BLIND FROM BIRTH, MOVE IN THE TURMOIL

OF THE WORLD: THEY KNOW NOTHING OF THE EVER-REVOLVING WHEEL OF CAUSES AND EFFECTS, NOTHING OF THE WORLD'S GREAT PAIN. BUT IN THE WORLD SO BLINDED BY IGNORANCE APPEARS THE HIGHEST OF THOSE WHO KNOW ALL, NAMELY, THE TATHĀGATA, THE GREAT PHYSICIAN OF COMPASSIONATE NATURE."

• THE LITTLE WAIF •

Once upon a time there lived at Śrāvastī a woman who fell into a long, deep swoon during the travail of childbirth. Her relatives, thinking that she was dead, bore her to the cemetery and prepared to cremate the body. But a spirit prevented the fire from burning by stirring up a storm of wind and rain; and the woman's kinsfolk returned to their homes.

Now, the child, a baby boy, was born hale and hearty while the mother died. And the spirit, assuming human form, took the infant and placed it in the caretaker's house, nourishing it for a time with suitable food. After that, the caretaker adopted the child: and because of his birth in a cemetery, the boy became known as Sopāka—"the Waif."

When little Sopāka was seven years old it came to pass that Lord Buddha, early one morning, spread out his "net of knowledge" to contemplate which folk might be converted to the Dharma. Seeing what the net enclosed, Śākyamuni went to the cemetery to find the boy.

Now Sopāka, impelled by his store of merit brought over from a previous existence, approached the Master with a happy mind and prostrated himself before the master. And the Master taught him so skillfully that he asked admission to the noble congregation of monks. The formalities over, Lord Buddha assigned to little Sopāka as a subject of special meditation the study of brotherly love.

Sopāka, taking this exercise and dwelling in a cemetery, soon acquired the corresponding psychic absorption; and making that his base, he gained Insight and realized Arhatship. And then, by uttering a verse, the little waif revealed to the other monks dwelling there the principle of the loving-friendliness exercises, bidding them to make *no distinction* among those who were friendly, indifferent, or hostile.

Even as a mother is loving-kind
Toward her child, her only son,
So too should ye be loving-kind
Toward all the creatures everywhere.

For all alike their love should be one and the same in its nature, and should include all realms, all beings, and all ages. VERILY, LOVE CONQUERS ALL!

• VACCHAGOTRA'S QUESTIONS •

Once a wanderer by the name of Vacchagotra came to the Perfect One and greeted him with friendly salutation. After the exchange of mutual courtesies, Vacchagotra sat down at one side and said: "Well, Venerable Gautama, is it your opinion that the universe is eternal?"

"I am not of the opinion, Vaccha, that the universe is eternal," replied Buddha.

"Then it seems, reverend Gautama, that you believe the universe to be temporal."

"But, Vaccha, I do not hold the opinion that the universe is temporal."

"Well, is it your opinion that the universe is infinite?"

"No, Vaccha."

"That the universe is finite?"

"No, Vaccha."

"That life is the same as the body?"

"No, Vaccha."

"That life is other than the body?"

"No, Vaccha."

"That an Arhat exists after death?"

"No, Vaccha."

"That an Arhat does not exist after death?"

"No, Vaccha."

"That an Arhat both exists and does not exist after death?"

"No, Vaccha."

"That an Arhat neither exists nor does not exist after death?"

"No, Vaccha."

Vacchagotra's face twisted with a grimace of vexation.

"Well, reverend Gautama," he said, "what danger do you perceive in these opinions that you completely avoid them as you do?"

"To hold that the universe is eternal," declared Śākyamuni, "is an opinion, a thicket of opinions, a wilderness, a jungle, a tangle, a fetter of opinions, full of agitation, vexation, trouble, and distress. It does not tend to aversion, absence of passion, cessation, tranquility, higher knowledge, Enlightenment, Nirvāṇa. And so with all the other opinions which you mentioned."

"Well, has the Venerable Gautama any opinion on anything?"

"The term 'opinion,' Vaccha, has been discarded by the Tathāgata. What has been perceived by the Tathāgata is: body, feelings, perception, the predisposing formations, discriminative consciousness, and likewise their origin and disappearance. Therefore an Arhat, with the abandonment and utter extinction of all imaginary and befuddled inclinations to conceit in an ego-soul, or in anything belonging to an ego-soul, is truly released, I declare."

"But reverend Gautama," asked Vacchagotra the wanderer, "where is the person, whose mind is thus released, reborn?"

"To say that he is reborn, Vaccha, does not fit the case," replied the Perfect One.

"Then he is not reborn?"

"To say that he is not reborn does not fit the case."

"Then he is both reborn and not reborn?"

"To say that he is both reborn and not reborn does not fit the case."

"Then he is neither reborn nor not reborn?"

"To say that he is neither reborn nor not reborn does not fit the case."

Vacchagotra was beginning to redden with impatience and perplexity.

"When you are asked, Venerable Gautama, where the person whose mind is released is reborn, you deny every logical possibility. In regard to this matter I have fallen into ignorance and bewilderment; and whatever faith I had before in the reverend Gautama has quite disappeared."

"Verily, Vaccha, you have more than just a little ignorance and bewilderment! THIS DHARMA, VACCHA, IS PROFOUND, SUBTLE, HARD TO SEE, HARD TO COMPREHEND, BEYOND THE SPHERE OF MERE LOGIC, TO BE UNDERSTOOD ONLY BY THE WISE. For you, holding other views, trained in a different way, it is difficult to understand. Therefore, Vaccha, I will reverse the process and ask questions of you. Answer as you see fit. Now, what do you think? If a fire were burning in front of you, would you know it?"

"Yes, Venerable Gautama, I should know it."

"And if someone were to ask you what was causing the fire to burn, how would you explain it?"

"I should say that the fire was burning because of its fuel of grass and sticks."

"If, Vaccha, the fire burning before you were to go out, would you know it?"

"Yes, Venerable Gautama, I should know it."

"And if someone were to ask you in what direction the element of fire had gone—to the east, west, north, or south—how would you reply?"

"It does not fit the case, reverend Gautama, for the fire was burning on account of its fuel of grass and sticks, and through the consumption of that, not getting any more, it had become extinct."

"In just the same way, Vaccha, that body by which one might denote an Arhat has passed away, it is cut off at the root, been made nonexistent, not capable of arising again in the future. So also the feelings, perception, predispositions, and the discriminative consciousness by which one might denote an Arhat. A released person, Vaccha, is released from what is named body, feelings, perception, the predispositions, and discriminative consciousness. He is profound, immeasurable, hard to fathom, like the great ocean. To say that he is reborn does not fit the case, or that he is not reborn, or both reborn and not reborn, or neither reborn nor not reborn."

"But Venerable Gautama," protested Vaccha, "what about the soul of the released person? What happens to that?"

Buddha sighed, knowing full well that Vacchagotra was incapable of understanding the matter.

"Venerable Gautama," insisted Vacchagotra, "have you nothing to say about the existence of the soul? Does the soul exist?"

At these words the Perfect One was SILENT.

"How is it, Venerable Gautama? Is there no such thing as the soul?"

The Perfect One was SILENT.

Then Vacchagotra the wanderer rose up from his seat and went away in disgust. And not long after he was gone, the blessed Ānanda said to the Perfect One: "How did it happen, Lord, that the Perfect One made no reply to the question asked by Vacchagotra, the wandering ascetic?"

"If, Ānanda, when asked 'Does the soul exist?' I had replied, 'The soul exists,' then that would be to side with those recluses and brahmins who are ETERNALISTS. But if, when asked, 'Then the soul does not exist?' I had replied, 'No, the soul does not exist,' then that would be to side with those recluses and brahmins who are NIHILISTS.

"Then again, Ānanda, if when asked, 'Does the soul exist?' I had replied, 'The soul exists,' would that reply be consistent with my knowledge that ALL THINGS ARE IMPERMANENT?"

"No, Lord, it would not," said Ānanda.

"Then again, Ānanda, if when asked, 'Then the soul does not exist?' I had replied, 'No, the soul does not exist,' then that would have increased the bewilderment of Vacchagotra the wanderer, already bewildered. For he would have said, 'Formerly I had a soul, but now I have a soul no more.' "

• THE BLIND MEN AND THE ELEPHANT •

Once upon a time, while the Perfect One was staying at the Jetavana Monastery in Anāthapiṇḍada's Park near Śrāvastī, a large number of recluses and brahmins, who were wandering ascetics holding diverse dogmas, entered Śrāvastī to beg alms.

Those wandering ascetics were tolerant of certain things, favored certain things, and were inclined to rely on certain things. Some of them held the view that the world is eternal, that this is the truth, that any other view is rank heresy. Others held that the world is not eternal, that this view is correct, and other views mere foolishness. Some maintained that the world is finite, others that it is infinite; some held that life is the body, others that life is one thing and the body another; some asserted that the soul is beyond being affected by death, others that the soul is destroyed at death, others that it both is and is not beyond being affected by death, still others that it neither is nor is not beyond being affected by death.

"This opinion is truth; any other opinion is delusion and infatuation!"

So they, by nature quarrelsome, contentious, and disputatious, lived scorching one another with the fire of the tongue.

"True doctrine is such and such; true doctrine is not such and such; it is, it is not!"

Now, many of Śākyamuni's monks, taking bowl and robe, also entered Śrāvastī to quest for alms. And after making their rounds and eating their morning meal, they went to the Perfect One and told him about the wrangling ascetics who squabbled so violently.

"O monks," declared Buddha, "those wanderers holding other views are blind, unseeing. They know neither things profitable nor things unprofitable. They do not know what is the Dharma and what is not the Dharma. In their ignorance of these things they are by nature quarrelsome and argumentative.

"Formerly, monks, in a bygone age, there was a certain king of this same Śrāvastī. And that king called to a certain man, saying: " 'Come, good fellow, go and gather together in one place all the men in Śrāvastī who were born blind.'

" 'As you say, O king,' replied that man; and in obedience to the king gathered together in a field near the royal palace all the men in Śrāvastī who were born blind.

" 'Now, my good man,' commanded the king, 'show the blind men an elephant.'

" 'As you wish, O king,' said that man; and when he had brought an elephant into the field, he said to the blind-born men, 'O blind ones, such as this is an elephant.' To one man he presented the head of the elephant, to another an ear, to another a tusk, to another the trunk, the foot, the back, tail, and tuft of the tail, saying to each one that that was the elephant.

"Now, monks, that man, having thus presented the elephant to the blind men, came to the king and said: " 'O king, the elephant has been presented to the blind men. Do whatever is your pleasure.'

"Then, monks, that king went up to the blind men and said to each, 'Well, blind one, have you perceived the elephant?'

" 'Yes, O king.'

" 'Then tell me, blind men, what sort of thing an elephant is.'

"Thereupon those who had been presented with the head answered, 'O king, an elephant is like a pot.' And those who had observed only an ear replied, 'An elephant is like a winnowing basket.' Those who had been presented with a tusk said it is like a plowshare. Those who knew only the trunk said it is like a plow. Others, knowing only the body, thought it like a granary; the foot like a pillar; the back like a mortar; the tail like a pestle; the tuft of the tail like a broom.

"Then they began to quarrel, shouting, 'Yes, it is!' 'No, it is not!' 'An elephant is not that!' 'Yes, it is like that!'—and so on, more and more heatedly until they came to blows over the matter.

"Then, monks, that king rocked with laughter at the spectacle.

"Just so are these wandering ascetics holding other views, ignorant of Dharma, by nature quarrelsome, contentious, and disputatious, each maintaining his own narrow view."

Whereupon the Master concluded his parable with this verse:

Oh, how they cling and wrangle, some who claim
Of brahmin and recluse the honored name!
For, quarrelling, each to his view they cling.
Such folk see only one side of a thing.

In a few weeks' time the Perfect One changed his residence to the storied monastery built by Viśākhā, "Mṛgāra's mother," in East Park. And it happened at that time that Viśākhā's granddaughter had died. So Viśākhā, with clothes and hair still wet, came very early in the morning to see the Perfect One; and on coming to him greeted him with a respectful salutation and sat down at one side, striving to repress her grief.

"How is it, good woman," said Buddha, "that you come here with clothes and hair still wet at an unseasonable hour?"

"Master, my little granddaughter is dead!"

"Viśākhā," said Lord Buddha, "would you like to have as many sons and grandsons as there are men in Śrāvastī?"

"Yes, Master, I would indeed!"

"But how many men do you suppose die each day in Śrāvastī?"

"Many, Lord," answered Viśākhā. "Śrāvastī is never free from men dying."

"What do you think, Viśākhā? In such a case, would you ever be without sorrow and grief?"

"Surely not, Master! Enough for me, Lord, of so many sons and grandsons!"

"Dear woman," said the Perfect One, "those who have a hundred things dear to them have a hundred sorrows. Those who have twenty or ten things dear to them have twenty or ten sorrows. Those who have but one thing dear to them have but one sorrow. But those who have not a single thing dear to them have no sorrow at all, I declare."

• BUDDHIST BREATHING EXERCISES •

Once when the Perfect One was staying in the storied monastery of "Mṛgāra's mother" in the Pūrvārāma (East Park) near Śrāvastī, many of the elder monks were instructing and advising hundreds of novices. And those young monks, thus instructed and advised, were realizing a great and gradually perceptible result. And on the full moon day in the middle of the month, Buddha addressed those novitiate monks, saying: "I have become perfect in this Path, O monks. I have become perfect of Mind in this Path. And you, O monks, must continue to perfect yourselves to achieve what remains for you to achieve, to attain what remains for you to attain, to realize what remains for you to realize. About a month from now, on the day following the last autumnal full moon day, I am going to leave Śrāvastī."

Now when the monks living in the country heard that the Perfect One was going to leave Śrāvastī, they set out to visit the Perfect One. And when the day of the last autumnal full moon had come, Buddha took his seat in the midst of the assembly of monks under the star-spangled canopy of heaven. Looking out over the calm, silent assembly of monks, Buddha addressed the congregation, saying: "Not even a whisper disturbs this assembly, silent and pure is this assembly. Verily, O monks, such an assembly as this, such a Saṅgha as this, is an unsurpassed field in the world for merit, worthy of offerings and gifts, of adoration and worship. This is the noblest community in all the world, I declare: its like cannot anywhere be found.

"Among you, O monks, are some who persevere assiduously in gaining mastery of mindful respiration. Mindful respiration, practised and cultivated—peaceful, sublime, pure, bestowing happiness—suppresses all ill and every immoral state which is apt to arise.

"But how, monks, is this concentration of mindfulness as to respiration developed? How, being repeated, can it suppress all ill and every immoral state which is apt to arise?

"Well, monks, a monk goes into a forest or to the foot of a tree or to a solitary place in the mountains and there sits down cross-legged, holding his body straight, and fixes his attention in front of him. Then:

"Attentively he breathes in, attentively he breathes out. And then:

> *1. "Breathing in a long breath, he knows, 'I am breathing in a long breath.' Breathing out a long breath, he knows, 'I am breathing out a long breath.'*
>
> *2. "Breathing in a short breath, he knows, 'I am breathing in a short breath.' Breathing out a short breath, he knows, 'I am breathing out a short breath.' Thus he trains himself. Continuing:*
>
> *3. " 'Conscious of the passage of breath, I breathe in. Conscious of the passage of breath, I breathe out.*
>
> *4. " 'Calming the passage of breath, I breathe in. Calming the passage of breath, I breathe out.*
>
> *5. " 'Feeling serenity, I breathe in. Feeling serenity, I breathe out.*
>
> *6. " 'Feeling happiness, I breathe in. Feeling happiness, I breathe out.*

7. " 'Conscious of the sequence of thoughts, I breathe in. Conscious of the sequence of thoughts, I breathe out.

8. " 'Calming the sequence of thoughts, I breathe in. Calming the sequence of thoughts, I breathe out.

9. " 'Perceiving the mind, I breathe in. Perceiving the mind, I breathe out.

10. " 'Elevating the mind, I breathe in. Elevating the mind, I breathe out.

11. " 'Concentrating the mind, I breathe in. Concentrating the mind, I breathe out.

12. " 'Liberating the mind, I breathe in. Liberating the mind, I breathe out.

13. " 'Discerning the impermanence of all composite things, I breathe in. Discerning the impermanence of all composite things, I breathe out.

14. " 'Conscious of the absence of passion, I breathe in. Conscious of the absence of passion, I breathe out.

15. " 'Conscious of the extinction of craving desires, I breathe in. Conscious of the extinction of craving desires, I breathe out.

16. " 'Conscious of the otherness of craving desires, I breathe in. Conscious of the otherness of craving desires, I breathe out.'

"In this way, O monks, must mindful respiration be practised and cultivated—peaceful, sublime, pure, bestowing happiness—that it suppress all ill and every immoral state which is apt to arise. In this way, O monks, must a monk train himself."

Thus spoke the Enlightened One, and well content were the monks with his instruction. And on the morrow Buddha left Śrāvastī with several hundred monks to go to Rājagṛha.

XIII

THE RETURN TO RĀJAGṚHA

• BUDDHA AND THE TWO YOUNG BRAHMINS •

Journeying east through Kośalan country, Śākyamuni came one day to the village of Manasāketa, in which lived many wealthy brahmins of renown. Now, among these brahmins were two youths, Vāśreṣṭha and Bhāradvāja, who were assailed by doubts as to the path of conduct which leads to union with the god Brahmā.

"There is a Recluse named Gautama now staying in the mango grove nearby," said Vāśreṣṭha to Bhāradvāja. "This venerable Gautama has a most excellent reputation. They even say of him that he is a Wholly Awakened One, blessed and worthy of veneration, abounding in wisdom and goodness, happy, with knowledge of all worlds, unsurpassed as a guide for erring mortals, a teacher of gods and men, a Supreme Buddha. Come, friend Bhāradvāja, let us go to the place where the Ascetic

Gautama is staying, let us present our difficulties to him, and let us bear in mind whatever he says."

Bhāradvāja consented, and so the two young men went straightway to the mango grove where Buddha was staying. And when they had arrived, they exchanged the customary greetings and seated themselves at one side.

"As we were walking up and down exercising ourselves," began Vāśreṣtha, "there arose a discussion between us as to which is and which is not the true path to union with Brahmā. I said that the straight way which leads one directly to Brahmā is the one taught by the brahmin Pokharaśrādi. Bhāradvāja, however, said that the direct way is the one taught by the brahmin Tārukṣa. Hence the dispute which we wish you to settle for us, reverend Gautama."

"But wherein, Vāśreṣtha," asked the Perfect One, "lies your difference of opinion?"

"About what is and what is not the path that leads to union with Brahmā, reverend Gautama," replied Vāśreṣtha. "Do the various ways that the brahmins teach all lead to the same salvation, the same union with Brahmā, much as different roads may lead to the same town?"

"Well, Vāśreṣtha, do you really think that any of those several paths lead to Brahmā?"

"Yes, Venerable Gautama, I believe that they do lead to Brahmā."

"But, Vāśreṣtha, is there even a single brahmin versed in the three Vedas who has himself seen Brahmā?"

"Certainly not, Venerable Gautama."

"Well is there a single teacher of those brahmins who has seen Brahmā face to face?"

"Certainly not, Venerable Gautama."

"Well, is there a single one as far back as the seventh in the succession of teachers who has seen Brahmā face to face?"

"No, Venerable Gautama."

"Well then, Vāśreṣtha, among the brahmins versed in the Vedas, among the ancient sages, among the composers and chanters of psalms, whose ancient hymns are still chanted, recited, and copied by the brahmins of today—intoning and reciting them as has been done for ages—is there a single one who ever said that he knew where Brahmā is, whence Brahmā came, or whither Brahmā goes?"

"Not a single one, reverend Gautama."

"Thus it seems, Vāśresṭha, that not a single one of all those brahmins knows what he talks about. Not a single one of them has seen Brahmā face to face. And yet they pretend to know all about Brahmā and how to attain union with him! Verily, Vāśresṭha, they do not know of any path that leads to union with Brahmā! Now, what do you think? Is not the talk of these brahmins, versed though they be in the three Vedas, just foolish babble?"

"Indeed, it would seem so, reverend Gautama."

"Verily, it is not possible that the brahmins, steeped in the Vedas, can teach the way to union with him whom they neither know nor see! They are just like a string of blind men clinging to one another. The first does not see, nor the middle one, nor the last. Truly, Vāśresṭha, the talk of these brahmins is ridiculous and foolish! Now, what do you think? Do the brahmins versed in the Vedas, as well as many others, see the moon and sun, and pray to them, praise them, and continually worship them with palms pressed together?"

"Yes, reverend Gautama, they do."

"What do you think, Vāśresṭha? Can those brahmins, versed in the Vedas, point out the way to union with the moon and sun and say, 'This is the straight way that leads anyone who takes it directly to union with the moon and sun'?"

"Certainly not."

"Thus it seems, Vāśresṭha, that those brahmins cannot point out the way to union with the moon and sun, which they can see. It seems that they have not seen Brahmā themselves, yet they pretend to point out the way to union with Brahmā! Are not their assertions just foolish talk?"

"Foolish and vain it would seem, reverend Gautama."

"Vāśresṭha, it is just as though a man should say, 'How I long for, how I love the most beautiful woman in the land!' And people should ask him, 'Well, good friend, this beautiful woman whom you love—is she a noble lady, a brahmin woman, a woman of the mercantile caste, or a serf?' and he should answer, 'Really, I don't know!' And when people should ask him, 'This woman whom you love—do you know her name, her family, whether she be tall or short, dark or of medium complexion, black or fair, which city or town she lives in?' and he should answer, 'No, I do not know!' And when people should say to him, 'How then, good friend, can you love and long for a woman whom you do not know and whom you have never seen?' and he should answer, 'Nevertheless, I love her.' Now, what do you think? Wouldn't that man's talk be the talk of a fool?"

"Yes, Venerable Gautama, it would indeed be the talk of a fool."

"Just so, Vāśreṣṭha, is the talk of the brahmins steeped in scriptures the talk of fools. Now suppose that this river Aciravatī were full of water up to the brim, overflowing, and that a man should come up and want to cross over because he had business on the other side. Suppose that he, standing on this bank, should begin to pray, saying, 'Come hither, O farther bank, come over to this side!' Now, what do you think, Vāśreṣṭha? Would the farther bank of the river, because of that man's invoking and praying and hoping and praising, come over to this side?"

"Certainly not."

"It is just the same with the brahmins, steeped in the scriptures. Neglecting those things that a brahmin ought to do, and practiing those things that a brahmin ought not do, they pray continually, saying, 'Indra, we call upon thee! Soma, Varuṇa, Iśāna, Prajāpatī, Brahmā, Mahiddhi, Yama, we call upon thee!' Verily, Vāśreṣṭha, that those brahmins, because of their invoking and praying and hoping and praising, should go after death to the world of the Brahmās is utterly impossible.

"Now, Vāśreṣṭha," continued the Perfect One, "when you have been among brahmin priests, listening as they talked among themselves, what have you learned from them and about them? Tell me, Vāśreṣṭha, is the god Brahmā in possession of wives and wealth, or is he not?"

"He is not, Venerable Gautama."

"Is his heart full of anger or not?"

"It is free from anger, Venerable Gautama."

"Is his mind full of malice or not?"

"It is free from malice."

"Is his mind depraved or pure?"

"It is pure."

"Has he self-mastery, or has he not?"

"He has."

"Now, what do you think, Vāśreṣtha? Are the brahmins who are steeped in the scriptures in possession of wives and wealth, or are they not?"

"They are, Venerable Gautama."

"Have they anger in their hearts?"

"They have."

"Do they have minds full of malice?"

"They do."

"Are they depraved?"

"They are."

"Do they possess self-mastery?"

"They do not."

"Then you say, Vāśreṣtha, that there is little agreement and resemblance between the brahmins and Brahmā. Verily, it is impossible that these brahmins, steeped in the scriptures, should attain union with Brahmā after death when the body breaks up. These brahmins are really sinking while they rest in confidence. They think they are crossing over into some happier land, but because they are really sinking, they can arrive only at despair. The knowledge of the brahmins, based on the Vedas, is a waterless desert, a pathless waste; and their knowledge is their destruction."

Then the young brahmin said: "It has been told to me, Venerable Gautama, that the Venerable Gautama knows the way to union with Brahmā. Can you teach us?"

Thereupon the Enlightened One taught Vāśreṣtha and Bhāradvāja the Dharma, both in the spirit and in the letter. And when he had finished, he questioned Vāśreṣtha, saying: "Now, what do you think, Vāśreṣtha? Will the monk who lives according to the Dharma and discipline proclaimed by me be in possession of women and wealth, or will he not?"

"He will not, Lord."

"Will he be full of anger?"

"No, Lord."

"Will his mind be full of malice?"

"No, Lord."

"Will his mind be depraved?"

"No, Lord."

"Will he have self-mastery?"

"Surely he will, Lord."

"Vāśreṣtha, you say that such a monk is free from worldly conditions. Is there, then, agreement and resemblance between the monk and Brahmā?

"There is, Lord."

"Well said, Vāśreṣtha! Truly, it is in every way possible for the monk, free from worldly conditions, at death to become united with Brahmā, who is also free from worldly conditions. But union with Brahmā, Vāśreṣtha, I declare to be a low aim for the monk. Higher than union with Brahmā, higher than rebirth in heaven, is the attainment of the unsurpassable Goal of Nirvāṇa."

And when the Perfect One had spoken these words, the two young brahmins exclaimed: "Most excellent, Lord, are your words! The Truth in all its perfection has been made known to us today by the Perfect One! We betake ourselves, Lord, to the Buddha, the Dharma, and the Saṅgha for refuge! May the Happy One accept us as disciples from this day forward, as long as life shall last!"

• SUPRABUDDHA THE LEPER •

When the Exalted One reached Rājagṛha in the country of the Magadhas, he took up residence in the Veṇuvana Monastery in the Squirrels' Feeding Ground.

Now there lived in Rājagṛha at that time a leper named Suprabuddha, a poor, wretched, miserable being. And it came about one day that Śākyamuni was sitting in the midst of a great multitude teaching Dharma.

When Suprabuddha the leper saw from afar the great crowd of people, he thought, "It looks very much like an almsgiving of food. Suppose I join that crowd: I might be lucky enough to get something to eat."

So Suprabuddha approached the throng, and he saw the Master sitting in its midst preaching a discourse. Then Suprabuddha thought, "No, there is no almsgiving of food here. It is the Ascetic Gautama preaching a sermon to these people. Suppose I stay and listen to the preaching." And so he sat down at one side of the crowd.

Now, the Perfect One, grasping with his thought the thoughts of the entire assembly, considered, "Who, I wonder, of all these present, is able to understand the Dharma?" Then he saw Suprabuddha the leper sitting there; and at the very sight of him the Master knew: "This fellow is able to understand the Dharma!"

For the sake of Suprabuddha, therefore, the Perfect One preached a discourse dealing, in progressive order, with such topics as almsgiving, the religious life, and the worlds of heaven. And he pointed out, in the course of his teaching, the wretchedness and vileness of sensual desires and the benefits of freedom from the Poisons.

Now, when the Perfect One saw that the heart of Suprabuddha was softened, made pliant, set free, elated, and full of faith and confidence, he expounded to him that most excellent of Buddha-teachings, namely:

"This is Suffering; this is the Cause of Suffering; this is the Cessation of Suffering; and this is the Path which leads to the Cessation of Suffering."

Then, just as a white cloth free from stain readily takes dye, even so in Suprabuddha the leper there arose the pure and stainless Insight—*the certain knowledge that whatever has a beginning must also have an end. And Suprabuddha saw Truth face to face, perceived and attained Truth; and, immersed in Truth, crossed over beyond the sphere of doubts, was freed from the necessity of asking questions, won confidence, and became established in the Holy One's Teaching, needing nothing more.*

A few days later, however, a young calf charged Suprabuddha the leper and gored him to death. And when the monks heard of this untoward event, they went to Śākyamuni and told him the news.

"Lord, that leper by the name of Suprabuddha, after being taught, stirred, established, and made happy by the Perfect One's instruction, is now dead, having been gored to death by a young calf. Tell us, Lord, what is the nature of Suprabuddha's rebirth? What is his future lot?"

"Suprabuddha the leper," replied the Tathāgata, "was a sage, O monks. He lived in accordance with the Dharma. Suprabuddha, monks, by destroying the Defilements is a Stream-Entrant. He has escaped the downfall. He has won assurance. He is on his way to Enlightenment."

When Śākyamuni said this, one of the monks asked: "What, Lord, was the circumstance, what was the cause that made Suprabuddha the leper such a poor, wretched, miserable being?"

"Well, monk, once upon a time, in a former life, Suprabuddha was a rich man's son in this very town of Rājagṛha. One day, while strolling through his garden, he caught sight of a Pratyekabuddha entering the town to beg. And on seeing him, the rich man's son spat upon him in disdain, saying, 'What is this miserable leper doing here, roaming about?'

"Thereafter," continued the Perfect One, "that rich man's son went to the hells, to one hell after another, remaining in them for many a year, for hundreds, for thousands, for hundreds of thousands of years; and as a result of that deed, he was reborn again here in Rājagṛha as a leper, as a poor, wretched, miserable being. But as soon as he embarked upon the Dharma and discipline set forth by the Tathāgata, Suprabuddha acquired faith, entered upon the religious life, and took on the Precepts, Self-sacrifice, and Wisdom. Thus established, on the breakup of the body at death, he was reborn in the happy state, in the blissful world, in the Heaven of the Thirty-Three Palaces, and there he outshines all the other gods in glory and renown."

• VAKULA'S SICKNESS •

It was while Buddha was residing near Rājagṛha that the venerable Vakula, then residing in a potter's shed, became sick, afflicted with a grievous disease.

This Vakula was the same monk who, many years earlier, had been rescued from the brink of suicide by Śākyamuni.

Now, the venerable Vakula called to his attendants, saying: "My friends, I want you to go to the Master and, prostrating before him in my name, say to him, 'Lord, the monk Vakula is stricken with a grievous ailment. He prostrates at the feet of the Perfect One. It would be good if the Perfect One would visit the monk Vakula out of compassion.' "

Vakula's attendants duly delivered the message; and Buddha, by his silence, consented to visit the sick monk.

When Vakula saw Buddha entering the shed, he made an effort to sit up on his sleeping mat.

"Enough, Vakula!" said the Tathāgata. "Do not bestir yourself! There are seats made ready: I will sit here."

"Yes, Lord," answered the ailing monk.

"Well, Vakula, I hope you are bearing up. I hope you are enduring. Do your pains abate and not increase? Are there signs of their abating and not increasing?"

"No, Lord, I am not bearing up. I am not enduring. Strong pains come upon me. They do not abate. There is no sign of their abating, but, rather, they seem to be increasing."

"Have you any doubts, Vakula? Have you any remorse?"

"Verily, Lord, of doubts and remorse I have none."

"Have you nothing, Vakula, in which to reproach yourself in regard to morals?"

"No, Lord, there is nothing to reproach myself for in regard to morals."

"Then, Vakula, that being so, you must have some worry, you must have something to regret."

"Well—for a long time, Lord, I have been longing to set eyes on the Perfect One, but I did not have strength enough in this body to come to the Perfect One to see him."

"Hush, Vakula! What profit is there in seeing this vile body of mine? HE WHO SEES THE DHARMA SEES ME; HE WHO SEES ME SEES THE DHARMA. VERILY, SEEING DHARMA, VAKULA, I AM SEEN; SEEING ME, DHARMA IS SEEN."

And after reminding the venerable Vakula of the impermanence of all composite things, Śākyamuni returned to Bamboo Grove (Veṇuvane) in the Squirrels' Feeding Ground (Kalandakanivāpa).

• DHARMA FOR LAYMEN •

One day the Perfect One, rising early in the morning, went forth from the Veṇuvana Monastery to enter Rājagṛha with bowl and outer robe on alms-quest. And at that time there was a young householder by the name of Sigāla who went mornings just outside the city to worship the several quarters of space—the east, south, west, north, nadir, and zenith.

When Buddha saw Sigāla worshiping with wet hair and wet garments, and with clasped hands uplifted, he addressed the youth, saying: "Why are you worshiping the quarters, young householder?"

"My father, Lord, when he lay on his deathbed, told me to do so. Therefore I, Lord, honoring my father's injunction, respecting and holding sacred my father's word, rise early and worship the quarters."

"But, young householder," objected the Tathāgata, "the six quarters are not so worshiped by one who follows the discipline of the Āryas."

"How then, Lord, ought the six quarters be worshiped?" asked Sigāla. "It would be good, Lord, if the Perfect One were to teach me the Dharma according to which, in the discipline of the Āryas, the six quarters should be worshiped."

"Then listen and reflect upon my words, and I will teach you."

"Yes, Lord."

"Forasmuch, young householder, as the Āryan disciple has put away the four vices of action, forasmuch as he does no evil actions from the four motives, forasmuch as he does not pursue the six channels for dissipating wealth, he thus, avoiding these fourteen evil things, covers the six quarters and gains victory both in this world and in the next. With the dissolution of the body at death, he is reborn to a happy destiny in the world of heaven.

"Now, what are the four vices of action that he has put away? The taking of life, theft, deceiving, and unchastity."

Thus said the Master; and when he had thus spoken, he spoke yet again, saying: "Killing, stealing, lying, adultery—to these the wise award no word of praise. Now, by which four motives does he refrain from evil action? Evil deeds are done from motives of passion, anger, delusion, and fear. But because the Āryan disciple is not enticed by these motives, they do not lead him into evil action.

"And which are the six channels for dissipating wealth? Being addicted to drugs and strong liquor, roaming the streets at untimely hours, visiting carnivals, being addicted to gambling, associating with bad companions, and being addicted to idleness.

"There are, young householder, six dangers in being addicted to drugs and strong liquor, namely, loss of wealth, quarrelsome brawling, loss of good reputation, immodest behavior, susceptibility to disease, and impairment of intelligence.

"Six, young householder, are the dangers in roaming the streets at untimely hours: he, himself, is unguarded; his children and wife are unprotected, his property also; he is suspected of crimes; he becomes the victim of false rumors, and many are the troubles that descend upon him.

"Six, young master, are the dangers in visiting carnivals: everything is crowded out of his mind by preoccupation with such questions as, 'Where is the dancing going on?' 'Where is the singing?' 'Where is the orchestra?' 'Where is the playacting?' 'Where is the playing of tambourines?' 'Where is the playing of tom-toms?'

"Six, young friend, are the dangers in being addicted to gambling, namely, if a fellow wins he loses friends; if he loses he mourns his lost wealth; his substance is wasted; his word has no weight in a court of law; he is held in contempt by friends and officials alike; and he is not sought after as a husband because gamblers are believed to be poor providers.

"Six, young householder, are the dangers in associating with bad companions: gamblers, libertines, drunkards, cheats, swindlers, and violent men, all of whom produce woe for those who associate with them.

"Six, young master, are the dangers in being addicted to idleness. Says the lazy man, 'It is too cold,' and does no work, or 'It is too hot,' and does no work. 'It is too late,' he says, 'It is too early,' and does no work. 'I am too hungry,' he says, 'I am too full,' and does no work. And thus living with duties undone, his wealth not yet produced does not come in, and such wealth as he already possesses dwindles away.

"Four, O young householder, are they who should be regarded as foes masquerading as friends: he who is out to get all he can, he who merely talks, he who oozes flattery, and he who is anxious to waste wealth. These four, young man, are false friends, counterfeit friends.

"Consider the fellow who is out to get all he can. He is an out-and-out robber, he wants much for little, he does his duty only when forced, and he puts on a show of attentiveness for profit.

"Consider the fellow who merely talks. He talks about what a good friend he was in the past, he talks about what a good friend he will be in the future, he ingratiates himself with empty words, and when a favor is asked of him he points to his own bad luck."

"Consider the fellow who oozes flattery. He advises you to go ahead with a bad course of action; he does not advise a good course of action; he praises you to your face and disparages you behind your back.

"Consider the fellow who is anxious to waste wealth. He is your bottle-friend, he is your mate in roaming the streets at unseasonable hours, he is your mate in wasting time at carnivals, and he is your mate in wasting wealth at gambling.

"But four, O young householder, are friends to be regarded as true-hearted: he who helps you; he who remains constant through times of prosperity and adversity; he who tells you what is for your own good; and he who shows affection for you.

"Consider the friend who helps you. He takes care of you when you have been careless; he looks after your property when you have been slack; he is a refuge when you are afraid; and when the need arises he supplies you twice over.

"Consider the friend who remains constant through times of prosperity and adversity. He tells you his secrets; he keeps your secrets; he does not forsake you in trouble; and he is willing even to die for you.

"Consider the friend who tells you what is for your own good. He restrains you from going wrong; he sets you straight; he tells you what you did not know before; and he shows you the way to heaven.

"Consider the friend who shows affection for you. He does not rejoice in your misfortune; he rejoices in your good fortune; he defends you against those who slander you; and he commends those who speak well of you.

"And how, young householder, does the Āryan disciple worship the six quarters? These should be regarded as the six quarters: parents should be known as the east, teachers as the south, child and wife as the west, friends and comrades as the north, servants and workers as the nadir, and religious recluses and priests as the zenith.

1. "Now in five ways should a son minister to his mother and father as the east. 'Once supported by them, I will now be their support,' he says. 'I will do my duty by them. I will maintain the honor of my family. I will enter upon my inheritance worthily. I will keep up offerings in the memory of my ancestors.'

"And in five ways should mother and father, thus set in the east and ministered to by a son, show their affection for him. They restrain him from vice; they exhort him to virtue; they teach him a trade; they find him a suitable wife; and in due time hand over his inheritance to him.

2. "Now in five ways should a pupil minister to his teachers as the south. He rises up to greet them; he pays tuition to them; he is eager to learn; he looks after them; and he pays attention when they are teaching him.

"And in five ways should teachers, thus set in the south and ministered to by a pupil, show their affection for him. They educate him well; they show him how to grasp their teaching; they instruct him thoroughly in every science and art; they speak well of him to his friends and comrades; and they continually have his safety in mind.

3. "Now in five ways should a husband minister to his wife as the west. He respects her, is kind to her, remains faithful to her, lets her have charge of the household, and provides her with finery.

"And in five ways should a wife, thus set in the west and ministered to by her husband, show her affection for him. She performs her duties diligently; she receives the relatives of them both in a hospitable manner; she remains faithful to him; she carefully guards what he earns, and she goes about her work cheerfully.

4. "Now in five ways should a gentleman minister to his friends and comrades as the north. He is liberal, agreeable, benevolent, impartial, and honest.

"And in five ways should a gentleman's friends and comrades, thus set in the north and ministered to by him, show their affection for him. They take care of him when he is careless; they guard his property on such occasions; they are a refuge to him in times of danger; they do not forsake him in his troubles; and they show respect for his family.

5. "Now in five ways should an employer minister to his servants and employees as the nadir. He assigns them work according to their ability; he provides them with food and wages; he takes care of them in sickness; he gives them a share in unusual profits; and he gives them rest and vacations at the proper times.

"And in five ways should servants and employees, thus set in the nadir and ministered to by their employer, show their affection for him. They get up before him; they go to bed after him; they do not steal; they do their work well; and they sing his praises everywhere.

6. "Now in five ways should a gentleman minister to religious recluses and priests as the zenith. He shows them friendliness in deed, friendliness in word, and friendliness in thought; he does not close his doors against them; he provides for their temporal needs.

"And in five ways should religious recluses and priests, thus set in the zenith and ministered to by a gentleman, show their affection for him. They restrain him from evil and exhort him to good; they love him with kindly thoughts; they teach him what he had not learned before; they make clear what he has already learned; and they show him the way to heaven.

"Thus, O young householder, are the six quarters of space worshiped, protected, and made safe and secure."

When the Perfect One had thus spoken, Sigāla praised and lauded the Perfect One, and asked to be received as a lay disciple—as one who has fled to Buddha for safety and refuge "from this day forward as long as life shall last."

• FIRST CLOUD OF THE APPROACHING STORM •

Came the morrow, a full moon day. And before the first glimmer of dawn, while the darkness of night still lingered, Devadatta, the evil-minded monk (son of Amṛtodana and cousin to both the venerable

Ānanda and to Śākyamuni, himself), rose up from his bed, troubled by bad dreams, and wandered restless through Bamboo Grove.

As he paced to and fro in the gloom, his mind seething with discontent and wicked ambition, Devadatta glanced up at the window of the Perfect One's chamber. A little oil lamp flickered there, burning perfumed oil, for the Perfect One was sitting up, rapt in deep meditation.

"A Buddha he calls himself!" thought Devadatta. "A charlatan is he, grown soft and easygoing! Better fitted am I to lead this Saṅgha than is Siddhārtha!"

A cold blast of wind suddenly screamed in the bamboo thickets; and the little lamp in the Perfect One's chamber flickered briefly and went out.

When dawn came, the blessed Ānanda arose and robed himself to go into Rājagṛha in quest of alms-food. And when Devadatta saw Ānanda leaving the monastery with bowl and outer robe, he went up to him and grasped his arm.

"Well, cousin Ānanda," said Devadatta, "do you suppose that cousin Siddhārtha will be able to wash and dress himself this morning without your assistance?"

Ānanda flushed with astonishment.

"It is not proper, cousin Devadatta, it is not fitting to speak of the Master as 'cousin Siddhārtha.'

Devadatta's mouth twisted in a grin.

"Come now, Ānanda, you are not speaking to a novice! Surely you are not so childish as to believe that Gautama is leading this Saṅgha properly! Small wonder that the brahmin ascetics find fault with us, so lax is Gautama with the rules of discipline! You know as well as I, cousin Ānanda, that this Saṅgha should be led by someone more capable than cousin Siddhārtha."

"Your words are shameful and wicked, evil-minded one!" exclaimed Ānanda. "This Saṅgha would not be willing to be led by anyone except the Lord, for who else could lead this Saṅgha?"

"Poor Ānanda, has it never occurred to you that you or I could lead this Saṅgha? Are not we Gautamids too? Why should all the honor and glory redound to Siddhārtha alone? Now if you will listen to me—"

"I do not care to listen to you, wicked one!" cried the blessed Ānanda. "I am the servant of my Master, the Buddha Supreme in the world; and I will follow his leading, not yours!"

Devadatta, releasing the Perfect One's favorite disciple with a rough thrust, angrily declared: "From this day forth, Ānanda, regardless of your Master, and regardless of the monks, I shall follow my own rules in regard to the discipline!"

Ānanda did not reply, but went on his way as he wiped the tears from his eyes.

Now, when the blessed Ānanda had returned from his begging rounds and had eaten his morning meal, he went up into Śākyamuni's perfumed chamber to bring food and to make ready the Perfect One for going out to preach.

"This morning, Lord," said Ānanda, "Devadatta accosted me and declared that he would henceforth observe only his own discipline, regardless of the Perfect One and regardless of the monks."

"Yes, Ānanda," replied Buddha, "I know. Last night, as I sat in meditation, I read Devadatta's thoughts with my thought. Just as if, Ānanda, Devadatta's mind were an open book, a manuscript of palm leaves written in large letters, easy to see, easy to read—just so, Ānanda, did the mind of Devadatta appear to me. So great was the evil in Devadatta's heart, Ānanda, that the gods of the winds, in astonishment and dismay, stirred up gusts which extinguished my little lamp and shook this entire Veṇuvana at the end of the third watch. So greatly were those gods horrified by the evil in Devadatta's heart, Ānanda, that they fled away not to return till monsoon time."

Thereupon the Perfect One uttered a stanza, saying:

Easy to do for the righteous are righteous things,
But hard to do are righteous things for the wicked.
Easy to do for the wicked are wicked things,
But impossible to do is wickedness for Arhats.

XIV

THE PLOT OF DEVADATTA

• POWERS AND CONFIDENCES • OF THE TATHĀGATA

The seasons came and went, and the years fell tumbling like the dead leaves of autumn into the silent reservoir of the past. Śrāvastī, Kauśambī, Rājagṛha, Vaiśālī, Vārāṇasī—these and many other cities and towns were visited by the Perfect One time and again, for the words of Dharma never ceased to flow from his lips like living water from the Fount of Truth. Friend to poor and rich alike, at home in the huts of the lowborn and in the magnificent palaces of kings, Buddha, even in his old age, continued to turn the Wheel of Dharma and to lead the Saṅgha of monks and the Saṅgha of nuns.

Over the years the five hills of Rājagṛha had become dotted with monasteries of the Saṅgha; and one of these hills, Gṛdhrakūṭa (Vulture Peak, about two miles from the city of Rājagṛha), was blessed as Buddha's favorite place of retirement from the noisy throngs of the city. It was on Gṛdhrakūṭa's sylvan slopes that the Blessed One often discoursed to the monks about the deeper things of Dharma and taught the holy Mahāyāna, namely, that all sincere and pure-hearted disciples are, in reality, Bodhisattvas on their way to ultimate Buddhahood.

On a certain occasion during the thirty-seventh year after the Supreme Enlightenment, when Śākyamuni was seventy-two years old, he preached to a congregation of monks assembled on Mount Gṛdhrakūṭa. Now, among those monks was Devadatta, the evil-hearted one, who, with increasing boldness, was stirring up discord within the Saṅgha.

"I, monks," declared Lord Buddha on that occasion, "do not dispute with the world. It is the world that disputes with me. No one who professes Dharma disputes with the world. Whatever the learned in the world agree upon as 'it is not,' I too, monks, say of that, 'It is not.' And whatever the learned in the world agree upon as 'it is,' I too, monks, say of that, 'It is.'

"And what, monks, is agreed upon by the learned in the world as 'it is not,' and of which I say, 'It is not'? That the body is permanent, stable, eternal, not liable to change—the learned in the world agree that it is not, and I too say of it that it is not. So also with feeling, perception, the predisposing formations, and discriminative consciousness.

"And what, monks, is agreed upon by the learned in the world as 'it is,' and of which I say, 'It is'? That the body is impermanent, a mass of suffering, liable to change—the learned in the world agree that it is, and I too say of it that it is. So also with feeling, perception, the predisposing formations, and discriminative consciousness. Keep this in mind, O monks.

"Now why, monks, is the Tathāgata called the Ten-Powered One? These are the Ten Powers of the Tathāgata, endowed with which the Tathāgata claims his place as Leader, roars the lion's roar in assemblies, and turns the Wheel Supreme.

1. "In regard to this the Tathāgata knows beyond likelihood of

error what is possible as possible and what is impossible as impossible.

2. "Again, the Tathāgata knows beyond likelihood of error the ripening of karmas past, present, and future.

3. "Again, the Tathāgata knows beyond likelihood of error where all paths of action and conduct lead beings.

4. "Again, the Tathāgata knows beyond likelihood of error the nature of the cosmos with its universes of manifold concatenations and elements.

5. "Again, the Tathāgata knows beyond likelihood of error the various dispositions of individuals.

6. "Again, the Tathāgata knows beyond likelihood of error the characteristics of the faculties of all beings.

7. "Again, the Tathāgata knows beyond likelihood of error the impurity or purity and the development of the absorptions, releases, concentrations, and psychic attainments of beings.

8. "Again, the Tathāgata knows beyond likelihood of error his own various kinds of previous existences as far back in the past as he wishes to remember them.

9. "Again, with his supernormal vision, purified and more than human, the Tathāgata sees beings passing away and being reborn according to their karma.

10. "Again, with the destruction of the Poisons (lust, existence-infatuation, false view, ignorance), the Tathāgata has of himself in this very life with higher knowledge realized and attained release of mind and release by Wisdom free from the Poisons, and there abides.

"Anyone who should say of me that the Ascetic Gautama does not possess superhuman qualities and truly Āryan Knowledge and Insight, and that he preaches a doctrine beaten out by mere logic, thought up by himself as a mere theory—if that misguided, ignorant person does not renounce those words and abandon that view, he will find himself taken and thrown into hell.

"Just as a monk endowed with morality, concentration, and full knowledge will attain perfect Insight in this very life, I declare that a misguided, ignorant person who holds such views as I have named, if he does not renounce those words and that thought and abandon that view, he will find himself taken and thrown into hell.

The eyes of the Perfect One were fixed upon Devadatta; and that evil monk knew that the Perfect One's warning was addressed particularly to him.

"These, O monks," continued Buddha, "are the Four Confidences, endowed with which the Tathāgata claims his place as Leader, roars the lion's roar in assemblies, and turns the Wheel Supreme.

1. "I see no ground for anyone, be he man or god, to reproach me with validity for not having perfect comprehension of these things which I, as All-Enlightened, claim to comprehend.

2. "I see no ground for anyone, be he man or god, to reproach me with validity for not having destroyed the Poisons which I, as All-Enlightened, claim to have destroyed.

3. "I see no ground for anyone, be he man or god, to reproach me with validity for not having correctly stated as the Hindrances and Fetters which hinder from spiritual maturity which I, as All-Enlightened, have stated.

4. "I see no ground for anyone, be he man or god, to reproach me with validity for not teaching the eternal Dharma that leads to the complete destruction of suffering for those who practice it, which Dharma I, as All-Enlightened, have taught.

"And never having seen such grounds, O monks, I have reached the state of calm, of fearlessness, of confidence. Just as a blue lotus or a white lotus, born in the water, comes to full growth in the water, rises to the surface of the water, and stands unspotted by the water—just so, monks, the Tathāgata, having been born in the world, having come to full growth in the world, passing beyond the world, abides unspotted by the world."

When the Master had finished speaking, Ānanda, Śāriputra, and Maudgalyāyana approached him and sat down at one side.

"Lord," said the venerable Maudgalyāyana, "the monk Devadatta harbors evil desires. He intends to take over leadership of the Saṅgha; and several of the monks, deceived by him, have gone over to his support. It would be good, Lord, if the Perfect One were to rebuke Devadatta before the assembly."

"Have you heard the jackal, monks, who barks by night and at early dawn?" asked Buddha.

"Yes, Lord," replied the three disciples.

"That jackal, monks, is a decrepit jackal suffering from mange. Well, that jackal roams about wherever he pleases, stays and squats and lies down wherever he pleases, no matter how cold be the wind that blows upon him. It would be well for a certain monk, vowed to the Son of the Śākyas, if he were fortunate enough to attain such a state of birth as that. But it may be, monks, that the sense of thanks and gratitude felt by that decrepit jackal is lacking in that certain monk vowed to the Son of the Śākyas."

• PRINCE AJĀTAŚATRU • MURDERS KING BIMBISĀRA

Devadatta straightway left Mount Gṛdhrakūṭa and stole unobserved into Rājagṛha, where he went to the palace of King Bimbisāra and performed a miracle of magic power before the eyes of Prince Ajātaśatru.

Having won Ajātaśatru's favor by his display of magic, Devadatta then made clear his intention to wrest leadership of the Saṅgha from the Perfect One. And the prince approved and offered Devadatta his support.

"Today my father the king and his court are going to the monastery in the Veṇuvana to hear the Great Ascetic preach to the monks," said Ajātaśatru. "Now is the time, therefore, to approach the Great Ascetic and ask him to hand over leadership of the Saṅgha to you. An opportunity to do so in the presence of my father the king may not come again right away."

Thereupon Devadatta went away dressed in fine garments given to him by Prince Ajātaśatru; and later in the day, when Buddha had come down from Mount Gṛdhrakūṭa and had commenced to preach a discourse in the Veṇuvana, surrounded by a great company which included

King Bimbisāra and his court, the wicked monk seized the opportunity to present his demands.

Rising from his seat and throwing his outer robe over one shoulder, Devadatta bowed toward Śākyamuni with palms pressed together and said: "My Lord, the Perfect One is now grown old, is aged and far gone in years. He has come to life's end. Let my Lord now live without worry. Let him now dwell given to such happiness as this life offers. Let him hand over the care of the Saṅgha to me, and I will take charge of the Saṅgha."

"Enough of that, Devadatta!" said Buddha. "Do not seek leadership of the Saṅgha!"

But Devadatta did not abandon his ambition. A second and even a third time did he make his improper request, and each time he received the same reply. Then said the Perfect One: "Not even to Śāriputra or Maudgalyāyana would I hand over the Saṅgha, and much less would I to one like you, a vile lickspittle!"

On hearing this rebuke, Devadatta became angry and humiliated.

"In the very presence of the king and his court Siddhārtha refuses me, calls me a vile lickspittle, and extols Śāriputra and Maudgalyāyana!"

Thus thinking, the evil-hearted monk turned his back to the Perfect One and walked out of the assembly.

When Devadatta had gone, Buddha spoke to Śāriputra, saying: "I appoint you, Śāriputra, to make it known to all concerned that in anything said or done by Devadatta from this day forward, neither the Tathāgata nor the Dharma nor the Saṅgha is to be recognized, but only Devadatta. From this day forward, Śāriputra, Devadatta is not to be encouraged or instructed by the monks any more."

Devadatta was thereby expelled from the Saṅgha, excommunicated from the noble Brotherhood of Saints.

Now, Devadatta, together with several hundred of the apostate monks led by him, set up a counterfeit saṅgha supported by gifts donated by Prince Ajātaśatru.

A number of monks, learning that the son of King Bimbisāra was aiding the schism of Devadatta, came before the Perfect One, saluted him, and announced the news, saying: "Prince Ajātaśatru, Lord, is supporting Devadatta late and early with five hundred carts, conveying in them food brought in five hundred cooking pots."

"Do not yearn for gains, favors, and flattery, O monks!" Śākyamuni warned them. "So long as Prince Ajātaśatru thus supports Devadatta, it is ruin that may be expected of Devadatta, not growth in good conditions. Just as if, monks, one were to crumble liver on a mad dog's nose, the dog would only become madder—even so, monks, as long as Prince Ajātaśatru supports Devadatta late and early with five hundred carts, conveying in them food brought in five hundred cooking pots, it is ruin that may be expected of Devadatta, not growth in good conditions.

"Once upon a time, monks, there was a great pool in a tract of forest, and elephants lived there beside that pool. Plunging into the pool they pulled up the stalks of lotuses. They washed them clean, and when they were free from mud, snatched them up and swallowed them. This practice was for them a source of health and strength. As a result of this practice, they did not come by untimely death or any mortal pain.

"Now, monks, the young calf-elephants, attempting to imitate the big elephants, likewise plunged into that pool and pulled up lotus stalks. But without washing them clean, they snatched them up, mud and all, and swallowed them. This practice was not for them a source of health and strength. As a result of this practice, therefore, they came by mortal pain and death. Even so, monks, will Devadatta die, that wretched man, by copying me.

"To his own harm, O monks, have gains, favors, and flattery come to Devadatta, leading to his downfall. Just as a plantain brings forth fruit to its own loss, to its own destruction, just as a mule brings forth young to her own loss, to her own destruction—just so have gains, favors, and flattery come to Devadatta.

"Terrible, O monks, are gains, favors, and flattery! They are a bitter and painful hindrance to the attainment of the Peace Secure that surpasses all. Therefore, monks, you must train yourselves thus: 'When gains, favors, and flattery befall us, we will reject them, they shall not lay hold of us, they shall not become established in our hearts.' "

Several weeks later Prince Ajātaśatru went secretly to Mount Gayāśīrṣa to visit Devadatta at the monastery appropriated by the wicked monk for the use of some five hundred novitiates of Vaiśālī whom Devadatta had persuaded to secede from the Saṅgha headed by Śākyamuni Buddha.

"My father the king," said Ajātaśatru, "disapproves of my supporting you and your followers, Venerable Devadatta."

Worried by the opposition of the king, Devadatta conceived a bold plan. He, himself, was to kill the Perfect One. Ajātaśatru was to kill his father, King Bimbisāra. Then the honor and glory for supporting and leading a world-famous order of ascetics would go to them both. Ajātaśatru agreed to the plan.

Returning to the royal palace in Rājagṛha, Prince Ajātaśatru went to Śrenika Bimbisāra with the intention of forcing the good king to support Devadatta, murdering him only if he refused.

"Surely, O king," said Ajātaśatru, "you cannot object to serving the Venerable Devadatta with gifts as you have served the Ascetic Gautama, that Recluse who has become lax in the discipline!"

"Do not ask such a thing of me, my son!" exclaimed King Bimbisāra. "It is not fitting that I serve with gifts and royal favor that evil monk who has instigated discord and schism in the Saṅgha led by the Perfect One! Gifts are rightly bestowed only upon those teachers who have the weal and profit of the people at heart. Such a one is the Perfect One. Not such a one is Devadatta."

A flush of anger colored Ajātaśatru's cheeks; and because royal ministers were present, he was unable to perform the act of murder. Instead, he went out from the royal chamber with the resolve to induce Bimbisāra to hand over the throne to him.

The evil plan succeeded, for Bimbisāra, old and tired, willingly resigned the kingdom to his son. He nevertheless continued to support the Saṅgha of the Perfect One; and Ajātaśatru, not daring to arouse the wrath of the people by ordering the beloved king to be put to death, cast his father into prison.

And Śrenika Bimbisāra, the righteous king, sitting constantly by the little window of his prison-cell in order to see the abode of Lord Buddha on Mount Gṛdhrakūṭa, soon died of a broken heart. Thus came about the rumor that Ajātaśatru had murdered Bimbisāra.

• DEVADATTA ATTEMPTS TO KILL BUDDHA •

Meantime Devadatta, having received skilled archers from King Ajātaśatru, concealed them along a path frequented by the Tathāgata. But when the time came to kill the Blessed One, the archers, suddenly overcome by remorse, threw down their weapons and fell at the Buddha's feet and implored forgiveness for their intended crime. Lord Buddha smiled upon them with compassion and converted them to the Dharma.

Now when Devadatta learned that the archers had been unable to carry out their deadly mission, he let loose on the highway by which Śākyamuni entered Rājagṛha a fierce elephant that had been crazed by intoxicating liquor.

When the elephant charged toward the Master, trampling down the trees in his fury, Ānanda ran ahead of the Perfect One, saying: "Let this elephant kill me first, Lord!"

In the twinkling of an eye Buddha reached out his arm and thrust Ānanda to one side out of harm's way. And then the Perfect One suffused and pervaded the elephant with loving kindness. The huge animal instantly became docile and followed Buddha like a gentle pet.

Having failed twice, Devadatta decided to kill Buddha himself.

Devadatta knew of a certain large boulder poised on a high cliff above the path leading up to Mount Gṛdhrakūta. Going up to it, the wicked monk discovered that the rock could easily be sent crashing down upon the path frequented by the Perfect One.

Seizing his chance, Devadatta crouched out of sight behind the boulder and waited for the Perfect One to pass by. Minutes lengthened into hours before Devadatta caught sight of the saffron-robed Buddha, followed by Ānanda, on the path below. But as soon as the Perfect One was in full view, the evil-hearted monk pushed the boulder with all his strength. The great rock began to roll, not to be held back.

Frightful was the thunderous roar made by that mass of rock as it bounded down the cliff, pulverizing into fragments the stones that lay in its path. Down went the boulder, crashing against ledge, smashing down bushes, and leaving a wake of dust in its trail.

The rock bore down upon the Perfect One before Ānanda could cry out in warning.

Just before the huge boulder reached the Tathāgata, it struck an outcrop of ledge that split it in twain with a loud noise. The two halves hurtled past Buddha, one on each side, without striking him. In a moment all was silence again.

The Perfect One stood still. Ānanda, trembling from the shock of the narrow escape, ran up to him.

"Are you unhurt, Master?"

The Perfect One did not reply, but only looked down at his feet. A line of scarlet trickled out from a cut inflicted in one toe by a flying splinter of rock.

"The blood of a Buddha!" said Ānanda with dismay.

The Exalted One raised his eyes up to the brow of the cliff where Devadatta, dazed by astonishment and chagrin, peered down.

"Great demerit, evil man," declared Śākyamuni in a loud voice, "great demerit have you produced for yourself, in that with murderous intent you have caused the blood of a Tathāgata to flow!"

Maddened by the failure of his third attempt to kill Buddha, the evil-hearted monk made other plans to harm Śākyamuni. Worried by the viciousness of Devadatta's attacks, the monks suggested that a bodyguard be provided for the Perfect One. But the Perfect One replied: "It is impossible, monks, for anyone to deprive me of life, for Tathāgatas reach Parinirvāṇa in the ordinary course of events. Impossible, monks, is the murder of a Buddha."

Resorting to slander, Devadatta went about the country and maligned the Perfect One by saying: "The Ascetic Gautama is no ascetic, my friends. He is an impostor, lax in discipline, and given to abundance and luxurious habits. No follower of the religious life is he, even though he claims to be perfect in morality. No Buddha is he, even though he claims to be perfect in wisdom."

• DEVADATTA'S FALL •

One day the blessed Ānanda approached a group of monks who had been consorting with Devadatta's partisans.

"O monks!" said Ānanda.

"Venerable One!" answered those monks.

"As you know, brothers, Devadatta is going about the country slandering Lord Buddha. Communion with bad men, brothers, is wrong. The wise man has nothing to do with slanderers, with men of wrath, with the mean-hearted and malign. The wise man associates with spiritual persons, with gentle and learned men. For blessed is communion with the good."

Thereupon those monks praised Ānanda for his good advice and ceased associating with the apostates who had gone over to Devadatta's counterfeit saṅgha.

Now, when a congregation of monks had assembled in the Veṇuvana to hear a discourse, the Perfect One spoke to them concerning Devadatta, saying: "Devadatta, O monks, being overcome by eight evil conditions, with mind obsessed by them, is doomed to the Downfall, to hell, to the state of woe for the whole eon without hope of remedy. What are those eight evil conditions?

"He is overcome, with mind obsessed, by love of gain and loss of gain, by love of fame and loss of fame, by love of honor and loss of honor, by evil desires and by evil friends. Such, monks, are the eight evil conditions.

"Overcome by evil desires, with mind obsessed thereby, Devadatta is doomed. Overcome by evil friends, with mind obsessed thereby, Devadatta is doomed. Overcome by pride in lesser attainments, causing him to come to a standstill though much remained for him to do in order to reach perfection, Devadatta is doomed. The Hell Avīci awaits Devadatta; and there he will remain lodged beyond hope of remedy for a full eon."

When word of Buddha's prediction of Devadatta's terrible fate spread through the district, the wicked monk's gains and eminence began to wane.

Now, it came to pass that a band of Jainas dwelling in Rājagṛha sought to use this prediction as a means of confounding and discrediting the Perfect One. So they summoned one of their supporters, a prince by the name of Abhaya, and said to him: "Go to the Ascetic Gautama and ask him if he would utter speech that is unpleasant and disagreeable to others. If he says 'yes,' then ask how he differs from the common people, for the common people utter speech that is unpleasant and disagreeable to others. But if he says 'no,' then ask why he said of Devadatta that he is doomed to hell to stay there without hope of release for a world-cycle; for at that speech Devadatta was angry and displeased. If the Ascetic Gautama is asked this question, he will be unable to swallow either up or down."

Abhaya accordingly went to the Master and invited him to a meal the next day. And on the morrow, after the Perfect One had finished eating, Abhaya came forth with the question he had been told to ask.

"Does the Ascetic Gautama utter speech that is unpleasant and disagreeable to others?"

"Not absolutely," replied the Tathāgata.

"The Jainas have heard so," declared Prince Abhaya.

"What do you think, O prince?" asked Śākyamuni. "If a baby boy, through the carelessness of his nurse, should get a stick lodged in his mouth, what would you do?"

"I should remove it from his mouth, sir," replied Abhaya, "and if I could not get it at once, I should seize his head with my left hand and, bending my finger, I should remove the stick with my right hand even if it caused the boy to bleed. And why? Because I have compassion on the boy."

"Similarly, prince," said Buddha, "speech that the Tathāgata knows to be untrue, false, and useless, and also unpleasant and disagreeable to others, he does not utter. That which he knows to be true and real, but useless, and also unpleasant and disagreeable to others, that, too, he does not utter. But that which he knows to be true, real, and useful, and also unpleasant and disagreeable to others—in that case he knows the right time to express it.

"Speech that he knows to be untrue, false, and useless, and also pleasant and agreeable to others, he does not utter. That which is true and real, but useless, and also pleasant and agreeable to others, that, too, he does not utter. But that which he knows to be true, real, and useful, and also pleasant and agreeable to others—in that case he knows the right time to express it."

One evening Devadatta gathered his five hundred followers together on Mount Ṛṣigili in order to preach to them. The Perfect One, however, sent Śāriputra and Maudgalyāyana to Devadatta's monastery to win back the apostate monks.

When Devadatta's servitor, Kokālika, saw these two of Śākyamuni's chief disciples approaching, he whispered a warning into his master's ear.

"O reverend Devadatta! Śāriputra and Maudgalyāyana have entered the monastery and are sitting in the midst of our congregation. They have undoubtedly been sent here by the Ascetic Gautama to win back our monks. Take heed, Venerable One, and send Śāriputra and Maudgalyāyana away!"

Devadatta looked out upon the congregation and saw Śāriputra and Maudgalyāyana chatting amiably with the apostate monks.

"Nonsense, Kokālika! Those two disciples have surely become disgusted with Siddhārtha and have come hither to join us."

Thus thinking, Devadatta began to address the assembly with an unworried mind, believing that he had won over Śāriputra and Maudgalyāyana. And so he talked on and on, far into the night; and Śāriputra and Maudgalyāyana listened to the evil monk's discourse in silence.

When the night was far advanced, Devadatta became weary and could speak no more. So he asked Śāriputra to address the assembly while he, himself, sat down to rest.

Both Śāriputra and Maudgalyāyana came forward, and both preached to the monks by turns. At first they spoke in general terms; but as soon as Devadatta had fallen asleep, they elucidated the profound Truth, taking the Triple Gem—Buddha, Dharma, and Saṅgha—as their theme. They exposed the wickedness of Devadatta and pointed out the folly of schism. So persuasively did they preach, and with such mighty power of eloquence and insight, that every one of the five hundred apostate monks repented of his secession and returned to Śākyamuni Buddha's Brotherhood of Monks.

As the last monk was departing from Devadatta's monastery to return to the Perfect One with Śāriputra and Maudgalyāyana, Kokālika woke Devadatta from his sleep.

"It was as I told your reverence!" exclaimed Kokālika. "Those venerable ones, those mighty monks Śāriputra and Maudgalyāyana, were sent hither by the Ascetic Gautama to brighten the assembly with the pure radiance of Dharma!"

"But the assembly hall is empty!" stammered Devadatta. "Where, pray, are my disciples?"

"They have gone, reverend sir."

"Gone? Whither have they gone?"

"They have gone back to the Ascetic Gautama, your reverence."

Devadatta rose to his feet and stared into the empty hall with astonishment and chagrin. And at that very moment, hot blood gushed forth from his mouth; and he sank down upon the floor quite unconscious.

Now, when Devadatta had first tried to wrest leadership of the Saṅgha from the Master, his supernormal powers began to fade away. And when he had first tried to kill Lord Buddha, his supernormal powers vanished completely. Seeing that the wicked monk was no longer able to perform wondrous feats of magic, King Ajātaśatru became disgusted with Devadatta and withdrew his support. When informed of this, the evil-hearted monk lay supine and silent, having been made speechless by the shock of the calamities which had befallen him.

After abandoning Devadatta, King Ajātaśatru went to the roof of his palace one night and sat down there surrounded by his royal ministers. And as he sat there looking out over the hill-fortressed city of Rājagṛha, and gazing rapt at the splendors of the heavens above him (it was the night of the autumnal full moon), he said: "Pleasant indeed is the bright night! Lovely indeed, fair indeed, pleasing indeed, auspicious indeed is the bright night! To what ascetic or brahmin may we pay homage today, so that having paid homage to him our mind may find peace?"

Sitting beside the king was Jīvaka, the royal physician. Now, Jīvaka was a lay disciple of the Perfect One, and was famed for his gifts of robes to the monks. Although he was bursting to suggest to King Ajātaśatru that homage be paid to Lord Buddha, he remained silent, thinking that the monarch was still on friendly terms with Devadatta.

Ajātaśatru, however, turned to the physician and said: "How is it, friend Jīvaka, that you are silent?"

"O king," replied Jīvaka eagerly, "the Perfect One, the Arhat, the Supreme Buddha is dwelling just now in our mango grove with a great assembly of twelve hundred and fifty monks. Let the king pay homage to Lord Buddha! Verily, if the king pays homage to the Perfect One, his mind will find peace!"

"In that case, friend Jīvaka, make ready the riding-elephants."

Jīvaka straightway made ready a number of she-elephants and one royal riding-elephant; and with his wives and a procession of torches, King Ajātaśatru left Rājagṛha and set out accompanied by his royal retinue for the mango grove where Śākyamuni was staying.

When the king drew near to the mango grove, fear and consternation swept over him, and his hair stood on end. And so the king, agitated and apprehensive, and overcome with panic dread, said to Jīvaka: "Surely, friend Jīvaka, you are not deceiving me? Surely, you are not duping me? You are not delivering me into the hands of my enemies, are you?"

"Fear not, O king," Jīvaka replied. "I am not deceiving your majesty, nor am I betraying your majesty to an enemy. Go forward, O king! Those are the chapel lights shining over there."

"How is it, then, that there is no sound of sneezing or coughing or talking to be heard in all that assembly of monks numbering, as you say, twelve hundred and fifty?"

So the king went on as far as the path allowed the elephants to go, and then, dismounting, he went on foot to the door of the chapel.

"Where, friend Jīvaka, is the Perfect One?"

"Yonder, O king, is the Perfect One, sitting up near the middle pillar, facing east and surrounded by the monks."

Thereupon the king made his way past the congregation of monks, each of them silent and calm like a pure translucent lake; and when he had come to the Perfect One, he bowed with clasped hands and sat respectfully at one side.

"Lord," said King Ajātaśatru, "I wish to ask the Perfect One about a certain matter, if the Perfect One gives me the opportunity of having an explanation."

"Ask whatever you wish, O king," said Buddha.

"Is it possible, Lord, to show in this very life a visible fruit of the life of an ascetic?"

"Do you admit, O king, that you have asked this question of other religious teachers?"

"Yes, Lord, I do."

"Well now, listen carefully to what I am going to tell you."

And so the Perfect One explained to Ajātaśatru how a recluse under the training of a Buddha attains contentment and the highest happiness here and now in this very life. In addition, the Master expounded the Dharma in full, explaining the Three Characteristics (Transience, Suffering, and Soullessness), the Law of Dependent Origination, the Four Āryan Truths, the Āryan Eightfold Path, etc., the practice of meditation, the attainment of psychic powers, etc.

And when the Master had finished speaking, Ajātaśatru exclaimed: "Wonderful, Lord! I go, Lord, to the Perfect One for refuge, to the Dharma for refuge, and to the Saṅgha for refuge! May the Lord receive me as a lay disciple from this day forward as long as life shall last! My misdeed overcame me, who was so foolish, so infatuated, so wicked, that for the sake of lordship I deprived my righteous father, the righteous king, of life. May the Perfect One accept this confession of my misdeed for restraint in the future."

"Verily, O king," declared the Tathāgata, "your misdeed overcame you, who were so foolish, so infatuated, so wicked, that you deprived your righteous father, the righteous king, of life. And in that you, O king, seeing the misdeed as misdeed, make amends in a right way—*that* do we accept of you. For it is increase, O king, in the discipline of the Āryan disciple who, seeing his misdeed as misdeed, makes amends in a right way and exercises restraint in the future."

At these words Ajātaśatru, the Magadhan king, said: "Well now, Lord, we go. We have much to do and many duties to attend to."

"As it seems good to you, O king."

So the king, having expressed delight and approval, rose from his seat, saluted the Lord by walking around him with his right toward him, and went away.

Then the Blessed One, after the king had gone, addressed the monks, saying: "Uprooted, monks, is the king. Damaged, monks, is the king. If, monks, the king had not deprived his righteous father, the righteous king, of life—why! in this very session the pure and spotless eye of Dharma would have arisen in him, and he would have attained the Peace Immortal. But as things are, monks, the king's destructive karma has begun to ripen. Because of his wicked crime, the king is doomed to the Downfall, there to remain for an eon until his evil karma is exhausted."

Devadatta, completely defeated, never recovered from his sickness. As the months passed, he repented of his evil deeds and expressed a desire to see Śākyamuni; but the Perfect One declared that Devadatta's desire was impossible of fulfilment.

Devadatta, however, discounted Buddha's words and had himself carried on a litter to where the Perfect One was staying. But no sooner had he come within sight of the monastery when an earthquake began to shake the ground with a loud roar. A wide fissure suddenly opened up in the path; and the litter-bearers, anxious for their safety, fled away, leaving Devadatta lying abandoned on the road.

With a grinding rumble another great crack split the earth: it passed directly beneath the abandoned litter. Devadatta's scream of terror rent the air but for an instant, for when he had been swallowed up into the depths of the earth, the gap closed shut. And then Devadatta, life ended on earth, reappeared among the nameless horrors of frightful Avīci, the Waveless, the uttermost hell possible for a human being.

But Devadatta was not destined to *eternal* punishment. The Perfect One made it clear to the monks that there is no *eternal* life in any realm of conditioned existence, neither in a heaven nor in a telluric world, nor yet in a hell.

"Devadatta, at the end of the eon," said Buddha, "will be reborn in a higher hell than Avīci, a less painful hell. Then, at the end of many eons, he will be reborn again as a man. And when a hundred thousand eons have elapsed, he will be reborn as a Buddha named Devarāja, and as such will attain the immortal bliss of Nirvāṇa free from the pains of death and rebirth."

XV

JOURNEY'S END

• ADVICE TO THE SAṄGHA; • ŚĀRIPUTRA'S DEATH

Seven years after the death of Devadatta, when the Master was seventy-nine years old, the Perfect One was staying at Śrāvastī at East Park (Pūrvārāma) in the monastery built by Viśākhā, "Mṛgāra's mother."

And late one afternoon Buddha was sitting in the westering sun, letting it warm his back.

The blessed Ānanda then came to Buddha to massage his limbs. And while he was doing so, dismay and sadness came to him.

"It is a strange thing, Lord! The Perfect One's complexion is no longer clear and glowing. All his limbs have become flabby and wrinkled. Formerly his body was radiant, but now is seen a change of every organ, of every faculty of sense. All is changed, Lord!"

A smile flickered over the peaceful face of the aged Buddha.

"Yes, Ānanda, all is changed. *We begin to die from the moment we are born, for birth is the cause of death. The nature of decay is inherent in youth, the nature of sickness is inherent in health, in the midst of life we are verily in death.* Accordingly, Ānanda, my complexion is no longer clear and glowing, and all my limbs have become flabby and wrinkled. Formerly my body was radiant, but now is seen a change of every organ, of every faculty of sense."

Having stayed at Śrāvastī as long as he wished, the Enlightened One journeyed again to Rājagṛha and took up residence on Mount Gṛdhrakūṭa (Vulture Peak). And there, on a certain occasion, he addressed the monks, saying: "O monks, I am a brahmin given to begging; my hands are always pure; I am wearing my last body, incomparable Physician and Surgeon am I. You are my own true sons, born of the words of my mouth, born of the Dharma, created anew by the Dharma, heirs of spiritual things, not heirs of worldly things.

"There are two gifts, O monks, the worldly and the spiritual. Of these two gifts the spiritual gift is preeminent. There are these two mutual sharings, O monks, the sharing of the worldly and the sharing of the spiritual. Of these two mutual sharings the sharing of the spiritual is preeminent. And there are two acts of kindness, O monks, the worldly and the spiritual. Of these two acts of kindness the spiritual is preeminent."

Now, the blessed Ānanda was standing behind Lord Buddha the while, fanning him. And when Śākyamuni had spoken these words, he turned to Ānanda and said: "What do you think, Ānanda? Have you ever heard that the Vṛjis repeatedly assemble together, and in large numbers?"

"I have heard so, Master," replied Ānanda.

"Well, Ānanda, so long as the Vṛjis shall assemble repeatedly and in large numbers, just so long may the prosperity of the Vṛjis be looked for, and not their decay. So long, Ānanda, as the Vṛjis assemble in harmony and disperse in harmony; so long as they conduct their affairs in harmony; so long as they introduce no revolutionary ordinance, but abide by the established Vṛji ordinances as ordained; so long as they honor and worship the elders among them and deem them worth listening to; so long as the women and maidens of the Vṛji families dwell without being violated or abducted; so long as they respect and worship the Vṛji shrines; so long as they do not neglect their religious duties; so long as the customary watch and ward over the Arhats that are among them is maintained, so that they may have free access to the realm, and having entered may dwell pleasantly therein—just so long as they do these things, Ānanda, may the prosperity of the Vṛjis be looked for, and not their decay."

Thereupon the Tathāgata cleared his throat and again spoke to the assembly of monks.

"I will teach you seven things that prevent decay, monks. Listen carefully, apply your minds, and I will speak."

"Yes, Lord," said the monks.

"So long, O monks, as the monks shall assemble repeatedly and in large numbers, the prosperity of the monks may be looked for, and not their decay. So long, monks, as the monks assemble in harmony and disperse in harmony; so long as they conduct the business of the Saṅgha in harmony; so long as they introduce no revolutionary ordinance, but live in accordance with the appointed precepts; so long as the elder brothers are honored and worshiped; so long as the monks do not fall subject to that craving which leads back to rebirth; so long as there shall be monks who are fond of the forest life and solitude; so long as the monks shall establish themselves in attentiveness, thinking, 'Let goodly co-mates in the holy life come hither in the future, and let those that have already come live happily'—so long as these seven things that prevent decay shall stand fast among the monks, and the monks are instructed therein—just so long may the prosperity of the monks be looked for, and not their decay."

Now it came to pass that the venerable Śāriputra, chief of those who teach the Dharma, experienced a premonition that he was soon to die. So the following day he taught the monks for the last time; and having obtained permission from the Perfect One, he set out for Nālandā, his hometown, near Rājagṛha.

Śāriputra's mother, the brahmin lady Rūpaśārī, prepared his room for him—the very same room in which he had been born. And while he lay sick, he preached the Dharma to Rūpaśārī and established her in the fruit of "Entering the Stream."

The night before he died, Śāriputra assembled a small group of monks in his room and asked pardon for anything he had done that had displeased them. Then he said: "I hanker not for life and I am not impatient for death. I await the hour like a servant expecting his wages. I am going to lay down this body of mine at last, foreknowing, recollected. I have done all that was to be done; I have lived the life religious; I have cast aside all attachments to the lower existence; and I have won the goal of Nirvāṇa."

And then, dawn being at hand, the great Arhat passed away with that supreme, utter passing-away that leaves no ęlements to go to birth again. Deathless and beyond time's toilsome current, Śāriputra entered Parinirvāṇa, the ineffable and incomprehensible Peace.

The venerable Cunda took the extinct Arhat's bowl, robes, and water strainer together with the ashes of the cremated body to Śākyamuni; and the Perfect One had a stūpa (memorial edifice for relics) made for them.

Now, Ānanda was so distressed and saddened by the death of Śāriputra that he became melancholy and bemoaned the transience of things.

"Ānanda, it is not right that you should become dejected because a beloved friend has passed away," declared Buddha. "We shall indeed miss the venerable Śāriputra; but you must bear in mind that death inevitably comes to every living thing.

"Ānanda," continued the Tathāgata, "have I not shown you in divers ways that all that comes to be must change and pass away? Are those persons who are dear to us an exception? That is impossible, Ānanda! How is it possible to say of that which is born, has become, is composite and liable to dissolution, 'Oh, let that never be dissolved'? Such a condition of things, I declare, cannot exist!

"Ānanda, as one of the larger branches might fall from a great, stable, and pithy tree, in just the same way has Śāriputra attained full Nirvāṇa in this great, stable, and pithy Saṅgha. Therefore, Ānanda, go along having yourself as your lamp, yourself as your refuge, and no other refuge. Go along having Dharma as your lamp, Dharma as your refuge, and no other refuge. In this way, Ānanda, you will become a peak in the mighty mountain range of Immortality—if you are willing to train yourself."

• DEATH OF MAUDGALYĀYANA •

Late in the autumn of the Perfect One's seventy-ninth year, while he was living in the Veṇuvanārāma near Rājagṛha, certain members of another faith met in conclave. And in the course of the meeting, a certain ascetic asked: "My esteemed fellows, do you know the reason why the alms and honor given to the Ascetic Gautama have increased?"

"No, we do not know. What is the reason?"

"Well, it is due to Maudgalyāyana, alone. For he goes by supernormal power to heaven and questions the gods concerning their previous karma, and then returns and tells it to men: 'It is by having done such and such good deeds that they now enjoy such good fortune.' Also, he asks those who have been born in hell concerning their karma, and then, returning, tells it to men: 'It is by having done such and such evil deeds that they now experience such great misery.' And the people, when they have heard him, shower alms and attentions upon him. If only we can kill him, the alms and honor that go to Gautama will then be ours."

This suggestion met with unanimous approval. By some means, it was decided, Maudgalyāyana must be killed. So those men obtained a thousand pieces of money from their supporters and summoned bloody-handed highwaymen to whom they said: "A monk of the Ascetic Gautama's Saṅgha, Maudgalyāyana by name, is staying on Mount Ṛṣigili. Go find him and kill him."

The highwaymen snatched up the money greedily and went and surrounded the Arhat's dwelling in order to kill him.

Concealing themselves in a thicket, the assassins sprang out and captured the venerable Maudgalyāyana as he was leaving his lodging. They pounded him with clubs until his bones had been broken into fragments the size of rice grains; and when they supposed he was dead, they threw him into the bushes and departed.

Maudgalyāyana expired not long afterward; and upon the dissolution of his body at death, he passed utterly away into Parinirvāṇa.

Now the report that Maudgalyāyana had been murdered by highwaymen spread all over India, and King Ajātaśatru of Magadha sent out spies to find the culprits. And as the highwaymen happened to be drinking together in a tavern, and became quarrelsome, they were overheard by the king's spies who arrested them there and then.

Then the king, when the highwaymen had been brought, had them summoned into his presence.

"Do you admit," asked Ajātaśatru, "that you killed the venerable Maudgalyāyana the Great?"

"Yes, your majesty," replied the assasins, trembling with fear.

"Who instigated you to this crime?"

"The naked ascetics, your majesty."

Thereupon the king seized five hundred naked ascetics and buried them, together with the highwaymen, up to their navels in pits dug in the palace courtyard. Then he covered them over with straw, which was set on fire; and after thus burning them, he took iron plows and plowed them into bits.

In the chapel of the Veṇuvana Monastery the monks assembled in discussion, saying: "Verily, Mahāmaudgalyāyana met a death unworthy of him."

The Perfect One, when the monks had informed him of the subject of their discussion, said: "Monks, the death of Maudgalyāyana the Great was unsuited to his present existence, but appropriate to the karma of a previous existence."

"What was that karma of his, Lord?" asked the monks.

"Once upon a time, monks, there lived a certain high-caste youth who took care of his blind old parents. But when he got married, his wife waited on the old people for a few days and then became so disgusted with them that she could not bear the sight of them.

"She accordingly induced her husband to kill the two old people. The highborn youth, who was Maudgalyāyana in a previous existence, took his blind parents to a forest. There, posing as a robber, he pounded his mother and father to death.

"Monks, the fruit of this one deed of Maudgalyāyana's was torment in hell for an eon and death by pounding in a hundred existences, as appropriate to the nature of his crime. Maudgalyāyana's death is therefore suited to his karma. The highwaymen and the five hundred heretics have likewise met with a suitable death for doing harm to my innocent son."

The monks were visibly saddened by the loss of Śāriputra and Maudgalyāyana, the two chief disciples.

"Truly this Saṅgha seems empty, O monks," declared the Perfect One. "This Saṅgha has become empty on the attainment of Complete Nirvāṇa by Śāriputra and Maudgalyāyana, O monks. We cannot discern any quarter of space in which Śāriputra and Maudgalyāyana might be faring along.

"Those who in past time became Perfected Ones, Utterly Awakened Ones, Buddhas—those Tathāgatas had just such a pair of chief disciples as Śāriputra and Maudgalyāyana were to me. And those who in time to come will become Perfected Ones, Utterly Awakened Ones, Buddhas—these Tathāgatas will have just such a pair of chief disciples as Śāriputra and Maudgalyāyana were to me.

"O monks, it is a strange and marvelous thing about disciples, that they become doers of the Teacher's bidding, promoters of his instruction. They become affectionate toward the four companies of monks, nuns, and male and female lay devotees, loved by them, revered, esteemed, and worshiped by them.

"O monks, it is a strange and marvelous thing about a Tathāgata, that on the attainment of Parinirvāṇa by such a pair of chief disciples as Śāriputra and Maudgalyāyana, there is for the Tathāgata neither grief nor lamenting."

• THE LAST JOURNEY TO VAIŚĀLĪ •

Late in the hot season the Master decided to journey forth once again. The fact that he had turned eighty years of age did not deter him, for the faithful Ānanda, he knew, would take good care of him.

Forty-five years had passed since Śākyamuni had sat as a young man under the Bodhi tree in the grove at Buddhagayā. For forty-five years the Wheel of Dharma had revolved once more in the world of men. And during those years the number of monks and nuns had swelled to hundreds of thousands, and the number of men and women lay disciples to millions. Success had crowned the Perfect One's holy mission. The Saṅgha had been established, not to decay until the dark age of iron in the dim future. The Truth had been proclaimed for all to hear—that Buddha-knowledge which sets free from every fetter, both human and divine.

Buddha set out to the north with a large company of monks. And when he had reached the outskirts of Rājagṛha, the Light of the World looked back for his last look at the capital city of the Magadhas.

Passing through the village of Ambalasṭhikā and the town of Nālandā, the Perfect One went on to the fortress city of Pāṭaliputra (Patna) on the south bank of the river Gaṅgā.

Pāṭaliputra was just then in process of being rebuilt by Ajātaśatru, the Magadhan king, as a defense against the Vṛjis. And having arrived there, the Perfect One was welcomed by vast throngs of enthusiastic Buddhists to whom he preached elevating sermons.

Now at that particular time large numbers of gods and angels were occupying the building sites in the new city. And the Perfect One, with divine sight purified and superhuman, beheld those spiritual beings. Said he to Ānanda: "Ānanda, pray who is building this new city here in Pāṭaliputra?"

"Lord, it is Sunīdha and Varṣakāra, important officials of Magadha, who are building up the city under the direction of King Ajātaśatru."

"It would seem, Ānanda, that they are doing so after taking counsel with the gods of the heaven of the Thirty-Three Palaces. I have just seen, with superhuman vision, a large number of gandharvas occupying the building sites. So far as the sphere of the Āryas extends, Ānanda, so far as merchants travel, this shall become the chief of towns, the place where men shall open up their bales of merchandise. But, Ānanda, three misfortunes shall befall Pāṭaliputra, namely, by fire, by water, and by the breaking of alliances."

Now, it happened that Sunīdha and Varṣakāra, the Magadhan officials, came to visit Buddha. And after exchanging the usual compliments and seating themselves at one side, they invited the Master and the monks to their house for the morning meal.

When Buddha accepted the invitation, Sunīdha and Varṣakāra returned to their house and made ready choice food, both hard and soft, afterward announcing the time to the Master.

So the Tathāgata, robing himself in the forenoon and taking bowl and outer robe, started out for the house of Sunīdha and Varṣakāra. And when he arrived the meal was served. Then Sunīdha and Varṣakāra, perceiving that the Perfect One had finished eating and had rinsed his hand and bowl, took low seats at one side. As they sat there, Buddha returned thanks to them, saying: "In whatsoever place the prudent man shall make his home, let him there offer food to well-controlled men who live the holy life, and let him there make offerings to all the gods and angels dwelling there. Thus honored, they will honor him. Thus worshiped, they will worship him. As a mother lavishes kind attentions upon the child that she has borne, he who lavishes kind attentions upon the gods and angels will always see good luck."

"But Venerable Gautama," asked Sunīdha, "is it really true that gods exist?"

"That is certainly known to me, Sunīdha," replied the Perfect One. "Gods really do exist."

"But can you be sure about that?"

"Verily, Sunīdha, there are gods. If anyone is asked and should say that there are gods, or should say, 'It is certainly known to me that gods exist'—then this is indeed the conclusion to be reached by intelligent men."

"I have heard much of your Teaching, Venerable Gautama, but I recall nothing about a belief in gods. Why did you not explain this matter at the beginning, reverend Gautama?"

"But this is acclaimed everywhere in the world," replied Buddha, "that is to say, that there are gods."

So saying, the Tathāgata rose up from his seat and went away with the assembly of monks.

Now, Sunīdha and Varṣakāra followed behind in the footsteps of Śākyamuni with this thought in mind: "By whatever gate the Ascetic Gautama shall depart, that gate shall henceforth be called Gautama Gate."

Accordingly, the gate by which Buddha left the city was called Gautama Gate.

When the Perfect One came to the river Gaṅgā, a fisherman was standing selling fishnets beside a huge pile of dead and dying fish on the river bank.

Śākyamuni turned to the monks.

"Do you see that fisherman, monks, who, having slaughtered a haul of fish, is selling fishnets?"

"Yes, Lord."

"Well, monks, I have never seen nor heard of a fisherman who, as a result of his karma, as a result of his mode of living, goes about in the manner of respectable persons or is welcomed in the society of decent people. Why is that? It is because he gloats diabolically over fish being slaughtered. It is the same with a butcher who kills and sells cattle or sheep or pigs or forest beasts or other animals. It is because he gloats diabolically over their being slaughtered that he does not go about in the manner of respectable persons or is welcomed in the society of decent people.

"Truly, monks, he who slaughters animals or condones their slaughter can make no claim to respectability. And he who slaughters or condones the slaughter of human beings shall reap torment and anguish for many a long day. For at the dissolution of his body at death, the merciless and cruel man with bloodstained hands will arise in the Waste, the Horrid Destiny, the Downfall, in HELL."

After crossing the Gaṅgā, the Perfect One and his monks proceeded northward, passing through the towns of Koṭigrāma and Nādika. And in no long time the rooftops of Vaiśālī, chief city of the Vṛjis and Licchavis, came into view.

• THE LAST RETREAT •

At Vaiśālī the Perfect One and the monks who had come with him took up residence in a mango grove belonging to Amrā, a beautiful but notorious courtesan. Now, Amrā, overcome by the realization that her frivolous life was a spiritually barren one, made haste to go to Buddha.

Alighting from her carriage she went through the grove on foot until she came to where the Master was and threw herself at his feet. Buddha gladdened and encouraged her with a religious discourse, and Amrā showed her gratitude by inviting the Light of the World and his monks to a meal at her palace on the morrow.

The Licchavi princes of Vaiśālī were outraged by Amrā's temerity; but despite their threatening and pleading, the beautiful courtesan refused to give the Licchavis the chance of serving Śākyamuni first.

"My lords," said Amrā to the princes, "were you to offer me all Vaiśālī together with its suburbs, I would not give up so great an honor."

The next day was indeed the dawn of a new day in the life of Amrā. Not only did she serve the Perfect One and the monks with her own hands, but after the meal was finished, she gave to Buddha and his disciples her beautiful park.

Buddha, accepting the gift, directed the monks to take up abode there for the rainy season retreat.

"O monks," said the Exalted One, "let a monk dwell mindful and self-possessed. This is my advice to you. And, how, monks, is a monk mindful?

"In regard to this, a monk, realizing that the body is a composite thing, remains enthusiastic for spiritual things, composed and mindful by controlling that hankering and discontent that characterize worldly life. That, O monks, is how a monk is mindful. And how is a monk self-possessed?

"Well, in regard to this, a monk is serene in all his comings and goings. He is serene in looking ahead and in looking back. He is serene in bending or stretching his body. He is serene in wearing his robes and carrying bowl and robe; in eating, drinking, chewing, and swallowing; in answering the calls of nature; in going, standing, sitting, sleeping, waking, speaking, and in keeping silence. That, O monks, is how a monk is self-possessed.

"During this retreat, therefore, let all of you dwell mindful and self-possessed. This, monks, is my advice to you. As for myself, I intend to keep the retreat in Beluva village."

Taking the blessed Ānanda with him, the Perfect One went to the hamlet of Beluva not far from Vaiśālī, and took up his abode in a little hut given to him by a lay follower of that place.

Now when the Perfect One had thus begun to keep the rainy season, there came upon him a grievous dysentery. Strong pains racked him, as though to end in death. But the Perfect One, mindful and self-possessed, endured those pains unflinchingly and without complaining.

"I am seriously ill," thought Buddha, "but it is not fitting that I should pass utterly away without notifying my supporters, without saying farewell to the Saṅgha. Suppose, now, that I were to hold down this sickness by an effort of will and stay on for a while by holding fast to the aggregates of conditioned existence."

So Buddha held down that sickness and stayed on, holding fast to the five factor-groups of conditioned existence—the aggregates of corporeality, feeling, perception, predisposing mental formations, and discriminative consciousness.

Then that sickness of the Perfect One was subdued. He arose from his sickness; and not long after so arising, he went out of his lodging and sat on the western side of the hut on a seat prepared for him by the blessed Ānanda.

Ānanda looked up at the pale disk of the mist-swathed sun and let his eyes wander over the restless clouds driven toward Himālaya's snowy slopes by the monsoon winds. And as the billows of fog swirled in the sky, tears swirled in his eyes and beclouded them.

"Lord," said Ānanda, "I have seen the Perfect One in health and I have seen him in endurance. And though my body, Lord, became as if drugged, and my bearings were confused—though things were no longer clear to me because of the sickness of the Perfect One—yet, Lord, I found some comfort in the thought that the Perfect One surely will not pass utterly away until he has made some pronouncement concerning the Saṅgha."

Buddha fixed his gaze upon his favorite disciple.

"What do you mean, Ānanda? Does the Saṅgha expect *that* of me? Now, I have always proclaimed the Truth to you without making any distinction between exoteric and esoteric doctrine. The Tathāgata is not like those teachers with the closed fist who keep back the best, Ānanda!

If, then, anyone thinks that he should lead the Saṅgha, or that the Saṅgha depends on him—let *him* make some pronouncement! As for me, I am now a broken-down old man, aged, far gone in years, kept going by medicines and spared pain only by mental concentration. I have reached the journey's end, Ānanda; I have come to life's limit. My age has now turned eighty years."

For the remainder of the rainy season the Perfect One, by directing energy toward the will to live, kept his illness in abeyance. And when the rains had come to an end, and sky and earth brightened with the pellucid blue and gold splendor of autumn, the Perfect One returned to Vaiśālī, staying a few weeks at Amrā's Park and a few weeks in the Hall with the Peaked Roof (Kūṭāgāraśālā) in Great Grove (Mahāvana).

And on a certain occasion, while he was staying in the Kūṭāgāraśālā, the Tathāgata called Ānanda, saying: "Go, Ānanda, and assemble in the council hall all the monks who are dwelling in Amrā's Park and round about Vaiśālī."

And after assembling the monks, the blessed Ānanda approached the Master and said: "The congregation of monks is assembled, Lord. Now is the time for doing whatever pleases the Perfect One."

Thereupon Buddha went into the council hall and sat on the appointed seat. Thus seated, he addressed the monks with these words: "I will teach you, O monks, the Incomposite and a way that leads to the Incomposite. What is the Incomposite? Whatever is the destruction of passion, the destruction of hatred, the destruction of delusion—this is called the Incomposite. And what is a way that leads to the Incomposite? Mindfulness in regard to body. And another way that leads to the Incomposite is tranquility and insight. Thus, monks, I have taught you the Incomposite and a way that leads to the Incomposite.

"Whatever may be done by a teacher, out of compassion, seeking the welfare of his disciples, that have I, through compassion, done for you. Therefore, monks, those teachings which have been understood and taught by me, you should grasp, follow, practice, and cultivate in order that the religious life may be lasting and widely published, that it may be of advantage to many, of happiness to gods and men. And what are those teachings? They are the disciplines and the moralities that I have taught you, namely: "The four Fundamentals of Attentiveness (i.e. dispassionate analytical contemplation of body, feelings, mind, and mental states).

"The four Right Efforts (i.e. preventing bad thoughts that have not yet arisen, dispelling bad thoughts that have already arisen, producing good thoughts that have not yet arisen, and developing good thoughts that have already arisen).

"The four Roads to Psychic Power (i.e. meditation combined with concentration of will, with concentration of energy, with concentration of mind, and with concentration of investigation).

"The five Faculties (i.e. of confidence, energy, mindfulness, concentration, and full Knowledge).

"The five Powers associated with the five Faculties.

"The seven Limbs of Wisdom (i.e. attentiveness, investigation of the Dharma, energy, joy, serenity, concentration, and equanimity).

"The Āryan Eightfold Path (i.e. Right View, Right Thought, Right Speech, Right Action, Right Livelihood, Right Effort, Right Attentiveness, and Right Concentration).

"These things, O monks, tend to profit in the present world, to happiness in the present world, to profit in a future state, to happiness in a future state.

"Come, monks, keep this always in mind: 'Impermanent are all composite things, unstable, untrustworthy, subject to change. Enough of collecting compounds! Enough of holding back!' Therefore, monks, after my passing-away, those things that tend to profit in the present and future should be grasped, followed, practiced, and cultivated by you out of compassion for the world, for the gain of many, for the joy, for the bliss, for the welfare of gods and men."

• ŚĀKYAMUNI PREDICTS OWN DEATH •

Early in the morning the Sugata, the Happy One, rose up and dressed himself; and taking bowl and robe went into Vaiśālī for alms-food. And after returning and eating his morning meal, he called to Ānanda, saying: "Ānanda, take a mat. I wish to go to Cāpāla Shrine for the noonday rest."

"Very well, Master," said Ānanda, taking up a mat and following the Perfect One.

Now when the Perfect One reached Cāpāla Shrine, Ānanda prepared a seat for him. And Buddha sat down and said to his favorite disciple: "Delightful, Ānanda, is Vaiśālī! Delightful are the shrines of Vaiśālī! Delightful is Cāpāla Shrine!

"Whosoever, Ānanda," continued the Tathāgata, "has developed, cultivated, applied himself to, made a basis of, stood upon, increased, and fully understood the four Roads to Psychic Power (meditation combined with concentration of will, of energy, of mind, and of investigation), such a person, if he wishes, may remain on earth for the full eon, or for what is left of it.

"Now, Ānanda, the Tathāgata has developed, cultivated, applied himself to, made a basis of, stood upon, increased, and fully understood the four Roads to Psychic Power. If he chooses, he can remain on earth for the full eon, or for what is left of it."

Even though so broad a hint as this was dropped by the Perfect One, even though his meaning was clear and plain, yet Ānanda was unable to understand what he meant. So he failed to beg Śākyamuni to stay on in his body.

Then a second and a third time, too, the Perfect One repeated his words. But Ānanda still failed to grasp Buddha's meaning, so far was Ānanda's mind misled by Māra, the Evil One.

Thereupon the Perfect One said: "Go, Ānanda! Do that for which you deem it the proper time."

Thus dismissed, Ānanda rose from his seat, bowed to the Perfect One, and went away and sat down at the foot of a tree not far off.

Not long after Ānanda had gone, Māra, the Evil One, came into Śākyamuni's presence.

"Now let the Perfect One pass away!" said Māra to Buddha's mind. "Now let the Buddha pass utterly away! Now is the proper time for the utter passing-away of the Perfect One! For thus it was spoken aforetime by the Perfect One: 'O Māra, I shall not pass away until my monks are trained disciples, disciplined and confident, having won freedom, who have heard the Teaching, who know the Dharma by heart, who fare on in accordance with Dharma, who fare on with diligence, living in accordance with Dharma, taking it as their very own teacher until they are able to proclaim, teach, show forth, establish, open up, analyze, and make it clear; until they are able to refute any wrong view which may well be refuted by right reasoning; until they are able to teach the Dharma that brings salvation with it.'

"And now, Ascetic," continued Māra, "all this has come to pass. And it was also spoken by the Perfect One: 'O Māra, I shall not pass away until I have nuns, lay brothers, and lay sisters as my disciples, followers who shall be trained and disciplined to show forth the miracle of the Dharma.'

"And now, Ascetic, all this has been fulfilled. Moreover, the Perfect One also said, 'O Māra, I shall not pass away until this religious life taught by me is powerful and prosperous, widespread and widely known, made popular, proclaimed abroad by gods and men.'

"And now indeed, Ascetic, this aim has been realized. Therefore, Ascetic, let the Perfect One pass utterly away, according to the word of the Perfect One! Now is the proper time for the complete, utter passing-away of the Perfect One!"

Thus spoke Māra; and the Perfect One replied to the Evil One, saying: "Do not become anxious, O Māra! The complete, utter passing-away of the Tathāgata shall take place in no long time. At the end of three months from now the Tathāgata shall pass utterly away."

Thereupon Buddha, mindful and self-possessed, discarded the will to live and rejected his aggregates of life there and then at Cāpāla Shrine. And at the very moment when he rejected his aggregates of life, the great earth rumbled and shook, and loud thunder boomed heavily in distant storm-clouds. Then the gods, with voices like thunder, uttered the following verse:

Things that had come to be,
Things gross and fine,
The aggregates of life—
These the Sage cast off.
With inward calm, composed,
He burst asunder,

Like shell of armor,
The self that had become.

Ānanda, alarmed by the earthquake, ran to where the Perfect One was.

"Strange it is, Lord, that the earth should quake and tremble so violently! What, Master, is the cause of it?"

"Ānanda," declared Buddha, "there are eight occasions which cause earthquakes. The first is the occasion of natural causes. The second is when a religious recluse who has acquired supernormal power, or a god of mighty power, practises unlimited earth-perception. In such a case the recluse or god shakes the earth. The third is when a Bodhisattva is conceived. The fourth is when a Bodhisattva is born. The fifth is when a Bodhisattva attains Enlightenment and becomes a Buddha. The sixth is when a Buddha first turns the Wheel of Dharma. The seventh is when a Buddha shakes off the aggregates of his life. *And the eighth is when a Buddha attains Utter Nirvāṇa with no aggregates remaining to go to birth again.*"

The Perfect One then told Ānanda how Māra had tempted him just after his Enlightenment, and he related the request Māra had just presented to him, and the rejection of his life's aggregates, causing the earthquake.

Ānanda's eyes widened with anxiety.

"O Lord," he exclaimed, "let the Perfect One not pass away! Let the Perfect One remain for the full eon! Let the Buddha remain for the rest of the eon for the gain of many, for the happiness of many, out of compassion for the world, for the joy, for the bliss, for the welfare of gods and men!"

"Enough, Ānanda!" replied Buddha. "Do not ask that of the Tathāgata! The time is now past, Ānanda, for asking that of the Tathāgata!"

But a second and yet a third time did Ānanda beg the Perfect One to remain in the world. And after making his request the third time, the Perfect One said: "Ānanda, do you have confidence in the wisdom of the Tathāgata?"

"Yes, Master, I do."

"Then why do you importune the Tathāgata, even to asking him a third time?"

"But, Lord," Ānanda protested, "face to face with the Perfect One I heard the Perfect One say, 'Whosoever has developed the four Roads to Psychic Power can, if he so desire, remain on earth for the full eon, or for what is left of it.' Now, the Perfect One has certainly developed the four Roads to Psychic Power. He could, therefore, remain on earth, if he so desired."

"Then, Ānanda, you believe that I am able to do that?"

"Yes, Lord, I believe that the Perfect One has this power."

"That being the case, Ānanda, yours is the fault and yours the transgression, insofar as, when so broad a hint was given, when such an illuminating remark was made by the Tathāgata, you could not penetrate it so as to ask the Tathāgata right then to remain on earth for the full eon, or for what is left of it. For if, Ānanda, you had begged twice, the Tathāgata might have rejected your petition; yet at the third time of asking, he might have consented. Therefore, Ānanda, yours is the fault and yours the transgression."

Śākyamuni then returned to Vaiśālī to the Hall with the Peaked Roof, and addressed the monks, saying: "Here it is now late in September, the lovely autumn time. In no long time, monks, the Tathāgata's entrance into Parinirvāṇa will take place. At the end of three months from now, the Tathāgata will pass utterly away. Ripe is my age, O monks, and limited my span of life. Leaving you, having made my Refuge hence, I go hence.

"Be vigilant, O monks, be mindful and steadfast in your aim. Keep in mind that all composite things are subject to decay. Practise concentration, guard your thoughts. And whosoever shall abide in this Dharma and discipline with vigilance, abandoning both birth and death, shall thereby reach the End of Pain."

Now, the nun Yaśodharā, who had been married to Siddhārtha Gautama in Kapilavastu before his attainment of Buddhahood, heard of this prediction and came to the Perfect One to beg permission to enter the uttermost Nirvāṇa before him. The Tathāgata assented.

Bowing humbly before him, Yaśodharā, then wrinkled by old age, asked the Light of the World to forgive her for any faults she might have committed. With deep appreciation the Perfect One told her that she had aided him on his quest for Enlightenment, and that her unfailing faith and encouragement made easier for him the path that led to his supreme Victory.

And as the radiance of perfect happiness illuminated her face, Yaśodharā passed utterly away never to come to birth again.

Early the next morning the Perfect One went again into Vaiśālī on alms-quest. And when he had returned to the monastery and finished his meal, he gathered up his bowl and robes and went out, accompanied by Ānanda and a large number of monks, to Vaiśālī Forest just outside the city.

The Perfect One ascended to the brow of a hillock with Ānanda at his side. A gust of chill wind, sharp and pure, came down from the blue northern sky and fluttered the saffron robes of the aged Buddha as he stood there in the sparkling autumnal sunshine looking out over Vaiśālī with steady gaze, turning his body as he looked with an "elephant look."

"Not without a cause," said Ānanda, "not without a reason, Lord, do Tathāgatas, Arhats, Supreme Buddhas look with an elephant look. What is the cause, what is the reason, Lord, of the elephant look?"

"Well said, Ānanda. Not without a cause, not without a reason, do Tathāgatas, Arhats, Supreme Buddhas look with an elephant look! This, Ānanda, is the Tathāgata's last sight of Vaiśālī. No more, Ānanda, will the Tathāgata come to Vaiśālī."

Ānanda lowered his head and bit his lip to repress the tears that were coming to his eyes.

"Come, Ānanda," said the Master, "let us go to Bhaṇḍa village."

• THE LAST MEAL •

From Bhaṇḍagrāma Buddha journeyed in a northwesterly direction, passing through the villages of Hastigrāma, Ambagrāma, Jambugrāma, and Bhoganagara. After staying nearly three months at Bhoganagara, the Master entered the country of the Mallas and came to Pāpā village, where he stayed in the mango grove of Cunda the Smith.

Now, Cunda the Smith heard the news that Buddha had come to

Pāpā with a great company of monks, and he accordingly went straightway to visit the Perfect One.

Prostrating at the feet of the Perfect One, Cunda said: "Let my Lord accept from my hands tomorrow's meal, together with the assembly of monks."

Buddha accepted the invitation by remaining silent; and Cunda, seeing the Lord's acceptance, bowed respectfully and returned to his house.

Cunda the Smith arose early the next morning and prepared with his own hands choice food, both hard and soft, together with a quantity of mushrooms that had been hurriedly gathered for the meal by servants. So excited and thrilled was Cunda that he could scarcely keep from dropping the cooking pots; but long before midmorning the meal was ready, and he forthwith sent word to the Tathāgata.

"It is time, my Lord: the meal is ready."

Thereupon Śākyamuni robed himself, took bowl and robe, and started off with the assembly of monks to Cunda's house.

When the Perfect One arrived, he sat down on a seat made ready. There sitting, he perceived danger with his Buddha-eye of Insight. "At the risk of offending Cunda the Smith," he thought, "I must see to it that the monks are not harmed."

"Friend Cunda," said Buddha, "as to the dish of mushrooms you have prepared, serve me with that. As to the other food, both hard and soft, which you have prepared, serve the monks with that."

"Very well, Lord," replied Cunda; and he served the food in accordance with the Perfect One's instructions. The mushrooms were placed in the Master's bowl. And those mushrooms were eaten by the Master.

After the Perfect One had finished eating, he called to Cunda the Smith and said: "Cunda, whatever remains of the dish of mushrooms, bury that in a hole dug in the ground: for I can see no one in this world, together with the world of gods—I can see no one by whom that food when eaten can be digested, save only by the Tathāgata."

"As you say, Lord," replied Cunda, who promptly went outside and buried the remainder of that dish of mushrooms in a hole dug in the ground.

When Cunda returned, Buddha delivered a discourse on the Dharma, after which courteous greetings were exchanged and the guests departed.

Not long after the Perfect One had eaten the food given him by Cunda the Smith, a severe sickness assailed him, and grievous pains accompanied by a bloody flux set in as if to end in death. But Śākyamuni remained calm and composed, enduring those excruciating pains without being overcome by them.

After having purged, the Master called to Ānanda and said: "Ānanda, let us be on our way. I wish to go on to Kuśinagarī."

• THE JOURNEY TO KUŚINAGARĪ •

On the way to Kuśinagarī, at a place where a brook crossed the road, the Perfect One stepped aside and went to the foot of a certain tree.

"Come, Ānanda! Make ready a seat for me by folding my extra robe in four. I am weary. I wish to sit down for a while."

"Yes, Lord," said Ānanda, and folded the robe to make a seat for the Master.

When he had seated himself, Buddha said: "Ānanda, bring me a drink of water from that brook. I am thirsty and wish to drink."

"Just a moment ago, Lord," replied Ānanda, "as many as five hundred carts crossed over that brook. The water has been stirred up by the wheels; and being shallow, it flows foul and muddy. But not far from here, Lord, is a river called Kukuṣṭhā with water sparkling and refreshing, cool and clear, easy of access and delightful. If the Perfect One will wait a little while, he can drink from the Kukuṣṭhā and bathe his limbs in it."

The brook was indeed turbid and muddy, having been stirred up by the cart wheels; but as soon as Ānanda approached, it flowed bright and pure, fresh and unmuddied.

"What an amazing thing!" thought Ānanda. "Just a moment ago this brook was muddy, but now it has suddenly become pure and transparent!"

Taking a bowlful of the pure water to Buddha, Ānanda said: "A marvel indeed, Lord! It is verily a miracle wrought by the mighty power and majesty of the Tathāgata! Why, the brook is now flowing fresh and unmuddied! Let the Perfect One drink the water! Let the Happy One drink the water!"

And Buddha, not reproving Ānanda for his lack of faith, drank the water.

Now, while Buddha was resting under a tree, a Malla by the name of Kuśala, who had been a pupil of Ārāda Kālāma, came along and stopped to see the Perfect One.

"I hear, reverend Gautama," said Kuśala to Buddha, "that you were once a pupil of Ārāda Kālāma, but abandoned the tutelage of that excellent master. How was it, reverend Gautama, that you abandoned Ārāda's teaching?"

"Ārāda Kālāme, friend Kuśala," answered the Perfect One, "was not an Enlightened One, not an Omniscient One. Ārāda's teaching, friend Kuśala, conducted only to the Sphere of Nothingness, and not beyond. For that reason the Tathāgata abandoned Ārāda's teaching in disgust."

"But reverend Gautama," declared Kuśala, "Ārāda Kālāma was an adept in the art of meditation and trance! On one occasion he was sitting in trance in the open air, and neither saw nor heard five hundred passing carts, even though he was fully conscious and awake!"

"Well now, friend Kuśala," retorted Buddha, "once when I was sitting in meditation at Ātumā, it rained in a cloudburst, and it thundered and lightened—and what do you think? Two farmers and four oxen were struck by lightning; but this I did not know until I had inquired why a crowd of people had collected there. Though fully conscious and awake, I had seen and heard nothing."

On hearing this, Kuśala marveled and begged to be accepted as a lay disciple of the Perfect One. And after the Perfect One had accepted him, Kuśala brought forth two magnificent robes of gold cloth and presented them to Buddha.

"Clothe me with one, Kuśala, and Ānanda with the other," said the Tathāgata.

When Kuśala had gone, Ānanda noticed that the golden robe worn by Lord Buddha seemed to have lost its glow, so bright, so radiant, so clear was Buddha's skin.

"What, Lord, is the cause of the Perfect One's radiance? The robe of gold cloth, brought near to the skin of the Perfect One, has lost its glow and become dull in comparison with the golden radiance of the Perfect One!"

"Ānanda, the skin of a Tathāgata becomes bright, radiant, and clear on two occasions. On the night when a Tathāgata attains Enlightenment does that Tathāgata's skin become bright, radiant, and clear, and also on the night when a Tathāgata enters Parinirvāṇa with nothing remaining to be reborn."

Thereupon the Master arose from his seat and resumed the journey to Kuśinagarī.

As soon as the river Kukusṭhā came into sight, Śākyamuni went to its bank and bathed his limbs in its fresh, clear-flowing waters. And when he had finished bathing, Ānanda wiped him dry and clothed him with extra robes in order to protect him from chill. For it was then late December, and the air was cold.

Then Buddha went with the monks to a nearby mango grove and called to the venerable Cundaka, saying: "Come, Cundaka! Fold my robe in four and make a couch for me. I am weary, and wish to lie down."

"Yes, Master," replied Cundaka, who forthwith proceeded to get ready a couch for the Perfect One.

When the couch had been prepared, Buddha lay down upon it on his right side in the posture of a lion, resting one foot on the other, mindful and composed. And the venerable Cundaka sat down in front of the Perfect One to watch over him.

After lying down for a time, the Tathāgata sat up and called for Ānanda.

"It may happen, Ānanda, that someone will arouse remorse in Cunda the Smith by saying, 'It is a loss for you, friend Cunda, it is a thing portending ill for you, friend Cunda, that the Tathāgata passed away after eating his last meal at your hands.'

"Now, Ānanda, any remorse in Cunda the Smith should be dispelled by saying to him: 'It is gain to you, friend Cunda, it is a thing portending good luck for you, friend Cunda, that the Tathāgata passed away after eating his last meal at your hands. Face to face with the Master, worthy

Cunda, did I hear it said; face to face with him I received the word:

" ' "These two meals are of like fruit and result, far exceeding any other meal in fruit and result. What are the two? That meal after eating which a Tathāgata is awakened with the Supreme Enlightenment, and that meal after eating which a Tathāgata passes away with that utter passing-away that leaves no basis for rebirth. These two meals are of like fruit, of like result, far exceeding any other meal in fruit and result."

" 'A deed has been stored up by the worthy Cunda, a deed which results in long life, good looks, happiness, fame, power, and rebirth in the heavenly worlds.'

"With such words, Ānanda, should be dispelled any remorse which may arise in Cunda the Smith."

Then the Perfect One said: "Come, Ānanda, let us go on to Kuśinagarī across the river Hirajñavatī to the śāla grove of the Mallas."

Ānanda thereupon assisted Śākyamuni to his feet and picked up the robes. And as the sun was sinking low in the southwestern sky, the Perfect One and the company of monks again took to the road.

The blessed Ānanda shivered as the cool air penetrated his robe and touched his body with icy fingers. The sadness in his heart was intensified by the clumps of bare trees by the roadside, their fallen leaves rustling with forlorn softness in the undergrowth.

XVI

THE GREAT DECEASE

• RIGHT HOMAGE TO THE TATHĀGATA •

Crossing the river Hirajñavatī, the Perfect One and the company of monks drew near to the town of Kuśinagarī and to the śāla grove of the Mallas. And as night was falling, the Perfect One entered the grove and called to the blessed Ānanda, saying: "Be so good, Ānanda, as to spread for me a couch with its head to the north between those twin śāla trees." And Buddha then laid himself down on his right side in the posture of a lion, with one foot resting upon the other: and he remained mindful and self-possessed.

(Now, śāla trees never lose their leaves entirely; and even in midwinter a scattering of withered leaves cling tenaciously to the branches. Not until March does the new foliage appear, and not until April do the śāla blossoms burst forth into full bloom. It was then near the end of December.

When Śākyamuni lay down upon the couch, the twin śāla trees bestirred themselves as though caressed by a spring breeze, and all at once became covered with a mass of bloom with flowers out of season. And all over the body of the Tathāgata the blossoms dropped and sprinkled and scattered themselves out of reverence for the Successor of the Buddhas of old.

And heavenly mandārava flowers, too, and heavenly sandalwood powder came drifting down from on high; and all over the body of the Tathāgata they fell and sprinkled and scattered themselves out of reverence for the Successor of the Buddhas of old. And music celestial sounded in the heavens, and choruses divine wafted from the skies out of reverence for the Successor of the Buddhas of old.

Then the Perfect One addressed Ānanda, saying: "See, Ānanda, the twin śāla trees are all one mass of bloom with flowers out of season! They are scattering their blossoms all over the body of the Tathāgata, covering him with their petals. Heavenly mandārava flowers, too, and heavenly sandalwood powder fall from the skies! And divine music and celestial choruses come drifting down! In this way, Ānanda, all nature adores and worships the Tathāgata.

"But it is not by all this, Ānanda, that the Tathāgata is rightly honored or venerated. The monk or nun, the devout layman or devout laywoman, Ānanda, who continually fulfills all the greater and lesser ethical duties, who conducts himself with propriety and in accordance with the Five Precepts,—it is he who rightly honors and venerates the Tathāgata with the worthiest homage. Therefore, Ānanda, train yourselves to be constant in the fulfillment of all the greater and lesser ethical duties, and to conduct yourselves with propriety and in accordance with the Five Precepts."

Now it happened, just at that time, that the venerable Upavāna was standing in front of Buddha, tending him.

"Step aside, monk!" commanded the Perfect One harshly. "Do not stand thus in front of me!"

Upavāna accordingly retired to one side; and Ānanda said to Buddha:

"The venerable Upavāna, O Lord, has long kept himself at the Perfect One's beck and call. What, pray, was the reason that the Perfect One was harsh to the venerable Upavāna, saying, 'Step aside, monk: do not stand thus in front of me'?"

"Ānanda," replied the Perfect One, "almost all the gods throughout ten world-systems have gathered together here to see the Tathāgata. For an extent, Ānanda, of twelve *yojanas* about the town of Kuśinagarī and this śāla grove of the Mallas, there is not a spot of ground large enough to stick the point of a hair into, that is not pervaded by powerful gods. And these gods are angered, saying, 'From afar have we come to see the Tathāgata, for but seldom and on rare occasions does a Tathāgata, a Supreme Buddha, arise in the world. And now, this very night, in the last watch, the Tathāgata is going to pass into Nirvāṇa. But this powerful monk stands in front of the Tathāgata, concealing him, and we cannot get the chance of seeing the Tathāgata even though his last moments are near.' Thus, Ānanda, are these gods angered."

"What are the gods whom the Perfect One perceives doing, Lord?"

"Some of the gods, Ānanda, are in the air, and some of them are on the ground; and many among them have minds engrossed by worldly things. These gods, Ānanda, dishevel their hair and cry aloud, and stretch forth their arms and weep, and fall prostrate upon the ground, and roll to and fro in anguish, crying, 'Too soon will the Perfect One die! Too soon will the Happy One pass away! All too soon will the Light of the World vanish from sight!'

"But those gods, Ānanda, who are free from passion, mindful and self-possessed, bear it patiently, saying: 'Transitory are all composite things. How is it possible that what has been born, has come into being, is organized and liable to dissolution, should not dissolve? That is truly an impossible state of affairs!' "

"For a long time, Master," said Ānanda, "the monks have come and attended the Perfect One after keeping retreat. What is to be done after the Perfect One passes away?"

"There are four places, Ānanda, which the faithful disciple should look upon with religious emotion. And which are the four? The place, Ānanda, where the Tathāgata was born, the place where the Tathāgata attained supreme and perfect Enlightenment, the place where the Tathāgata first set rolling the unsurpassed Wheel of Dharma, and the place where the Tathāgata passed utterly away with that complete, utter passing-away which leaves nothing whatever to remain behind.

"These, Ānanda, are the four places to which devout monks, devout nuns, devout laymen, and devout laywomen will come with holy emotion. And whosoever happens to die with peaceful heart while wandering on pilgrimage to such shrines shall be reborn, when the body dissolves at death, in the blissful realms of heaven."

Ānanda then asked the Tathāgata: "How are we to act, Lord, with regard to women?"

"Not seeing them, Ānanda."

"But if we chance to see them, how are we to act?"

"Not speaking, Ānanda."

"But, Lord, suppose that we cannot help speaking to them?"

"In that case, Ānanda, you must remain mindful."

• BUDDHA'S PRAISE OF ĀNANDA •

"What are we to do, Lord," asked Ānanda, "with the remains of the Perfect One?"

"Do not worry yourselves with the body of the Tathāgata," answered Śākyamuni. "Do not hinder yourselves by performing last rites for the Tathāgata. Be zealous on your own behalf, I beseech you. Devote yourselves to your own good. Be earnest, enthusiastic, resolute! There are discreet laymen, Ānanda, among the nobles, among the brahmins, and among the heads of houses, who are sincere and devoted believers in the Tathāgata. They will see to the Tathāgata's funeral."

"But, Lord, what should be done with the remains of the Perfect One?"

"As men treat the remains of a king of kings, in exactly the same way, Ānanda, should they treat the remains of a Tathāgata," replied Buddha.

"And how, Lord, do they treat the remains of a king of kings?"

"They wrap the body of a king of kings in new cloth and carded cotton. When that is done, they place the body in an oil-vessel of iron and cover that tightly with another like it. Then they build a funeral pyre with all kinds of incense and burn the body of the king of kings. That, Ānanda, is how they treat the remains of a king of kings.

"And as they treat the remains of a king of kings, in the same manner, Ānanda, should they treat the remains of the Tathāgata. At the four crossroads a stūpa should be erected to the Tathāgata. And whosoever shall offer flowers or perfumes or paint there, or worship there, or become in its presence calm in heart, it shall be a profit and a joy to them for many a long day."

When the blessed Ānanda had heard these words, the painful realization that the Master was about to die swept over him. No longer able to suppress his tears, he ran to the little monastery at the edge of the śāla grove and stood leaning against the bolt of the door, weeping bitterly and crying: "Alas! I am still only a pupil, with much yet to be learned; and my Master will soon pass utterly away, he who was so kind to me!"

Then the Perfect One called to the monks standing beside his couch. "Monks, where is Ānanda?"

"Brother Ānanda has gone over to the monastery," they replied. "He is now standing at the door, leaning against the doorbolt and weeping."

"Go to him," said Buddha, "and call Ānanda in my name, saying, 'Brother Ānanda, the Master calls for you.' "

When Ānanda had returned to where the Perfect One was, he took his seat respectfully at one side, tears streaming down his cheeks.

"Enough, Ānanda!" said Śākyamuni. "Do not grieve nor weep! Have I not on many former occasions told you that in all things, even in those most near and dear to us, there is the element of transience, of separation, of otherness? How then can it be possible, Ānanda, that what is born, what has come to be, what is put together, what is of a nature to dissolve away, should fail to dissolve away? Verily, no such condition can exist!

"For a long, long time, Ānanda, you have been very near to me by acts kind and good, by words kind and good, by thoughts kind and good, with love that never varies and is beyond all measure. You have done well, Ānanda! Apply yourself to effort, and you too shall soon attain Nirvāṇa!"

Then the Perfect One addressed the assembly of monks and said: "O monks! Whatever Supreme Buddhas have lived in the past, all of them have had personal attendants just as devoted to those Tathāgatas as Ānanda has been to me. And whatever Supreme Buddhas there shall be in the future, all of them shall have personal attendants just as devoted to those Tathāgatas as Ānanda has been to me.

"A wise man, O monks, is Ānanda! He knows when it is the right time for the monks or for the nuns of the Saṅgha, for male and female lay disciples, for a king or for a king's ministers, or for other teachers or for their disciples to come and visit the Tathāgata.

"O monks, there are four wonderful and marvelous qualities in Ānanda. What are the four? If, monks, a number of monks of the Saṅgha should come to visit Ānanda, they are filled with joy on seeing him; and if Ānanda should then preach the Dharma to them, they are filled with joy on hearing the discourse; but when Ānanda makes an end of speaking, that company of monks is disappointed. So also if a number of nuns of the Saṅgha, or a number of male lay disciples, or a number of female lay disciples should come to visit Ānanda."

Turning to Ānanda, the Perfect One said: "O ĀNANDA, BE AN ISLAND UNTO YOURSELF, BE YOUR OWN REFUGE, WITH NONE OTHER. MAKE THE DHARMA YOUR ISLAND, MAKE THE DHARMA YOUR REFUGE, WITH NONE OTHER."

• THE CONVERSION OF SUBHADRA •

Then said Ānanda to the Master: "Let not the Perfect One die in this little backwoods town, in this settlement in the middle of the jungle, in this branch-village! For, Lord, there are other places, great cities such as Campā, Rājagṛha, Śrāvastī, Sāketa, Kauśāmbī, and Vārāṇasī. Let the Perfect One die in one of them! There are many wealthy followers in those cities who will pay due honor to the remains of the Perfect One."

"Do not say that, Ānanda!" exclaimed Buddha. "Do not say that this is only a little backwoods town, a settlement in the middle of the jungle, a branch-village!

"Long ago, Ānanda, there was a great king, a righteous man who ruled in righteousness, lord of the four quarters of the earth, victorious, the protector of his people. This Kuśinagarī, Ānanda, was the royal city of that great king. From east to west it was twelve *yojanas* in length, and from north to south it was seven *yojanas* in breadth. This city, Ānanda, was prosperous and flourishing, populous and thronging with people, and well provided with food.

"Therefore go now, Ānanda, and enter Kuśinagarī and inform the Mallas of Kuśinagarī, saying, 'This day, O Mallas, in the last watch of the night, the final passing-away of the Tathāgata will take place. Be favorable, worthy sirs, be favorable! Allow no occasion to arise for reproaching yourselves hereafter, saying, "In our own village did the Tathāgata pass into Nirvāṇa, but we did not avail ourselves of the opportunity of visiting the Tathāgata in his last hours." ' "

Now at that time the Mallas of Kuśinagarī were assembled in their council hall on some matter of business. And having arrived at the council hall, Ānanda repeated to the Kuśinagarī-Mallas the message which had been given to him by Śākyamuni.

The Mallas, on hearing the news, were grieved and heartbroken—they together with their children, their daughters-in-law, and their wives. They lost no time in going to the śāla grove where Buddha lay dying.

Then the blessed Ānanda thought: 'If I allow the Mallas of Kuśinagarī to pay their respects to the Tathāgata one by one, the whole of them will not have been presented to the Perfect One until the night brightens up into dawn. Suppose, now, that I cause the Mallas to stand in groups, each family in a group, and so present them."

And that is what Ānanda did. By the light of the flickering torches which the Mallas had brought with them, and which illuminated the whole śāla grove with soft radiance, the blessed Ānanda announced each family to the reclining Buddha as a group, saying, "Lord, a Malla of such and such a name with his children, his wives, his retinue, and his friends humbly bows down at the feet of the Perfect One." By this device Śākyamuni's favorite disciple succeeded in presenting all of the Mallas of Kuśinagarī before the first watch had elapsed.

Now, the report that Buddha was to pass into Nirvāṇa in the last watch of the night happened to reach the ears of a certain wandering ascetic named Subhadra, who was dwelling at Kuśinagarī at that time.

"Religious doubts have arisen in my mind," thought Subhadra. "Suppose I go to the Ascetic Gautama and ask him to explain the matter to me. For rarely indeed do Tathāgatas, Arhats, Supreme Buddhas appear in the world."

So Subhadra went directly to the śāla grove and approached Ānanda. And having drawn near, Subhadra introduced himself and said: "Venerable Ānanda, I have heard wandering ascetics who were old men, advanced in years, teachers, and teachers' teachers, declare: 'Rarely indeed do Tathāgatas arise in the world, they who are Arhats, Buddhas Supreme.' And here tonight, in the last watch, the Recluse Gautama is going to pass into Nirvāṇa.

"O reverend Ānanda, a doubt has arisen in my mind; and I have confidence that Gautama can so teach me the Dharma that I may dispel my doubt. If only I could have the opportunity of seeing the Ascetic Gautama before he passes utterly away!"

"Enough, enough, friend Subhadra!" replied Ānanda. "Do not trouble the Tathāgata! The Perfect One is weary."

But Subhadra persisted, and repeated his request even to the third time.

Now, the Perfect One chanced to overhear the conversation between Ānanda and the wandering ascetic.

"Ānanda, do not prevent Subhadra from coming to the Tathāgata," said Buddha. "Let Subhadra be permitted to see the Tathāgata. Whatever Subhadra shall ask of me, he will ask for the sake of information, and not from a desire to annoy me. And he will quickly understand my answers to his questions."

So Subhadra the Wanderer went into the presence of the Perfect One. And after the exchange of courteous greetings, Subhadra addressed the Tathāgata, saying: "Reverend Gautama, all those recluses and brahmins who have a large following and crowds of pupils and disciples—famous, renowned founders of religions, esteemed as holy men by the people, men like Pūraṇa Kāśyapa, Maskarin Gośālīputra, Sañjaya Vairūṭīputra, Ajita Keśakambala, Kakuda Kātyāyana, and the Nirgranṭha Jñātaputra—have all these, as they themselves say, realized the Truth by their own knowledge, or have only some of them or none at all so realized?"

"Brush that question aside for the time being, Subhadra," replied the Enlightened One. "Do not concern yourself with whether or not others have realized the Truth. I have no desire to make people neglect their religious obligations or give up their accustomed ways of life just to win converts. But false creeds are false views, Subhadra; and false views lead to confusion and states of suffering.

"There are bad things to be put away, Subhadra, things that involve corruption, things that drag one down again to rebirth, things causing pain, having pain for their fruit, things involving birth, decay, and death in time to come. It is for the rejection of these things that I teach the Dharma by which the things involving corruption shall be put away, wholesome things shall be brought to full growth, and by which even in this present life a man, by his own powers, shall realize and abide in the full knowledge and realization of perfect Wisdom.

"Subhadra, in whatever doctrine and discipline the Āryan Eightfold Path is not found, therein also are not found monks who have gained even the first stage of attainment, much less the second, third, and fourth! But in whatever doctrine and discipline the Āryan Eightfold Path is found, O Subhadra, therein also are found monks of the four stages of attainment. Now, in this Dharma and discipline of mine the Āryan Eightfold Path is found. Herein alone, Subhadra, are found monks of the four stages of attainment.

"I was twenty-nine years old when I left the world to seek the Highest Good. Now fifty-one years and more have passed since I renounced the world to range the Dharma, outside of which are found no adepts of the first stage of attainment, much less the second, third, and fourth! Destitute of genuine saints are all other creeds. But so long as men of good will live the holy life in this Dharma and discipline of mine, Subhadra, the world will not be destitute of Arhats."

At these words, Subhadra the Wanderer said to the Perfect One: "Wonderful, O Lord! Marvelous, O Lord! To the Buddha, to the Dharma, to the Saṅgha I go for refuge! Permit me to retire from the world under the Perfect One! Grant me ordination!"

Thus did Subhadra the Wanderer retire from the world under the Perfect One; and he received full ordination there and then without delay. And not long afterward, the venerable Subhadra began to live solitary and remote from the crowd, vigilant, strenuous, and resolute. In no long time he came to learn for himself and to realize and live in possession of the Highest Good to which the religious life conducts. And so the venerable Subhadra became another of the Arhats; and he was the last disciple to be converted by the Master.

• THE GREAT UTTER PASSING-AWAY •

As soon as the venerable Subhadra received ordination, at the end of the second watch, Śākyamuni turned to Ānanda and said: "It may be, Ānanda, that some of you will think, 'Gone is the word of the Master! We have no Teacher any more!' But you should not so regard it, Ānanda, for the Dharma and discipline which I have set forth and laid down for you all—let them, after I am gone, be your Teacher. By the way, if the Saṅgha so desires, Ānanda, let it abolish all of the lesser and minor rules and regulations after I am gone."

The brilliant December stars wheeled silently over the śāla grove like glittering diamonds strewn on purple velvet as the night entered the third watch.

"It may be, O monks," said the Perfect One to the entire assembly, "that in the mind of some one monk there is doubt or perplexity about the Buddha, or about the Dharma, or about the Saṅgha, or the Path, or the course of conduct. If that be so, monks, ask now. Do not be remorseful hereafter at the thought, 'Here was our Master face to face with us, and yet we did not have the heart to question the Perfect One, though we were in his very presence.' "

At these words the monks were silent.

A second and a third time the Perfect One uttered the same words, yet none of the monks spoke out.

"It may be, monks," said the Tathāgata, "that it is out of respect for me that you ask no questions. Speak to me, then, as one friend to another."

But even then the monks remained silent.

"Wonderful, Lord!" exclaimed Ānanda. "Verily, I believe that in this entire congregation of monks there is not a single monk who has any doubt or perplexity regarding the Buddha, the Dharma, the Saṅgha, the Path, or the course of conduct!"

"It is out of faith that you said that, Ānanda," declared Buddha, "but the Tathāgata has positive knowledge of the fact that in this whole assembly of monks there is not one monk who has any doubts as to these things. For even the most backward of all these many hundreds of monks, Ānanda, has become genuinely converted, is no longer liable to be born in a state of suffering, and is destined to supreme and perfect Enlightenment, to the bliss of Nirvāṇa."

Then Śākyamuni addressed the monks, saying: "Suppose, monks, that a man traveling in a forest, along the side of a mountain, should come upon an ancient road, an ancient path, traversed by men of olden times, and that he should proceed along it, and thus proceeding come upon an ancient city, a royal city of olden times, inhabited by men of bygone ages, laid out with parks and groves and reservoirs, and strongly fortified with a wall—an altogether delightful place.

"Then suppose, monks, that this man should inform the king of his discovery, saying, 'Pardon me, sir, but you may be interested to know that while traveling I came upon an ancient road which led me to an old-time city, a delightful spot. If it please you, sir, restore that city.'

"Then suppose, monks, that the king were to restore that city so that thereafter it became prosperous, thriving, and populous, crowded with inhabitants, and were to grow and increase even more.

"Just so, monks, have I discovered an ancient Path, an ancient Way traversed by the Buddhas of old. And what is that Path? Verily, it is this Āryan Eightfold Path.

"NOW THEN, O MONKS, I REMIND YOU: SUBJECT TO DECAY ARE ALL COMPOSITE THINGS. STRIVE DILIGENTLY FOR LIBERATION."

These were the last words of the Tathāgata.

Then the Perfect One entered into the First Absorption. And rising out of the First Absorption, he passed into the Second. And rising out of the Second Absorption, he passed into the Third. And rising out of the Third Absorption, he passed into the Fourth. And rising out of the Fourth Absorption, he entered into the Sphere of Boundless Space. And passing out of the Sphere of Boundless Space, he entered into the Sphere of Infinite Consciousness. And passing out of the Sphere of Infinite Consciousness, he entered into the Sphere of Nothingness. And passing out of the Sphere of Nothingness, he entered into the Sphere of Neither-perception-nor-nonperception. And passing out of the Sphere of Neither-perception-nor-nonperception, he entered into the CONDITION WHICH IS BEYOND ALL THOUGHT, BEYOND ALL IDEA.

Then the blessed Ānanda turned to the venerable Aniruddha and said: "Reverend Aniruddha, the Perfect One has passed into Nirvāṇa."

"No, reverend Ānanda, the Perfect One has not passed into Nirvāṇa. He has entered into that condition which transcends both thoughts and ideas."

Then the Perfect One, passing out of the condition which is beyond all thought and beyond all idea, entered into the Sphere of Neither-perception-nor-nonperception. And passing out of the Sphere of Neither-perception-nor-nonperception, he entered into the Sphere of Nothingness. And passing out of the Sphere of Nothingness, he entered into the Sphere of Infinite Consciousness. And passing out of the Sphere of Infinite Consciousness, he entered into the Sphere of Boundless Space. And passing out of the Sphere of Boundless Space, he passed into the Fourth Absorption. And descending from the Fourth Absorption, he passed into the Third. And descending from the Third Absorption, he passed into the Second. And descending from the Second Absorption, he passed into the First.

A smile flickered over the radiantly serene face of the dying Buddha just then. There was not a sound to be heard; and the monks, with palms pressed together, venerated the Paramount Victor in utter silence.

Rising out of the First Absorption, the Perfect One passed into the Second. And rising out of the Second Absorption, he passed into the Third. And rising out of the Third Absorption, he passed into the Fourth. And rising out of the Fourth Absorption, the Perfect One passed at once into Parinirvāṇa.

Śākyamuni Buddha died thus in his eightieth year in the month of Mārgaśīrṣa.

When the Perfect One died there occurred, at the moment of his passing out of existence, a mighty earthquake, tremendous and awful; and from the depths of the earth an upsurge of sound arose, sweeping through all nature in a crescendo of music that soared up in the sky and merged with the intonations of celestial orchestras echoing the dolors of ten thousand world-systems amid ear-shattering thunderings that gripped the universal chiliocosm in a paroxysm of grief.

"Too soon has the Perfect One died!" cried celestial beings from on high. "Too soon has the Happy One passed away! All too soon has the Light of the World vanished from sight!"

When the Perfect One died, at the moment of his passing out of existence, the god Mahābrahmā exclaimed:

All beings that have life shall lay
Aside their complex form, that aggregation
Of mental and material qualities
That gives them, in heaven or on earth,
Their fleeting individuality!
Even a Teacher such as he,
Man unrivaled in all the world,
Successor of the Buddhas of old,
Endowed with powers and Insight clear,
Has died!

Declared Śakra, governor of the gods:

Impermanent, alas, are all composite things!
They come to be, and then they pass away.
Having once arisen they cease in course,
And in their Extinction is utter bliss.

When the Perfect One died, those of the monks who were not yet free from the passions covered their faces and wept in anguish, saying: "Too soon has the Perfect One died! Too soon has the Happy One passed away! All too soon has the Light of the World vanished from sight!"

But those who were free from passion bore their grief collected and composed, thinking, "Impermanent are all composite things. How is it possible that they should not dissolve?"

Then the venerable Aniruddha exhorted the monks, saying: "Enough, my brothers! Do not weep and lament! Has not the Master formerly declared to us that the nature of all things, even things most near and dear to us, is such that we must divide ourselves from them, leave them, sever ourselves from them? How can anything born, brought into being, organized, and containing within itself the inherent necessity of dissolution—how can it be possible that such a compound should not be dissolved? No such condition can exist, brothers! If we err in this respect, even the gods will reproach us!"

On hearing Aniruddha's counsel, the monks composed themselves; but there were gods of worldly mind in heaven and on earth who would not be consoled, but disheveled their hair and wept, stretched forth their arms and wept, fell prostrate upon the ground and rolled to and fro in anguish, crying: "Too soon has the Perfect One died! Too soon has the Happy One passed away! All too soon has the Light of the World vanished from sight!"

• THE LAST RITES •

When morning came, the venerable Aniruddha went to Ānanda and said: "Go now, reverend Ānanda, into Kuśinagarī and inform the Mallas that the Master is dead."

Thereupon Ānanda, taking bowl and robe, and accompanied by an attendant, went into the village. And he found the Mallas of Kuśinagarī assembled in the council hall discussing that very matter.

"The Perfect One is dead," said Ānanda to the Mallan chieftains. "Do, O Mallas, whatever seems proper to you."

The Mallas accordingly took perfumes and garlands and all kinds of musical instruments and went to where the Tathāgata's body lay in the śāla grove. There they spent the whole day venerating and paying homage to Buddha with dancing and hymn-singing and instrumental music, and with incense and garlands of flowers. For six days they paid homage to the body of the Perfect One; but on the seventh day they carried it through the town of Kuśinagarī to a shrine of the Mallas called Makuṭabandhana on the east side. And as they did so, all Kuśinagarī, even down to the dustbins and rubbish heaps, became strewn knee-deep with mandārava flowers that fell from the sky.

After the body of Lord Buddha had been brought to Makuṭabandhana Shrine, the Mallas wrapped it in new cloth and carded cotton. Then they placed the body in an iron oil-vessel and covered that tightly with another like it. And after doing this, they built a funeral pyre of all kinds of incense.

Now at that time the venerable Mahākāśyapa was journeying along the highway from Pāpā to Kuśinagarī with a large company of monks. And they met a certain naked ascetic who had picked up a heavenly mandārava flower in Kuśinagarī. Pangs of grief pierced the hearts of those monks when the naked ascetic told them the news.

"The Ascetic Gautama has been dead a week this day. That is how I obtained this mandārava flower."

Now, a certain Subhadra in that assembly (but not the Subhadra whom Buddha had converted as his last convert) came forward and exclaimed to the grief-striken monks: "Enough of this grieving, my friends: we are well rid of the Great Ascetic! Too long have we been annoyed by being told, 'This befits you, this does not befit you'! We can now do as we please and refrain from doing what we do not wish to do."

The monks ignored the words of Subhadra; and Mahākāśyapa reminded the monks of Buddha's teaching concerning the transience of all composite things and the consequent inevitable separation from things near and dear to us in this world.

When Mahākāśyapa and the company of monks arrived in Kuśinagarī, they went to Makuṭabandhana Shrine and venerated the body of the Tathāgata. And as they did so, lo! the piles of incense of which the pyre was composed spontaneously burst into flame.

The body of the Perfect One burned up completely, leaving only the bones behind. And when the body of the Perfect One had been burned up, a shower fell from the sky and extinguished the fire. And in addition to the water caused by the gods to fall from the sky, the Mallas brought water scented with all kinds of fragrant perfumes and poured it upon the embers.

Then the Mallas of Kuśinagarī surrounded the pyre with a fence of spears stuck upright in the ground and venerated the relics of Lord Buddha for seven days with dance, song, and instrumental music, and with flowers and perfumes. And on the eighth day they took the bones of Śākyamuni into their council hall for distribution as relics to the messengers of kings and chieftains who had arrived to claim their share.

• ĀNANDA'S VICTORY •

The monks, in the meantime, were holding meetings in the monastery in the śāla grove of the Mallas. Now, at these meetings it was decided to hold a great council of the Saṅgha in Rājagṛha for the purpose of reviewing the rules of discipline for the monks and the teachings of the Perfect One. Because Ānanda had committed to memory a larger number of Buddha's sermons than had any other disciple, he was approached by the elders of the Saṅgha.

"You are very learned, reverend Ānanda. How many of the Master's discourses do you keep in mind?"

"I have learned eighty-two thousand discourses from the Perfect One himself," replied the blessed Ānanda, "and I have learned two thousand more from the monks. Hence I keep in mind eighty-four thousand discourses in all."

"Come then, reverend Ānanda, accompany us to Rājagṛha and recite the Master's discourses to the Saṅgha that Lord Buddha's holy word be kept alive among men even till the end of the eon."

Ānanda, however, had not as yet succeeded in becoming an Arhat, a Holy One who has attained Nirvāṇa. For this failure, and also because he had obtained the admission of women to the Saṅgha, had not asked the Perfect One at the proper time to remain in the world, and had neglected to ask the Perfect One which were the lesser rules that could be abolished, the monks were unfriendly toward the Lord's favorite disciple.

Thus chided and made sad by the monks, the blessed Ānanda did not remain to accompany them to Rājagṛha, but ran out of the monastery one evening at twilight and made his way alone to the funeral pyre of the Perfect One at Makuṭabandhana Shrine. And when he had come to the place where the body of the Master had been cremated, Ānanda sat down upon a rock and wept.

The ashes of the pyre were a black heap barely visible in the dusk; and the spears standing in barricade around the pyre glistened coldly as the dew of nightfall condensed upon their iron points. Grief overwhelmed Ānanda as tears blurred the remains of the pyre.

The glow of twilight had dwindled to a thin finger of ruddy luminescence skirting the western hills. Scintillating asterisms flashed forth with hard, prismatic radiance in the sky above it. And then, all of a sudden, Ānanda heard a voice in his own mind—the Master's voice!

"Ānanda, have I not taught you aforetime in divers ways . . . ?"

The beloved disciple knew that there was no need, no reason, to glance about. It was dark; yet in the darkness a light shone with surpassing glory, dispelling with its radiance the gloom that had shadowed his heart.

"I am the Tathāgata," declared the Self-Existent One, "the Arhat, the Buddha! Having myself traversed the ocean of life and death, I conduct others to the Farther Shore; being myself free, I make others free; experiencing comfort, I comfort others; being myself perfectly at rest, I lead others to rest.

"By my perfect Wisdom I know all worlds as they really are: I am omniscient; and there is nothing beyond the ken of my Vision. Come to me, O gods and men: hear the Dharma! I am he who indicates and shows the Path as one knowing the Path.

"As the Buddha Śākyamuni I went out from the land of the Śākyas and attained supreme Enlightenment at the town of Buddhagayā. But in reality I arrived at Enlightenment from beginningless time. Unlimited in the duration of my life am I, the Tathāgata.

"You are my child and I am your father who has removed you from pain, from the triple world of existence-and-nonexistence, and from fear and danger when you had been burning for many multimillions of eons."

Filled with amazement and rapture at the sudden influx of Insight, Ānanda exclaimed: "I am amazed and astonished, O Lord! I am charmed to hear the incomparable Voice of Dharma! Mine the fault, mine the offense, that I failed to understand! But now, Master, I am ripe for supreme Enlightenment!"

And there and then the spotless eye of Wisdom arose in the blessed Ānanda. He had lived the holy life, he had accomplished all that needed to be accomplished, he had won the uttermost Goal—Nirvāṇa. Thus the blessed Ānanda became yet another of the Arhats.

The venerable Ānanda then wiped the tears from his eyes and rose up from the rock. Picking up his begging bowl, he set out for Rājagṛha. And glancing for the last time at the pyre of the Great Sage, the venerable Ānanda said:

The Master has my fealty and love,
And all Lord Buddha's ordinance is done.
Low have I laid the heavy load I bore,
Cause for rebirth is found in me no more.

Epilogue

And this is why Fully Enlightened Buddhas manifest themselves in the world from time to time:

"I am the Eternal One, the Self-Born, the Healer, the Protector of all creatures. Knowing beings to be perverted, infatuated, and ignorant, I instruct them and reveal the path to Peace. And what is the reason for my repeated manifestation in the world?

"When men become unbelieving, unwise, uninformed, careless, fond of sensual pleasures, and from thoughtlessness get into trouble, then I, who know all things as they really are, declare that I am So-and-So, and consider: 'HOW CAN I INCLINE THEM TO ENLIGHTENMENT? HOW CAN THEY BECOME PARTAKERS OF BUDDHAHOOD?' "